D0251272

THEY ARE MY CHILDREN, TOO

CATHERINE
MEYER

They Are My Children, Too

A MOTHER'S
STRUGGLE FOR
HER SONS

PublicAffairs *New York*

Chapters 1-17 were previously published in 1997 in Great Britain under the title
Two Children Behind a Wall: The true story of a family torn apart, by Random
House UK Limited.

Book design by Jenny Dossin.

The Germans and the au pair in this book are not identified with their real names
apart from Catherine Laylle Meyer's ex-husband and his family, her friends, and her
lawyers Herr Struif and Frau Stadler-Euler.

All photographs belong to the author apart from the final photograph in the section
© Gamma/F. Reglin.

LIBRARY OF CONGRESS CATALOGING-IN-PUBLICATION DATA
Meyer, Catherine (Catherine Laylle)
    They are my children, too : a mother's struggle for her sons / Catherine Meyer.
  — 1st ed.
        p.   cm.
    Includes bibliographical references.
    ISBN 1-891620-15-0
      1. Meyer, Catherine (Catherin Laylle)   2. Kidnapping, Parental—Germany—
Case studies.   3. Kidnapping, Parental—Great Britain—Case studies.   4. Custody
of children—Germany—Case studies.   5. Custody of children—Great Britain—
Case studies.   6. Conflict of laws—Custody of children.   7. Ambassadors'
spouses—Great Britain—Family relationships—Case studies.   I. Title.
HV6604.G42   M495   1999
362.82'97'092—dc21
  [b]   99-18192
                                                                                   CIP

FIRST EDITION
10 9 8 7 6 5 4 3 2 1

To my darling sons,
Alexander and Constantin.

There is not a moment of the day when I do not think of you, not a moment of the night when I do not dream of you. You are always with me. My love for you cannot be destroyed.

Europe: Our Homeland

This is why we are channeling all our energy into creating an integrated Europe, because Europe includes our own homeland, because Europe—in a broader sense—is our homeland, and because it is only by taking this step that we can give our children the chance to live in peace and happiness.

—KONRAD ADENAUER, *Leader of the Christian Democratic Union and Chancellor of West Germany 1949–63, speech at Recklinghausen, September 1, 1957*

CONTENTS

ACKNOWLEDGMENTS

There are so many people who have contributed to this book by supporting me in my cause. Without their love, sympathy, and help, I would never have been able to muster the strength and belief in myself to keep going.

Above all, I must thank my parents and friends: Maurice and Olga Laylle, Irene Commeau, Sir John Craven, Ginette Hiait, Amelie Knecht, John McLaren, Brigitte Pahl, Lila Rachidian, Charlotte Stratos, Anne Swift, Sheelagh Taylor, Valérie Woodmansey, Joachim von Bonin, and particularly, Alan Kingston, Leonard Louloudis, Nicolette Narten, Erica Thoma, and Claudine Ward.

I would also like to acknowledge with deep gratitude those in the British and French governments who have taken a personal interest in my case: British Prime Minister Tony Blair and his wife, Cherie Booth, QC; French President Jacques Chirac, and his former European adviser, Pierre Ménat; Justice Minister and Garde des Sceaux Elisabeth Guiguou and her adviser, Michel Debacq; former French Justice Minister and Garde des Sceaux Jacques Toubon; French Foreign Affairs Minister Hubert Vedrine and his adviser, Gérard Castex; British Ambassador in Bonn Sir Paul Lever; former British Ambassador in Bonn Sir Nigel Broomfield; French Ambassador in Bonn François Scheer; British Consul General in Hamburg Michael Sullivan and Vice Consul Alex Brown; French Consul in Hamburg Bruno Perdu; and Head of Consular Division, Foreign and Commonwealth Office, London, Duncan Taylor.

My thanks also go to members of the British, French, and European Parliaments, Mary Banotti, Pierre Cardo, Bill Cash, Daniel Hoettel, Kate Hoey, Bill Olner, Sir John Stanley, Catherine Urban, and Xavier de Villepin; Denise Carter and everyone at Reunite; and the National Center for Missing and Exploited Children in Arlington, Virginia.

And, of course, to my darling husband, Christopher. His love and support brought me back to life. I am no longer alone.

Foreword

by Sally Quinn

I first met Catherine Meyer at a small dinner the week she arrived in Washington. Her husband Christopher had just been appointed the British ambassador to the United States. They had also just gotten married the day before they left for America. Catherine joined in the conversation with gusto, interjecting thoughts, joking, teasing, laughing, and most impressively, never hesitating to ask a question if she didn't know what we were talking about.

I was impressed, not only with her intelligence and her sense of fun, but her gameness. She was definitely a player. She also seemed like a thoughtful and kind person, which was what really drew me to her. Christopher, by the way, was equally attractive but it was Catherine I couldn't stop thinking about on the way home. I even mentioned to my husband how much I liked her.

But there was something I had picked up about her that troubled me. The way she laughed a little too hard, jumped into the conversation when there was the slightest lull as if to fill the empty space, smoked too many cigarettes . . . I don't think it was particularly noticeable to the others but it haunted me. I saw her again some weeks later at a ladies luncheon, and the same quality was there.

It was later that afternoon, when almost everyone was gone, that I asked her about her children. I had heard she had two boys and I thought perhaps I could get them together with my son.

It was then that she told me. Her children had been kidnapped by her German husband. She had barely seen them in four years. But that was impossible, I said. That can't happen. What about the laws? What about the Hague Convention? Surely she could get them back. After all, she was their mother. There was no country, certainly no civilized country in the world that would deprive children of their mother and vice versa unless she had held their feet in tubs of boiling water and burned them with cigarettes.

I was filled with questions. Why didn't she just go over there and spend time with them? Why wasn't she living in the town where they were and dogging her husband every day? Why couldn't she get the courts to agree to visitation? I didn't say it but I must admit I thought privately that she must not have done all she could to get them back. She must not have fought hard enough.

I wondered if there was something in her past that I didn't know, some reason why a court—any court—would reach such a harsh and cruel judgment against a mother unless she had done something horrendous to her children or proven herself to be so unfit that they had no choice. A mother whose children were taken away from her and refused visitation rights and the courts upheld this? There had to be two sides to the story.

I could tell that Catherine saw the horror and pain in my eyes, then the skepticism and doubt. I left that day feeling completely outraged by her story but also curious. One thing I knew for certain. If my children had been kidnapped by my ex-husband, I would not be in Washington going to dinner parties. I would be camped out on their doorstep, fighting and doing everything I could to get them back. Something just didn't make sense here.

My husband sat next to her at dinner shortly after our conversation, and the next day she sent him a copy of her book, which had just been published in England. I immediately grabbed it and began reading. I needed to find some explanation for why this was happening.

I was completely shocked by what she wrote.

The fact was that one summer, two years after her separation and after she had been awarded custody, she put her two children on a plane for Germany for their holiday visit with their father and they never came back.

The fact was that she had spent every moment of the ensuing years fighting for them to the point where she lost her job, her home, all of her money, her health, and at some points, her sanity.

The fact was that a German court with German lawyers in a tiny German town in which her husband's family and friends were prominent refused to allow her even visitation rights, and turned a blind eye to her husband absconding with the children.

The fact was that her children, having been told repeatedly she had abandoned them, became hostile and uncommunicative on the few occasions over the years when she was allowed to visit them (always supervised) in her husband's home.

I could go on. But rest assured that Catherine Meyer did and is still doing all that is humanly possible to get her children back, to visit them, to talk to them.

It is not an exaggeration to say that this situation is Kafka-esque. And the system, the German system that has prevented her from being with her children is nothing if not evil.

The lunacy of the German legal reports are enough to make anyone with respect for decency simply crazy. The skewed logic in one of the last reports was that because she hadn't seen her children for several years they wouldn't be comfortable with her and they would be terrified that she would re-abduct them.

As Catherine writes, "The report had its own logic. But behind the logic was a set of twisted and perverse assumptions: that a child does not need two parents; that it is better for a child's development to live in Germany and be exposed to German culture; that German blood is superior to others; and that nationalities are transmitted by blood, not by birthplace or residence. Alongside this was the belief that a biological parent has no entitlement to her children. All this is the legacy of the German legal system of the late 1930s. Much of the family law of that period has still not been revised and is still a part of today's German legal system."

Hearing those words and reading this book sends chills up and down one's spine. Images of a master race and "Deutschland über alles" rear their ugly heads. And it's not as if the German government has not been besieged by other governments. Cherie Booth, wife of British Prime Minister Tony Blair, and French President Jacques Chirac have intervened with the German government and its ambassadors. They have been greeted with shrugs and weak excuses that these matters are in the hands of the German courts and that nothing can be done to help.

What is Germany thinking? Doesn't it understand that this evil is also a public relations disaster? Taking children away from their mothers is what happened fifty years ago! Not today.

How can modern Germany allow these laws still to exist and not do anything about it? There is no excuse for this in a civilized and humane country. Every German who sits back and lets this happen should feel an immense sense of shame.

And it's not just Catherine Meyer's children who have been taken away. Recently three German thugs cut off a mother and her two toddlers on a French backcountry road, tore the screaming babies out of their mother's arms, and drove them across the border to their German father. She hasn't seen her children since. And all the outrage and complaints from the French government have fallen on deaf ears. So much for the Hague Convention.

To this day Catherine Meyer spends her time trying to get her children back, working with lawyers and friends and doing everything she can to help others who are in the same position. She is actively involved in the National Center for Missing and Exploited Children and will continue to lobby everyone she can to reinforce what the Hague Convention should already be doing.

I read this book in one sitting. I have to admit that I cried the entire time I was reading it. I cried with anguish at her loss. I cried with frustration at her failed attempts to rescue her children, to visit them, to talk to them. I cried with outrage that her children, anyone's children, could be ripped away from their mother and then have that heinous deed supported by anyone's law. And I cried with despair at the horrible pain her children must have gone through and must still be going through now, not only because they lost their mother but because they were told and came to believe that she had abandoned them and didn't want to see them anymore. I only pray for their sake and for her sake that irreparable damage has not been done. I laid awake nights after I read the book, plotting revenge against the father and his family, the entire village, the German legal system, the Germans themselves. I refought World War II.

And when I saw Catherine again after I had finished reading her book I almost didn't know how to greet her. I felt the way so many people feel when confronted with enormous pain. It was almost a fear that if something so horrible could happen to her it could happen to me and my child too. And I thought too of how tragic it was that something that had started with such youthful gaiety and insouciance and love as her marriage had could end with such ugliness and hate and deception and cruelty.

Mostly though, I felt guilty. I felt guilty that I ever questioned her fitness as a mother, her determination to get her children back, her commitment to save them from permanent damage, and her deep involvement in trying to help every other parent whose children have been abducted.

The one thing that keeps Catherine going, and her friends too, is the hope that there will be a happy ending. Her children are growing up. And though she will have lost their childhood forever and there will always be an empty place in her heart for those years she won't ever recapture, she can be sure that one day they will know the truth. And they will know it because of this wonderful book. They will know that she loved them with all her heart and she did everything that was humanly possible to be with them. That she never ever gave up trying. They will know that, and they will have their precious mother back. And nobody will ever be able to take them away from her again.

These are our children, too.

CHAPTER 1
Cri de Coeur

My heart is filled.
It is filled with nothing but pain.
This is my last scene of our life together.

In our London home, the three of us were packing in Alexander and Constantin's bedroom. A few hours later my sons would be leaving for their summer holiday in Germany to stay with their father. Little did we know then that this would be the end of our happy and peaceful existence. Little did we know that this would be the very last day we would be free to talk, free to cuddle, and free to love.

"You won't touch anything, Mummy? Promise. I have cleared my desk and arranged my toys the way I want them for when I get back."

Alexander was always so meticulous. His collection of tube tickets was neatly held together with a rubber band in one drawer, his stamps in another, and on the shelf above, small boxes containing his secret treasures and souvenirs were tidily stacked. Everything had its special place, and no one, not even his younger brother Constantin, was allowed to disturb the private domain of his desk. In the large cupboard, his Legos were laid out very precisely, like a theater. On one shelf, he had arranged his medieval knights, shields and spears in hand, ready to venture forth on their next crusade. On the shelf beneath, pirate ships encircled a lone island, ready for imminent attack. The display was so carefully planned that the models looked almost real.

My Alexander: partly a serious boy and yet still partly a demanding baby. By nature, he was less levelheaded and even-tempered than Constantin. He was full of mischief, often given to embroidering the truth with his vivid imagination; he could be capricious sometimes, torn between the real world and fantasy.

But fate would throw him prematurely into adulthood. His father and I had separated when he was six and a half, and since then we have lived in different countries. His daddy stayed in Germany, and the three of us moved back to London, where he had been born. Living without a man around, he gradually assumed that role for himself. I never imposed it on him. In my eyes, he was still so tiny and vulnerable. But he cherished this new status, and at times he would almost take charge and be protective of me. Today was such a day.

"Do we still have time? We won't miss the plane?"

"There's plenty of time. We don't have to leave for another hour."

"And, Mummy, don't forget to buy the exercise books I need for the beginning of term. Here's the list from school."

He spoke to me in French, as he always did, French being his and Constantin's mother tongue. Both children had always attended French schools, but they were also fluent in German and would automatically speak to their father in it. It was wonderful to hear them switching so easily from one language to the other. Alexander was particularly gifted, and his English, too, was perfect now. English offered many fun expressions, which he loved to mix up, sometimes with a Rastafarian accent that he imitated well and that always made Constantin and me laugh. Both my sons were the perfect image of the new Europe. Brought up in London, with a German father and a French mother, they had, and still have, three passports and are trilingual. In a future Europe, this background would surely give them tremendous advantages. I was thrilled that they had this chance and terribly proud that both of them could rise to the challenge. Even given the opportunity, not all children are so adept at languages!

As I was packing their last items, I fell into thinking how lonely the next six weeks would be without them. I knew how much I would miss their cheerful voices, the constant to-ing and fro-ing and rampaging about the house. Without them, the house was always so silent: no one to greet me with a shower of kisses in the mornings. This is the harsh price of a broken marriage: schooldays with Mummy and most of the holidays with Daddy. But watching Alexander pack his rucksack, I realized that he was already halfway into his German forest.

"I think I've packed everything—my magnifying glass, my swimsuit, my goggles, and a few toys."

Alexander loved going to Germany, exploring the woods and the bird life, examining the insects under his magnifying glass. Alexander is an explorer, and his lively interest and curiosity were always a delight to watch. Verden had become a second retreat, offering him an assortment of mysteries to discover. He had two lives—one there, one here in London—and each offered its thrills, even though he was occasionally torn between them.

Alexander was, I think, the more complex of my two sons. Not a difficult child, but apprehensive and sometimes restless. He was a funny mix of tender emotion and anxiety, a will to please and obstinacy. Somehow I was always slightly worried about him and wondered whether he would eventually be at peace with himself. Alexander saw life as full of complications.

Constantin, on the other hand, was the steady and predictable one. He was even-tempered—almost never moody. At school he was exceptionally competent and at the top of his class; he did his homework without protest, was good at sports, and was popular with his schoolmates. Constantin had a calm, cheerful, robust disposition. This made him more independent and self-confident than Alexander.

But if Alexander and Constantin were so different, they were very compatible. One observed the world with solicitude, the other with serenity. One was already longing for peaceful country walks, the other looking forward to his return to London.

"Mummy, when are we coming back?"

Constantin had not packed a thing. Packing was boring, and besides, a holiday in the countryside did not hold the same fascination for him. It was just something that could not be bypassed, but soon he'd be back with his mummy and on holiday with her.

"Where are we going to go? To Valérie's, like last summer?"

"I am not saying. It's a surprise."

"Oh, Mummy!"

"If I tell you, it won't be a surprise."

I had arranged a trip to the theme park Alton Towers. The thought of their excited little faces as they discovered what the surprise was made me smile in anticipation. Little did I know that this was never to be. Little did I know that day—July 6, 1994—what a tragic turn our lives were about to take.

Had I had the slightest inkling of what was going to be inflicted on them, I would never have let them go. I would have protected them, protected their peace and, above all, their freedom. I never realized, never imagined . . . and because I was so naive, their lives have become a monstrous charade.

How can I ever explain to them the injustice of the law, the injustice of life, when it is they who are paying the ultimate price? How can I ever make them understand that they have become the victims of a bitter intra-European dispute when it is so far removed from their reality—two small, vulnerable boys who have no idea about justice or politics? How can I ever make them realize that they have been used as two puppets, that they have been denied their own mother, in order to make a point?

All day and all night, I dwell on the images of my children, the boys they were and the dark shadows of the two little prisoners they have become. I can feel their warmth close to my body, remembering how we used to read our ritual bedtime stories snuggling together in my bed. How many nights have I heard Constantin's calls, which woke me with a start, cold perspiration dripping on my face. Sometimes he felt so close I could almost feel him touching me. At other times his voice was far away, lost in a fog. These calls were the most agonizing because they were calls of despair.

With Alexander, I could only ever sense his silence and his fear. I only saw him confused and angry, a black cloud around him. I know that it is Alexander who is suffering more. It is he who is carrying the weight of remorse and guilt on his tiny shoulders. But there is no guilt to carry. It is not of his doing. He is only a tool. Alexander is the older, the more emotionally vulnerable, and this is why he was the one who was most used. If only I could take him in my arms, take away the pain and the enormous burden. If only I could speak to him, comfort him. . . .

"Mummy, let me carry the suitcase, it's too heavy for you."

How protective of me he was that day. Maybe in his young mind he is protecting me even now. Alexander was leaving. Constantin was just chugging along behind. He sat behind me in the car, his arms around my shoulders, his cheek against mine.

"When did you say we were coming back?" Constantin asked.

"In six weeks, Tini."

In the two and a half years we had been in London, they had made this trip many times, at Easter, at Christmas, and in the summer. Yet this time Constantin was set to endure it calmly, while Alexander was marching blindly on, driven inexorably by fate.

At the airport, the stewardess came to pick them up, attaching a British Airways folder around their necks containing their passports and plane tickets.

"Mummy, will you put the old one in my cupboard, please?" This was another of Alexander's collections. "The others are in the cupboard on the right."

Alexander always needed reference points and organization. This side of his character touched me. Tini, bolstered by his self-assurance, didn't need any extra organization around him. Life was already in crystalline order in his head.

Their departure to Germany was symbolic. I remember every detail, every word we said, every expression on their little faces. This was my last image of their freedom, the last time I could truly share my emotions with them, and they could share theirs with me, before an impenetrable wall would cruelly separate them from the world and from me, their mother.

Alexander was so grown-up that day, so solicitous in his responsibility as elder brother. He dutifully took Constantin by the hand and gave me their last instruction:

"And don't forget to buy the Legos."

This was another ritual of ours. A present would always be waiting for them on their return, and this morning they had each marked an "A" and a "C" next to the Legos they had chosen in the brightly colored catalog.

"Mummy, you won't be sad without us. We will be back soon, remember."

I felt tearful as Alexander hugged and kissed me good-bye, but I smiled.

"Of course I will be a bit sad, but as you say, it won't be long, and you will have fun in Verden and on the island of Juist."

Constantin was sad that day. He hardly spoke, but kissed me desperately instead. His arms were still tight around my neck when the stewardess interrupted us:

"Come on, time to leave."

Tini extricated himself from my arms. I stood up from kneeling on the floor, and he just walked away, led by Alexander, without turning back. Constantin never showed his intimate feelings, but I had never seen him so dispirited. It was precisely because he did not turn around that I realized how deeply upset he was. Now, looking back, I know he had a premonition, even before I did.

Alexander turned around, waving, blowing kisses at me, and calling, "Bye-bye, Mummy. Be good."

And there they were, two very small boys, each with his rucksack on his back, disappearing amid the crowd of adults into the transit area. They looked so vulnerable. Suddenly, I had an overwhelming desire to stop them, and I almost called out:

"Stop! Don't go. You can't go!"

Yet I told myself that it was irrational. In no time they would be back, and we would be off on our holiday together. Besides, their father would have been hysterical on the telephone:

"Are you mad? Why aren't the boys here? I need them as much as you do."

Was it a premonition? My younger son was experiencing the same, strange feeling. But, like Constantin, I could not show my emotions in public. Like him, I complied with the form, head high, ready to face reality. I said nothing but could not contain the tears in my eyes as I watched him walk away, proud and strong. Even from the back of his fragile little neck, I could tell that my Tini was biting his lip and sighing resolutely.

Alexander stopped at the last corner and blew a final kiss, then suddenly they both vanished, swallowed into the crowd of travelers.

This was my last image of them.

They were stepping into a trap their father had set. My little birds would be transformed into puppets on a string, controlled by their father's hands. They would be taught to fear their mother, to wipe all thoughts of her from their minds. Caught in this never-ending nightmare, I am no longer the woman I was: I have lost my sense of reserve and can no longer hide my feelings. I am in despair. Privacy no longer has any importance. I don't care who witnesses my emotions. All I care about is justice for my sons.

I am their mother. I am the one who gave birth to them, carried them inside my womb, feeling them grow inside my body as an intrinsic part of me. I could feel their kicks grow stronger by the day, already sensing their different identities. I fed them, cuddled them, calmed their fears. . . . Since the day I gave birth to them, my life has been devoted to them. How can I go on living when a part of me has been torn away?

But I will never abandon them. I will never be dragged into self-pity and resignation. I will stay strong and composed, otherwise I will never be able to release them.

My own mother wrote to them, "The years pass, and we pray that God will reunite us before we vanish from this earth. Hope is the last thing to die."

Hope has also become my only solace, my only resource. This is the story of a mother whose life relies on hope. A mother who cannot even talk to her sons, who has been wiped out of their existence. I do not know when they will be free again or when they will be able to read this book, but deep in their hearts they must know that I have not abandoned them, as I know they have not abandoned me. A mother cannot be rubbed out like a spelling mistake.

How deep and unquestioning a child's love is! No one can love so freely and so unreservedly, yet only a mother's love is boundless. This is what "they" are trying to eradicate. The only way this can happen is through systematic manipulation, because my children have always loved me, and because I am their mother.

"They" are a small-minded, bigoted, close-knit community in the heart of Europe, in a small provincial town in Lower Saxony in Germany. "They" are by no means typical of Germans in general, let me hasten to add. "They" would not have mattered at all had they not categorized me as a "foreign mother"—for them an unpardonable sin. Their xenophobia, which encouraged my husband to abduct my children when I had custody of them and then to refuse me all access, should alarm every citizen of the so-called civilized societies.

The story I have to tell is an outrageous one. Confronted by a wall of nationalism, corruption, and legal loopholes, I have used every avenue available to me: the media, embassies, European institutions. I have fought in England, France, Germany, and now even in the United States. So far, no politician, no senior official, no diplomat, no judge has been able to help me obtain the rights due to a mother. A German province and its courts have been allowed to victimize me as if the so-called new Europe did not exist.

I will not, cannot, remain silent before such a barbaric injustice. My only concession is not to name them, because above all I want this book to be published in Germany where my sons are living, a land that forms a part of the tapestry of Europe, a land that must review its system of justice in cases of child abduction.

We are citizens of a democratic society, and I want to see my children grow up in this free world. No one should be allowed to deny us the freedom to love and speak. No one should be allowed to separate a mother from her children in the name of a nationality.

I want everyone to hear my call. Alexander and Constantin are my sons. They were only nine and seven when they were abducted, and they are unaware of what has been done to them. Even their photographs of me have been destroyed, their mother tongue has been forgotten, and London has been erased from their minds. These are the lengths to which they have been manipulated, the extent of the wickedness perpetrated on them.

This book is like a bottle tossed into the sea. It will float away and, someday, reach my children. Only then will they finally know the true facts and understand how in spite of the justice and decency in which I naively believed, we are being kept forcibly apart. Only then will they realize how cruelly and unnecessarily we were separated and how this book is the only way I have left to communicate my undying love for them.

CHAPTER 2
Your Mother's Story

In the way that adopted children crave to know
their origins and who their natural parents are,
Alexander and Constantin, too, will want to know.
A wall of silence and lies now surrounds them, and
the remains of their mother's image must be
blurred and confused. This is why I must tell them
about myself and the other world—their world,
their heritage. The world they also belong to and
which has been mercilessly screened from them.

So here is my story—our story.

I was born in Baden-Baden, Germany, in the French occupation zone where my father was posted after the war. My sister, Véronique, who is nearly eight years older than me, went to kindergarten and learned to speak German fluently, but I was only a year old when my parents returned to Paris.

My father is French. He was born in Pau, in the Pyrenees. His mother died when he was only ten, and his father sent him to a Jesuit school where discipline was very strict. Pupils were not even allowed to talk in the corridors.

He became an officer in the French Navy, and between 1934 and the Second World War he traveled around the world. When I was a little girl, I used to love him telling me about all the French and British colonies he visited and the balls that were organized to receive the officers. At the outbreak of the war he was sent to what was then French Indochina. For his achievement against the Thai fleet (controlled by Japan) in January 1941, he was awarded the Croix de Guerre and the Légion d'Honneur, the highest awards for bravery that France can bestow on its citizens. In 1944 he was made a prisoner of war by the Japanese, but he would never tell us anything about this period. When the war ended on August 14, 1945, and he was freed, he went to look for my mother, whom he had met in Saigon a few years earlier.

My mother, Babusia, as the boys called her, is Russian-born. She comes from an old aristocratic Saint Petersburg family who fled Russia after the 1917 Revolution. Her father, a naval career officer, fought against the Bolsheviks as an artillery officer in Admiral Kolchak's army in Siberia. When the army dispersed, his regiment retreated to Harbin in China, where my mother spent her early childhood.

Harbin was a town built by the Russians, on the Manchurian branch of the Trans-Siberian railway. But after the "Chinese Generals' Wars" and the Japanese invasion of Manchuria in 1932, her family fled again, first to Peking and then to Shanghai. My mother married her first husband, but he died in action before my sister, Véronique, was born in Saigon.

Being such a mixture of nationalities and cultures, I always felt a citizen of the world. I was also soon exposed to living in different countries, as my father was transferred abroad by the American oil company he had joined in 1958. We lived in Gabon in French Equatorial Africa for two years, and when I was twelve, we moved to London. Here I went to the French Lycée in South Kensington; then I went to university at the School of Slavonic and East European Studies, part of King's College, London University.

I loved the Lycée and have many wonderful memories of my schooldays there. It is very international but has a strong, underlying French influence and method of instruction that has no doubt shaped my Cartesian way of thinking. However, my Russian inheritance and the English environment also deeply influenced my character, making me both rational and emotional, determined yet forbearing.

I had an old-fashioned and stricter upbringing than my school friends, as my parents belonged to an older and more organized world. I longed for my own freedom—to choose things for myself. Even then I remember thinking: "When I have children, I'll let them be independent and self-reliant, so their own personalities can flourish."

Knowing now that the exact opposite is being done to them fills me with horror. They were accustomed to think freely and be respected, and all of a sudden their world is narrow and restricted. I'm tortured by this thought because, from very early on in my life, I have realized that the most important thing in life is freedom. In Western Europe we take this for granted.

My Aunt Natasha, who had been a journalist in Shanghai, returned to Russia in 1948, following Stalin's active campaign to persuade children of émigrés to return to the Soviet Union. For the next twenty years she was cut off from my mother. It was only in 1961, when the "iron curtain" was partially lifted in the Khrushchev years, that they were finally reunited. I was eight, but I remember that day and the impression that Communist Russia left on me. I could never forget, either, how several years later my Russian friend cried on my shoulder because she would never be free to visit me abroad. Today it is my own little two boys who are behind an iron curtain, and I, their mother, cannot reach out to them.

I sit alone in silence and pain in the empty flat that once resounded with their laughter and happiness, trying to tell them more about myself, careful that nothing I say will be used as evidence against me by the German courts. Even through this book I cannot communicate freely with my own flesh and blood.

.   .   .

London.

London is where my happiest memories belong.

On my twenty-fourth birthday, on January 26, 1977, my parents announced that they would soon be returning to Paris, as my father was retiring. They understood that I was enjoying life in London but were worried about leaving me. What I needed, they felt, was a husband. Here our views differed. I still had romantic notions of marriage and dreamed of meeting the perfect man. My mother saw the world in much more practical terms:

"Katia, you live in a fantasy world. You will never find the man of your dreams. Reality is just not like that."

There was no one I particularly liked among the men I knew. My heart still belonged to Robin, my first adolescent love. He was American, and I had spent years writing passionate letters to him (although they were only sporadically answered). But when he eventually came back to England, he had fallen in love with someone else. Although I had some admirers, my heart was still broken by that first romantic disappointment.

While I was at university, I entered the world of finance. Merrill Lynch was an excellent company, and I felt appreciated and valued. I also enjoyed the excitement of the financial markets: each day was different and challenging. It demanded strong nerves and quick reactions. It involved politics, economics, and public relations, and I enjoyed them all. The nature of this unconventional business created a terrifically charged office atmosphere, and I felt very much a part of this male-dominated environment. I was particularly fascinated by the up-and-coming commodities markets, with their erratic price movements and mysterious novelty. The challenge of making it in a man's world excited me far too much for me to contemplate settling down to the demands of married life. Not at that point, at least.

But life is always unpredictable, and in no time Robert appeared. I met him in the City through a friend. He was working in the same business, commodity brokering, and was relatively successful, with a promising future as a partner in a private metal-trading venture.

Twelve years my senior, he was going through a crisis in his life, battling through a complicated divorce. Robert was tall, dark, and extremely charming, and his great sense of humor, unaffected ways, and social ease had caught my attention.

"Of course he's divorced. But at his age, most men are not free. . . . He has experience and you need a mature man." My mother could relax. Robert would offer her daughter security, and there was no need to worry about me any longer.

Robert's demand for marriage was expressive of his particular disposition. We went out to a Greek restaurant in Bayswater, which at the time was a favorite place of ours. We had dinner, and Robert drank a whole bottle of wine to summon up the courage:

"Well, I suppose I can pop the question now. Will you marry me?"

It came out of the blue, and I was taken aback. We hadn't been together for long, and he'd just got his divorce. The following day we were due to have dinner at my parents' house, and in the morning I called my mother from work to tell her what Robert had asked me. When I got home, there was champagne on the table and a list of guests had been prepared.

But it wasn't far into our marriage when I realized we had little in common. At first, Robert tried to change me, as I later tried to change him, but of course neither of us succeeded, and in time we drew further apart, both locked in our different cultural molds. Robert soon returned to his energetic and wild social life, and I felt increasingly disoriented. His friends were older and much more worldly than me. I would just tag along feeling out of place and insecure.

Robert and I simply could not create a life together. We had been drawn together through a misreading of what we thought we needed.

After spending months organizing the decoration of the house we'd bought, everything was finally ready. Robert was on yet another business trip, and I found myself separating his things from mine as I moved in alone. I knew then that the gap between our two worlds could not be bridged.

Whereas Robert was able to escape, I was left behind to face reality. The time had come to do something.

I wrote a long explanatory letter, which I presented to him as we went out to dinner. I knew this was the only way he would hear me out. Although I was capable of managing clients and their investments, I felt incapable of conveying my innermost thoughts. Robert read the letter in silence, folded it, and calmly put it in his jacket pocket. He was composed:

"Okay, how much do you want, and where will you sleep tonight?"

I couldn't believe it. Who was this man? I had understood so little about him. His restrained reaction was far removed from the reality of the event for me.

But our divorce was quick and uncomplicated, neither of us seeking unnecessary bitterness. We had simply made an error. He had wrongly celebrated the end of his first divorce, and I the end of romanticism.

Somehow I never doubted the soundness of my decision, but I felt confused and guilt-ridden. Our marriage had been a failure, and I had to reconcile myself to that.

"If you were silly enough to leave Robert, don't expect us to support you," my mother announced, after my explanatory lunch with her.

My mother still saw her role as a directing one, with me as a little girl. "Katia, the perfect union you still go on about is only in the movies. I've told you before—and now you've left a perfectly nice husband."

I was disappointed by her reaction and could not understand her down-to-earth wisdom. Half businesswoman, half dreamy child, I was incapable of abandoning my naive belief that somewhere out there existed a Prince Charming. My father, though, reacted in his usual gentle way: "Catherine, at least you had the courage to do what you thought was right. That is something to be respected."

I am my father's only child (my sister's father had been killed by the Japanese in the war), and—like most young people with their parents—I had not realized at the time that he respected and loved me very much. My father was extremely fair-minded and very principled but rather reserved and self-effacing. The education of us children had been entrusted to my mother, and my father would rarely interfere. My memories of childhood hardly included him, and I was rather intimidated by his conventional discipline.

This was the day I discovered my father. He no longer saw me as a child. My education was over, and the time had come for a new relationship between adults. We talked a lot, about all sorts of things, from current affairs to personal ones, but too many years had to be made up for in a single lunch.

My father was born in 1912, and the gap between our two generations had yet to be properly filled. My parents were now living in Paris, and I was too busy with my job for such an opportunity to occur—until a disaster brought us together.

The emotional failure led me to be totally engrossed in my work, and within a year of my separation from Robert, I became a successful broker at E. F. Hutton. My life was shaping itself after all, and I relished my independence and success. I was comfortable in an environment of instant decisions, constant movement, and practical colleagues. My best friend, Leonard, had recently joined the firm, and my office days were infinitely more gratifying than my weekends.

That is, until one summer's day, when I unexpectedly fell in love.

A series of coincidences created a curious encounter that would change my life. The future father of my children would uncannily take the same road that I did.

I had decided to take a short break. My job was very demanding, and I was tired; I seemed to work endlessly. I would stay in the office until the close of the U.S. markets, come in early for the opening of the London ones, read the news, write sugar reports, analyze charts, and trade, a telephone at each ear. In the past year my business had grown substantially, and I now had my own assistant.

These were the years when price volatility was enormous, and several of my clients used to "day trade" in the gold, silver, stock index, and currency markets. I had a few very large clients who demanded constant attention, and others for whom I managed accounts. When the markets got busy, the stress was high. Being a woman in a world almost exclusively male, I could not allow myself to fail and ended up working twice as hard.

August was traditionally a quiet month, and I set off in my newly acquired car. This had been a small, admittedly immature extravagance with which I had spoiled myself to reflect my new success. I had built up some savings in the bank and felt I had worked hard enough to deserve it.

A holiday plan with friends had fallen through at the last minute, and I decided to drive down to the South of France. This change of mind was the first coincidence in the chain of events that would bring Hans-Peter and me together. Why did I decide to go to that part of France, and stay at that particular hotel in Beaulieu? My original plan had been to holiday in the States.

I spent my time contentedly, reading beside the hotel swimming pool, relaxing, and enjoying my lazy days. One of the books I read was *Lady Chatterley's Lover*—an unusual choice for me, and I can't recall if I found it dated or daring!

After several days of peace and quiet I was getting bored with my books and the men who hovered hopefully around any single women. The inactivity started weighing on me. The following day, August 15, my brother-in-law was to celebrate his birthday:

"Why don't you come to La Baule to visit us?" my sister asked me over the telephone. I agreed instantly, packed my bags, checked out of the hotel at around four o'clock, and set off toward Brittany.

Night was falling on the deserted motorway. Luckily, I found a hotel close to Bordeaux. The next day, without any precise timetable, I was back on the road and eventually stopped to fill the car up. I decided to walk into the petrol station to have some coffee.

As I stood drinking the watery coffee, a tall, boyish-looking man wearing Bermuda shorts walked past me and stopped at the counter to buy some sweets. I looked at him mechanically, and he smiled—a broad, childlike smile, which lit up his face. Automatically, I smiled back. He looked very young. He took his sweets and headed out of the station.

I finished my coffee and walked outside to my car. Just as I stepped out, a navy blue Volkswagen Beetle drove right in front of me. The same youthful man was at the wheel, now smiling broadly at me. A man sitting beside him looked up, and I guessed he had just been told, "Hey, that's the girl I saw inside. . . . "

I was amused and secretly flattered by this impromptu success, though it had little significance. As their car drove away, I noticed the "D" for "Deutschland" above the registration plate.

After another hour's drive along the motorway, I turned west toward Nantes on the *route nationale*. The August traffic was thick with endless lorries one never seemed able to overtake. I switched on the radio, with nothing particular on my mind, concentrating on the music.

Two hours later the traffic was still awful. But because I was on holiday, it didn't matter. As I drove through yet another village blankly looking at the houses lining the road, my eyes suddenly widened in astonishment: they were there! The two Germans of the motorway were having a drink on the terrace of a café. They waved as I whizzed by.

The road stretched on. After another hour I wanted a break. Parking my car, I walked into a small café and sat down at a table by the window. As I drank the café au lait, staring aimlessly at the ribbon of cars threading by, my eyes were suddenly jolted as I caught sight of the navy blue Beetle.

This was definitely fate. Somehow the peculiarity and the blondness of this man resembled someone. It had struck me at the petrol station. He'd reminded me of Camelia, who had been my best friend until she died tragically when we were twenty.

Camelia was very beautiful and looked like Jane Fonda. I remember so well the first day she arrived in our class at the Lycée. She looked different—more beautiful, more interesting, more delicate than any of the other students—and everyone looked up at her in silent admiration.

Her life had been difficult. Her German father had fled Germany at the rise of the Nazis and became active in the Resistance movement operating from Romania. He married a Romanian; Camelia was born in 1953 under the Communist regime. Life became increasingly hard for her parents until eventually they managed to escape to France, later settling in England.

Camelia was much brighter and more mature than we were. I worshiped her and was proud to be her best friend. Until the car crash took her life away, we were inseparable. She died on December 23, 1973.

My world collapsed, and it took me over two years to reconcile myself to the injustice of God. Adolescent friendships are often intense and absolute. When she died, a part of me went with her. I could not accept that God had taken her life away at twenty but had allowed Hitler and Stalin to live.

Sitting behind the window of the café, seeing this blond man again for a third time, I thought of all this. There was no doubt that the material and spiritual aspects of life were often contradictory, but both existed and neither could be discounted. Such coincidences did not just happen. I considered.

What should I do? Catherine, this is quite ludicrous. A stranger passes by, and you think it's "fate." My mind was confused.

But what if. . . . What if this was written, and I simply ignore it?

I finished my coffee and half consciously, half in a dream, hurried out to join the trail of cars.

Looking back, I think I saw it as a sort of game. I was placing a bet on fate: if I bumped into him again, it was meant to be. If I didn't, it was just a fluke!

Yet, deep down, I already knew that I would find him. It was just a question of overtaking the few cars that separated us.

Soon enough, the Beetle with its "D" was in front of me, the back of his blond head on the left, his companion waving his arm as he recognized my car. Our little game lasted for a while across Nantes. At the traffic lights, smiles were exchanged. At times they were in front, at times I was. Coincidentally, we were following the same road signs. It was fun.

Finally, we found ourselves on a dual carriageway. Automatically, I accelerated.

Playing hide and seek with two strangers on French roads is quite ridiculous, I thought to myself as I disappeared at high speed.

My car was much faster than theirs, and as I glanced in the mirror I saw their little Beetle dissolving in miniature. It was shaking, nearly out of breath in its vain attempt to catch up with me. It was silly, but I felt rather sorry for it. I slowed down.

The game could have ended there, but they overtook me and signaled, turning into a parking bay. I told myself that the joke was a bit over the top now, but I followed them to the roadside and stopped. What a funny situation. I hesitated; the two young men had already stepped out of their car and were approaching mine.

They spoke good English. Wasn't it amazing we should meet three times like this? It transpired that they too were heading for La Baule. As I gave them my business card, on the back of which I scribbled my sister's telephone number, I thought, *Catherine, you are making a mistake. Why on earth did you let*

them have your office number as well? This is so unlike you.
They may not belong to the same world as you. What will you
do with them? The blond man looks so young and naive. He's
probably still a student on a camping holiday.

But it was precisely the youthfulness of this twenty-seven-
year-old man with his cheerful and enthusiastic manner that had
put me off guard. And it would be only a fun holiday encounter,
to be forgotten once I was back in London.

· · ·

His name was Hans-Peter Volkmann, and within four days
he had fallen in love with me. His love was youthful, platonic,
and exuberant, and it struck a maternal chord in me. Hans-
Peter was a wonderful breath of fresh air, an escape from the
demands of everyday life.

On the first evening I fell asleep thinking of him. The following evening we parted reluctantly, and on the third day we
kissed in the car like a couple of students. He left for Germany
on the fourth day. Three hours after waving good-bye to me
from the little Beetle, he telephoned. He called again that
evening, and the next day. I returned to London. He called
there, too, and then at the office. At the end of the week he
decided to visit me in London.

At the time I did not notice the forcefulness of his demands. I
only saw how much Hans-Peter was in love with me and found
myself falling in love as well.

However, on the Friday he was due to come I was beset with
doubts. This had just been a light holiday romance. Did I really
like him? And want to see him again? In my own environment?

But it was too late to stop him coming. I could hardly send
him back to Koblenz as soon as he stepped off the plane!
Instead, I asked some other friends to dinner that evening to
give me time to think and to neutralize the situation a little.

He arrived at the airport gate with his broad smile, and I
immediately forgot my anxieties. On the way home he talked
excitedly about his medical studies, his military service in

Koblenz, the last time he had been in London, and how much he loved it. His English was excellent. That was lucky, as none of us spoke any German.

He kissed me as if we had known each other forever, taking my hand in his and settling in among my friends. Nothing seemed to disconcert him. Hans-Peter had walked into my life, and I found myself encouraging him to stay.

The only one who observed us with a critical eye was my friend Leonard, but he was too polite and too perceptive to say anything. He was happy that his friend was happy and in love. This was reason enough to withhold judgment. Although I sensed his reserve, he was aware that it would have been pointless to criticize at this stage.

CHAPTER 3

The Blindness
of Love

After our weekend together, Hans-Peter went back to Germany on Sunday evening. I could sense that my friends didn't relate to him—perhaps they found him too demonstrative. His continuous need to kiss me in public to prove that I was his, and his alone, seemed cloying to them.

But I felt that Hans-Peter had temporarily transported me into a world of youthful fantasy. Now I returned to the adult world and my daily responsibilities to my clients, the news updates, and the market analysis. However, as soon as he had reached Koblenz, Hans-Peter began inundating me over the phone with declarations of his love and demands for mine. At times he would ring when I was in the middle of trading, concentrating on the erratic price movements appearing on the Reuters screen, one line connected to the U.S. exchange, the other to a client. He would become childishly impatient, and I would succumb to his pleas and ask my assistant to take over:

"Hello, Catherine? It's me."

"I really can't talk to you now. The gold market is in chaos, and I have a client on the other line."

"Do you still love me?"

"Of course I do. But, Hans-Peter, my client is waiting. I'll call you back when the market closes."

"I must talk to you now. . . . "

Hans-Peter could not accept my daytime priorities, and although I was often irritated by his brash intrusions, his loving voice would soon win me over. It was flattering to feel so wanted. Hans-Peter was like a ray of sunshine. He brought a carefree, cheerful radiance into my life.

By the following Friday, when Hans-Peter resurfaced in London, I was regressing to childhood. He would splash me in the bath, joyfully hug me, stretch out on the sofa, and turn my life into happy disorder. This was no sideshow anymore. These turbulent, carefree interludes became a part of my regular life. I slipped blissfully under his spell.

Hans-Peter's calls were so frequent that it became a sort of joke in the office.

"Cat, it's Hans-Peter!" my assistant would call out, ready to take over.

Shirley would attend to the client. She was efficient and capable. When Hans-Peter was calling from abroad, I could not make him wait on the line. His pleading made me feel alternately moved and guilty. Hans-Peter just could not accept my job getting between us in any way. Our love had to come first, and he managed to make me feel ashamed that, as a woman, I should be giving precedence to business responsibilities. I would find myself apologizing, even though it was he who was interrupting.

Soon my life had totally changed. I would come home in the evenings, and instead of accepting a friend's invitation out, I would wait for his calls. I would think of him as I was falling asleep and wait impatiently for the weekend. My life was becoming entirely dedicated to him. He managed to arouse in me irresistible feelings of devotion, mixed with a sense of guilt.

On the fourth weekend I flew to meet him in Koblenz. His flat startled me a little: it had white walls, thin, colorless curtains, plain furniture, and not a single painting to warm its impersonal mood. It was in such contrast to the homes I felt comfortable in, with their thick fabrics and warm colors. But what disconcerted me most was his untidiness, which was in such contrast to my meticulous order.

Hans-Peter was like an uncared-for child who needed constant attention. Had I had any sense then, I would have been more cautious, but I was drawn to his warm, carefree personality. Hans-Peter was intelligent and well read, and I enjoyed his inquisitive and enthusiastic character.

However, even though I was already too in love to heed these warning signs, meeting his mother should have raised the alarm. Gundel, who had come to inspect the foreigner her son was involved with, was a tall, blonde, severe-looking woman. We had nothing in common, and as she spoke very little English, our conversation was limited to banalities. She scrutinized me with an unmistakable expression of distrust that made me retreat into polite reserve.

I belonged to a cosmopolitan city that she considered overpowering and threatening. The gap between her secure provincial world, with its structured order, and my world was an unbridgeable one. Soon her attention centered on her beloved son, whom she had not seen in a month. They seemed so absorbed in the privacy of their conversation that Hans-Peter hardly bothered to translate. I had no choice but to offer only a strained smile. After all, it was Hans-Peter I was in love with, not his mother.

Hans-Peter seemed totally unconcerned about the disparity between the two women in his life, and I felt reassured by this.

He was on the verge of finishing his military service and would soon, I hoped, flee the maternal nest.

.   .   .

Hans-Peter had mentioned the possibility of moving to London once he was released from the Bundeswehr, the German army. Although I cannot recall having any say in it, in June 1983 he and two suitcases appeared in my flat. Within a month he told me he'd obtained a two-year research grant from Germany. From the little knowledge I had of the medical profession, this seemed amazing, and impressive. Being selected from hundreds of other applicants clearly suggested that Hans-Peter was very capable and had excellent career prospects. If he was disorganized and chaotic, this was obviously because he was a promising scientist constantly lost in his thoughts!

Living with this absent-minded professor, I had no choice but to be the practical one. In principle, I had no objection to being the breadwinner. My career was established so it seemed natural for our joint life to depend on my income to start with. I assumed Hans-Peter didn't earn much, on a grant, but in time he would take on more financial responsibilities. Medicine requires many years of training.

We started seeing less and less of my friends. Hans-Peter would tell me how much he would rather be alone with me than invite people over. In the name of love, Hans-Peter was isolating me, and in the name of love, he convinced me that we didn't need the outside world.

During our first year together Hans-Peter hardly ever spoke about his research work, gave evasive answers, and preferred talking about us and our perfect love.

This vaguely bothered me, but I assumed it was only a stage; once he was in a proper career, he would feel more involved. After all, the few times Hans-Peter mentioned his future plans, they were filled with ambition and high prospects. Some days he would talk about becoming a famous professor; at other times he saw himself running a high-profile medical general practice. He had not yet decided what direction he would take—but whatever it was, it would have a successful outcome. He knew nothing about the financial world, and I was ignorant of the path to success in his field.

Very soon Hans-Peter mentioned having children.

"It would be so cute!" he mused, cuddling me.

I could not disagree, but the timing was precarious. Hans-Peter was not established, and we were reliant on my income, which was not so lavish as when we first met.

The sugar market was my specialty, and I tended to be fairly accurate in my forecasts. In the summer of 1983 I predicted a rally out of the previous year's sideways price trend and advised my clients to invest in sugar. I was spot on. Very few had expected this move, and I was rewarded with reverent recognition. Brokers from our Bahrain and Beirut offices were calling me the new "sugar guru," seeking my advice and daily predictions. Should they buy now or wait for a price correction first? I wrote morning reports and was glued to my screens and charts.

This unexpected and sudden success caused me to be overconfident and bold. My clients were delighted and impressed at my performance. Such moves seldom occur and are difficult to anticipate. I felt that if I was such an inspired sugar trader, I, too, ought to share in the good fortune. So I started buying one contract of sugar, then another, and as the market continued up, I bought more.

There were, however, several problems. The first one was that by the time I got into the market I had already missed much of the upmove. Even in a bull market, prices do not rise consistently but have occasional setbacks, or "corrections," as they are known. These are often caused by some investors liquidating their positions, that is, selling in order to cash in their profits. The greater the number of sellers, the sharper the price decline.

When a particular market experiences a bullish trend, investors will rush to participate in the new profit opportunities.

This invariably causes greater price volatility, and this was what was happening to the sugar market. The price rise that had begun slowly attracted more and more participants, many of whom were speculators looking for a quick return. As more people bought, prices started shooting up. However, this created great market nervousness, as any dip would be interpreted as a possible reversal of the trend. Still glued to my charts, I was recalculating my upside objective daily, before the downward correction could occur.

The problem was that this correction took place three days too early. And it was sharp—involving a string of six consecutive "limit down" days. This meant that the maximum daily price "limit" move set by the New York Sugar Exchange was reached immediately on the opening, and the market would close—no one was allowed to sell until the following day. If the market opened "limit down" again one was simply stuck in a collapsing market, waiting for the day when trading would finally resume. Sugar traders, clients, and I were trapped for an agonizing week, unable to liquidate our positions while the losses mounted.

I tried to explain to Hans-Peter what was happening, but he was neither interested nor sympathetic.

"You have problems? Well, what do you expect with your type of job? It's just sheer gambling"—and he would change the subject.

In the meantime, I spent sleepless nights, worried to death about how to control the losses. Leonard and I tried to work out ways to improve the situation. He would listen to my anguish and carry some of its load on his shoulders.

I tried to hedge my position by selling in the cash market, which has no daily limit moves when trading is suspended. But even this did not help. On the third day the cash market remained static while the futures were still "limit down." The following three days, the cash prices actually went up! I was now losing on both sides.

In the space of a few days I saw all my profits disappear. By the time I was able to get out, I had incurred a huge loss. Unlike my clients, who had adequate funds to cushion the loss or who could ride out the correction, I had lost much more than I could afford. From then on, most of my income was taken up repaying my debt.

Hans-Peter considered the problem to be exclusively mine, so he dismissed it and criticized my working in this business. Today I realize that Hans-Peter did not so much object to the job itself but to the very fact that I was working. Only today do I understand that it was not a question of it being my problem rather than his, but that there *was* a problem.

In those early days, however, I had grasped little other than my immediate predicament, and I became disillusioned with the brokerage business. This job had been my passion and a source of great professional satisfaction. How many times had I spent eleven-hour days in the office, radiating happiness? Hans-Peter was right: commodities futures was sheer speculation. Only two days after I liquidated my position, prices rallied to their initial levels. The only players who seemed to profit were the unethical brokers who lived from "churning" their clients' accounts in order to earn more commissions, or the actual insiders who had proper market information.

Hans-Peter, however, had other preoccupations:

"Catherine, you know, at thirty-one it's high time you had children. Trust me, I'm a doctor. Late pregnancies carry risks. And just imagine how cute our baby would be."

Of course our children would be cute—but shouldn't Hans-Peter concentrate on getting a job for the next year if he wanted to assume the responsibilities of a father? Instinctively, I knew he was not mature enough for such a step, and I was right. But my maternal instincts were awakening. I found it increasingly difficult to remain uninterested in the idea, especially with Hans-Peter telling me how fulfilling it would be.

By the spring of 1984, less than a year after Hans-Peter had arrived on my doorstep with his amorous and insatiable passion, he finally convinced me:

"I love you, for sure. I need you. We should have children. Why not get married?"

After all, when two people are in love, marriage is a normal step. But before we had children, my finances had to improve or Hans-Peter had to ensure he had a job.

I thought I was in control. On the surface I was. Leonard was to be my best man. We would rush out from the office at lunchtime to visit hotels, choose the rooms for the reception, the menus for the dinner, the flower arrangements for the church. Both perfectionists, we went over every detail with a fine-tooth comb: Was the menu balanced? Would everyone like the choices of food? How would we seat the guests? There were so many considerations to take into account to blend the disparate groups, and we enjoyed the challenge. Hans-Peter steered clear of our deliberations but was happy to see the event shaping around him.

As the day drew closer, I was overwhelmed with premarital nerves, and like every bride, I managed to lose three kilos in a few days! The Volkmann clan was landing in London in ever-increasing numbers and needed immediate assistance. I was running to pick one lot up, drop another, draw maps, and plan sight-seeing routes while Hans-Peter, still locked away in his separate world, remained impervious to it all.

Most of Hans-Peter's Verden and Bremen relations were totally disoriented, alarmed by the traffic, and unable to find their way around. There was the aunt who hardly spoke English, the mother who needed constant attention, the sister who was arguing, the brother who went his separate way, uncles, cousins. . . .

The contrast between this overpowering clan and my own friends and family was striking. Even their physical appearance differentiated them. The men were all over six feet tall, and Hans-Peter's sister, Antje, was two heads taller than my father and brother-in-law. I felt small and brittle. The wedding portrait snapped in front of the Russian Orthodox Church in Ennismore Gardens would capture the oddness of this assortment: his tall and extravagantly large family and the four diminutive adult members of mine.

Besides my parents and my sister's family, I had no other relations, but my circle of friends was very large, and Hans-Peter's lack of friends surprised me. But our wedding was beautiful, with its inspiring ceremony at the Orthodox church in the warm June sunshine, the wonderful reception. . . . I felt loved and happy, yet disquieted by Hans-Peter's pride in the woman he was marrying: the perfect Catherine who loves him and gives in to his demands.

As I listened to Leonard's elegant and witty speech, recounting how he and I had arranged the entire wedding between our client calls, I thought about Hans-Peter's aloof ways with a mixture of loving indulgence and latent unease.

I had hung on to the belief that Hans-Peter would cut the umbilical cord. His family would shortly go home, and he and I would create our own independent world. Our Orthodox wedding, with its ritual of the crowns being held over our heads, symbolized exactly this.

Hans-Peter was different from his family. He was the only one who spoke fluent English, had worked in the United States and in England, and seemed fascinated by the cultural mix of London. At one stage, we had visited my aunt in Moscow, and he'd been so captivated by Russia that he intended to learn the language. Of course, the bond with his family was strong, and I respected this, but he expressed open-minded opinions, and his outlook seemed to be very different from theirs.

I thought I was marrying Hans-Peter. How desperately wrong I was! I didn't marry Hans-Peter—I took on an entire dynasty that was soon to engulf me in its grip and direct our lives.

CHAPTER 4

Responsibilities

We had been married less than three months when I discovered I was pregnant. At the very moment I expressed my suspicion, Hans-Peter rushed out to buy a pregnancy test. He hurried back in a state of great excitement.

"Here, we must find out. It would be so wonderful. . . . "

He sat and stared at the colored dots to see whether the chemical reaction would show positive.

He was ecstatic.

"Be careful now, you shouldn't move too quickly."

"But, Hans-Peter, I'm not sick. I've only just done the test!"

It was touching to see Hans-Peter's concern. He knelt in front of me, his hand on my stomach. His heir was inside, and the womb carrying it had become his most precious treasure.

He kissed me enthusiastically and then rushed to call his mother and sister. I could hear the excitement in his voice, mixed with exuberant exclamations: *wunderbar, fantastisch.* Within a few minutes his whole family had been informed of the happy news.

This revelation raises strong emotions in a woman, especially when it is her first child. I needed a little time to understand the meaning of our new existence. Soon I would be a mother. A small being was beginning its life inside my body. I was trying to absorb the implications of this sudden and unexpected turn of events.

But Hans-Peter's reaction was only to disorient me further. His endless advice on how to take care of myself was stifling, even harassing. He had already come into my life and taken it over. Now I had the strange feeling that I was not in control even of my own pregnancy. It was as if he had appropriated my womb. For him, the baby was an extension of Hans-Peter, and Hans-Peter alone. I had become simply his child bearer, the surrogate mother carrying what was his.

Maternity leave was only six weeks, and since Hans-Peter's hospital work would end in September, there was no question of my being able to take extra time off. I decided I would stay in the office until delivery day, to have as much time as possible with the baby later.

Hans-Peter phoned his mother all the time. I had no idea what they needed to discuss for hours on end. The baby? Future plans? Only they know. However, one day I did discover that Gundel had been regularly sending him money. Hans-Peter never said how much, and from then on he mostly talked to his mother when I was not about.

Our financial situation was not brilliant, but we were certainly not in any desperate need. My opinion was that we should keep our independence at all costs. Hans-Peter, however, dismissed my views and continued to accept his mother's handouts. His childlike exuberance began to worry and irritate me. However, I hoped that when he had settled into a regular job he would share my attitude toward dependency. After all, he was still completing his specialist training, and if he didn't object to his mother treating him like a child, why should it bother me? Youth is not eternal: one day Hans-Peter would grow up, and maybe I would miss his cheerfulness then!

In the meantime, though, it was I who was assuming the responsibilities of our life together. Hans-Peter relied on my sense of order and my ability to lead two lives simultaneously: as career woman and mother-to-be. I had always been organized and accustomed to hard work, and as I managed well under pressure, Hans-Peter gradually gave up almost all domestic duties.

As the months went by, my work gradually became less central in my life. I had put on well over thirty-five pounds in weight, tired easily, and work became a serious strain.

Being pregnant was a new and strange sensation. The baby was a part of me. Day and night I could feel him, sometimes with little unexpected kicks in the ribs that would make me hiccup just as I was telephoning an order through to the exchange.

It was wonderful to feel the baby grow and to experience the blossoming of my maternal instinct. I thought about what he would be like, what sort of a mother I would be, and how our life would be changed.

At times I minded looking large and tired. At other times I was transported into the blissful world of maternal love. But I was always conscious that a new being would soon come into this imperfect world, and a strange anguish would grip me: *Please, God, make him strong and healthy,* I prayed.

The baby was due toward the end of May 1985, and I was still in the office on Friday the twenty-fourth. The next evening Hans-Peter drove me to Westminster Hospital. As soon as we reached the maternity ward, Hans-Peter took over. In his capacity as medical practitioner and in the name of his child, he had decided that an epidural was out of the question.

"It can be harmful for the baby. We really should not run this risk," he announced.

I couldn't argue. He was a doctor, and I reminded myself that generations of women had had children without the help of pain relief. Although I have a very slight build, I have a high pain threshold. I can tolerate having my teeth drilled without an injection and usually ask not to have one. Having a baby would test my courage, but I did not particularly wish to show any suffering.

"What do you mean? Of course I won't leave the room."

"But, Hans-Peter . . . a woman giving birth is not a pleasant sight."

"Don't be stupid. It's just the way you've been brought up. I'm the father, and I'm a doctor. It's absolutely natural for me to be there."

Well, I suppose he's right, I thought to myself. My education has made me too shy and self-conscious. Although in the privacy of my home, I was natural and unreserved, I was very aware of my public appearance and even more of any display of emotions. Growing up in England had molded me this way, and I could not simply change overnight. I was torn between guilt and annoyance, and the pain had already become too acute for me to argue. Hans-Peter stayed.

No contractions occurred after my waters broke, so I was put on a transfusion. People say you forget the agony. I won't. There seemed nothing left around me besides this excruciating pain. The nurse, who had a dinner engagement, kept increasing the doses of the drip to accelerate matters. This led to practically uninterrupted contractions, and I couldn't even find the strength to beg her to stop. It seemed endless. I wanted to die.

Nine hours later Alexander finally appeared. He was a big, sturdy baby weighing 7.4 pounds. I had fought between the implacable nurse and Hans-Peter's gesticulations. We were both shattered. Later Hans-Peter was reproachful:

"And you didn't even react when the baby was put in your arms!"

In fact, I couldn't even properly remember what happened. Half conscious, everything seemed a blur. I remember Hans-Peter's emotional voice, though:

"Oh, what a beautiful baby. He's so big, so well formed. . . . "

My body had given up on me, and my mind was still suspended in a trance. Hans-Peter was enraptured with his new son. I fell asleep with the disquieting impression that Hans-Peter had not been there for me. He had only been concerned with protecting his property.

The next day I felt better and was holding happiness in both hands. A tiny being was lying next to me in his cot. I looked down to examine him, hardly daring to touch his minute hands. In the space of an instant I was completely convinced he was the most beautiful baby in the world. Maternal instinct is an extraordinary phenomenon that seizes you suddenly and completely. Only yesterday I was a pregnant woman: today I am a proud and protective mother.

I stood looking at him:

"You are so beautiful! My baby!"

That afternoon he was no longer mine. Hans-Peter arrived with flowers in hand, his mother behind him. He had contacted the whole clan to announce the news, and Gundel had taken the first flight to London and settled into our flat.

It was natural enough for a grandmother to rush in, but I was surprised that I hadn't even been given breathing space.

"Oh, Catherine! You are so fat!"

As I was sensitive about gaining so much weight, reminding me was rather unnecessary. But, as I found out later, this was Gundel's idea of being "honest."

Gundel and Hans-Peter rushed toward the cot, and I was no longer invited to take part in their conversation, which continued in German with exclamations from Gundel:

"*Er sieht genau wie du, mein Junge,* your nose, your eyes . . . ," except for what to her was one unfortunate detail: "Well, of course, he's dark like Catherine. . . . "

Rejected and still exhausted from the birth, I found solace in silence. After all, Gundel's favorite child had just given her a grandson. Her reactions were understandable. I should be tolerant and patient.

But it was exactly this lack of reaction and my eternal will to please that would become the source of my terrible fate and that of my sons. That day, had I felt stronger, I should have stood up and insisted to Hans-Peter, "Look, this is *our* son. Not your mother's. Don't let her boss you around. Don't let her control our lives."

But would Hans-Peter have listened to me? I doubt it. He seemed to belong to his mother, and when she was around, they were an indissoluble entity. Recently, I have spent many days, many months dwelling on the past, asking myself why I was so restrained and why I allowed mother and son to command my life. I blame myself for my lack of insight, yet I know this is not entirely fair.

At that time I understood little and was too ready to keep the peace by compromising. Relations with mothers-in-law are often uneasy. Gundel was particularly besotted with her son, and so we were competitors for his attention and affection. I was the woman who "stole" her son from her, keeping him in a foreign land. Gundel had no doubt seen me as a threat. With the additional language barrier that prevented us from establishing the affinity that can easily bond two women, I was unable to express my own fears.

But language was not the only barrier that separated us. Gundel simply did not like me. I wonder, though, whether I realized it then and whether I had formulated in my mind what really needed to be said: "Gundel, please cut the umbilical cord. Let go of your son and let him become a father."

Hans-Peter was Gundel's property, and his newborn son the extension of her rights. She couldn't accept that a child eventually becomes his own person and needs to be set free. She had hung on to her children and retained control over them. Hans-Peter, her favorite, had remained entirely hers: he still relied on her. Alexander was meant for her—never for me.

·   ·   ·

After a week in hospital, with Hans-Peter and Gundel paying daily visits, it was time for my baby and me to go home. They arrived, in my car, eager to claim their priceless possession. Gundel held her arms out, ready to take Alexander from me. It was then that I uttered my first no.

"Oh, of course. I simply wanted to help," she said, retreating immediately and withdrawing her hands.

My instinct to protect my baby had made me react automatically. But inexorably, Gundel and Hans-Peter took over my life, and postnatal depression set in. Even my flat felt alien. Things had been moved around, and it smelled different. Gundel's presence was everywhere, and I no longer felt it was my home. She slept in the sitting room, strategically positioned between Alexander and our bedroom.

Gundel sent me to rest: I looked tired and pale and should take advantage of her presence to recuperate. There was no need to worry, she and Hans-Peter would take care of the baby. He was a doctor, and she had been a nurse during the war. Alexander was in excellent hands. I was a businesswoman and could therefore not be competent. The only requirement was that I should breast-feed the baby.

"Breast-feeding is essential. It's the only way to ensure a child's healthy development. Alexander deserves a good start in life."

Nature gave me tiny breasts, and my inadequate milk production drove Gundel to despair, but she would not give in. She bought a pump, and by hook or by crook, she was going to extract her grandson's requirements! I felt completely demeaned, and my sense of insufficiency was accentuated by Gundel's sighs:

"The poor child hasn't had enough milk to satisfy him."

Tired, frustrated, and depressed, I was quite unable to stand up to her demands. She would feed Alexander, and her reproachful stare at the half-empty bottle threw me into gloom and a sense of inadequacy. Shocked by this violent intrusion, weakened by the birth itself, I felt myself a helpless observer of what was going on around me.

My friends who came to visit could not fail but notice.

"Catherine, what's going on? Your mother-in-law has taken over!"

Gundel's stay in London seemed an eternity. Rather than defend me, Hans-Peter was entirely swamped by his mother's behavior; they spoke German together, and I couldn't join in.

Alexander cried a lot and had trouble getting to sleep, but at my slightest movement, mother or son would rush to pick him up first. Doctor and nurse could attend to his needs; I had better regain my strength to increase my milk production.

When Gundel finally returned to Germany, there were less than three weeks before I had to go back to work. Kept from my baby, my day now became dedicated to him. But the hours were short, as Hans-Peter returned very early from the hospital. Whether Alexander was asleep or not, Hans-Peter would pick him up, hold him in the air as if he were a doll, and roll with him on the bed.

"Hans-Peter, please. He's much too small for that. You're being too rough, and he won't be able to go back to sleep."

Mornings were my heaven, finally alone with my Alexander. These are my happiest memories of our early months together. We used to sit on the sofa facing the large window that gave directly onto the communal garden. A large chestnut tree was in full blossom, beautiful in the warm June sunshine.

Alexander was mine, and I could sense how comfortable he felt in my arms. When he cried, I would immediately pick him up and hold him tight, and he was instantly comforted. I could feel the warmth of his little body, snuggling up to mine. This was his home, this was where he belonged, and he needed to feel the security of it enveloping him. People say that babies recognize the smell and the voice of their mother from the time they have been inside her. Alexander certainly did! His little gurgles of happiness made me wonder how deeply he had missed me in the past weeks.

He did everything with me when he was not sleeping, and even then I would not leave him in a different room from me. I took my bath with him beside me in his cot, I prepared the food holding him in my arms, I talked to him all the time—sometimes in French, but mostly in English. He was my little angel, the most beautiful baby in the world, so warm and cuddly.

Alexander was born with tiny muscles in his arms and legs. I was fascinated and extremely proud. All the other babies in the hospital had pudgy limbs. He was different and very special! He was adorable with his darkish tan and his brown eyes like his mummy's, but shaped like those of his daddy with his square face and well-shaped nose.

"No one will ever harm you. Your mummy will always be there to protect you. You'll see, your life will be different. You will not be raised so that everyone can walk all over you!"

Like many mothers, I would talk about all kinds of things to my baby—my love for him, my hopes, and even my fears.

In the meantime, a shadow had fallen over my love for Hans-Peter, and I was beginning to have doubts about our relationship. At night Hans-Peter was totally uncooperative and always pretended he could not hear Alexander's cries. Most men do not realize what physical and emotional stress the first months can be for a woman. I could not really blame Hans-Peter—he was working, and I wasn't. However, when I did return to the office and had to deal with the long hours, I resented Hans-Peter's excuses.

I tried to organize my day to spend as much time with Alexander as possible. Since I was mostly working on the U.S. markets, my assistant held the fort in the morning and I was able to leave home as late as twelve o'clock.

The mornings still belonged to us, and they were sheer delight. Day by day Alexander was developing into a little bundle of cheerful babbles and chirps. He started to grab things, sit in his baby chair, and loudly express his joy, a dimple appearing on his right cheek. At noon the Portuguese nanny would take over until his daddy's return.

At first, I found it hard to reconnect with the futures markets, world events, and statistics, but slowly I settled into my new life, being a mummy in the morning and a career woman in the afternoon. There was little choice. Hans-Peter's grant would run out in September.

"What will you do now?" I queried.

"I'm not sure. You know, I think it would be difficult for me to become a doctor in this country."

"What do you mean?"

"Well, I want to become a specialist, and since I haven't been trained through the National Health Service, it won't be possible."

"But I thought this was the reason why you got yourself a grant in a teaching hospital in London."

"You just don't know the system! I haven't done my training here, and it will be practically impossible to open a practice."

I was aware of the problems in the National Health Service and of how difficult it was for doctors and nurses. This was often in the national press. I could not argue with Hans-Peter's views.

"Okay, but what do you intend to do then?" I asked.

"Go into the pharmaceutical industry. In any case, one earns much more money. I'm thinking of applying for a job in research or in marketing."

I was taken aback. Hans-Peter had always said that medicine was his vocation, and now he was considering the business world of marketing! I presumed his experience at the London teaching hospital must have disappointed him. This was why he had been so detached and evasive. At least he realized it now, and I had no doubt that, with his medical training and a Ph.D., he would find a good position.

Days went by. Hans-Peter mentioned nothing. Weeks went by, and I began to worry. I did not want to pressure him, as I knew how frustrating job hunting can be, but his silence was disturbing. The only interview I remember was in south London, and I wonder now whether Hans-Peter actually ever looked for work in England.

Finally, he announced, "Hoechst is offering me a marketing job here, and they want me to fly to Frankfurt to meet the big boss."

Two days later Hans-Peter returned from Frankfurt looking sheepish and ill at ease.

"So, how did it go?"

"Well, I was offered a job in Frankfurt in marketing."

"What do you mean? I thought the offer was for their London branch?"

"Yes, but . . . it would only be for two years, and the salary is much better in Germany."

Hans-Peter was still standing, and I could sense some embarrassment. He started pacing nervously around the sitting room, waiting for my reaction. I was thinking aloud:

"Of course, getting a contract with head office is always a good idea and a better assurance of promotion . . . "

I hardly had time to finish my sentence when Hans-Peter threw himself at me, enthusiastically kissing me.

"So you agree! That's fantastic!"

This was typical of Hans-Peter—extracting a positive answer before I had even expressed my views. He had his desires, and nothing would deter him from getting what he wanted. Hans-Peter was so happy. He was hugging and kissing me. Already he was making plans, and I could not stop his flow of enthusiasm.

So many things were disturbing me about Hans-Peter after only two years of marriage. But no one is perfect. I must have been irritating, too, with my meticulousness and perfectionism.

The more I understand Hans-Peter now, the more I wonder. Had he contacted Frankfurt directly? For months he had been quiet about his search. I can't remember much correspondence either. If Hoechst-Frankfurt had known about a London contract, why had they offered him something?

But I was optimistic and supportive. His career was my main concern. Two years was nothing if it meant establishing the basis for his future. Furthermore, this could offer me an immediate way out of my financial situation. I could sell my flat and pay off my debts. By the time we returned, the flat would be too small, in any case. Leaving London and abandoning my work did not thrill me, but it would allow me to dedicate all my time to Alexander.

On the other hand, I knew Frankfurt would be difficult for me. I could not speak a word of German and knew no one there. Hans-Peter did not have these problems when he came to London. As he spoke English fluently, he could easily integrate himself and meet people through work.

"The office will keep my job open until we come back. . . . "

"*Ja, ja.* Frankfurt wants me to start on January the third."

"So soon."

My life was again running ahead of me. I felt there was nothing I could do to determine its course anymore.

.   .   .

It was bitter cold and gray on our arrival in Frankfurt. Modern, impersonal tower blocks rose imposingly against the wintry sky, and occasional pedestrians, wrapped in their thick coats, hurried along the half-deserted streets. My first impression of "Bankfurt" was disheartening.

Every flat we were shown seemed sterile. Unable to understand what the estate agent was saying and irritated by Hans-Peter's blind enthusiasm for completely unsuitable flats, I chose one that seemed to be in the most central part of the town, next to the attractive Palm Garten. I felt as if I were in a movie, that this reality was not mine, that I would never actually live here.

We returned to London, and I sold my flat. The last of my London roots had disappeared. After the loading of the removal van, I walked back into the empty sitting room, with its high ceilings, cornices, warm-colored curtains . . . and a strange sensation overtook me. Everything had happened so quickly that there had been no time to think. A chapter was ending, and the unknown future was alarming. I was overcome with apprehension. As I closed the door I thought: *Catherine, you're closing the door on your freedom.* I was giving up my friends, my career, and, above all, London, the soul of my existence. So many memories belonged here. Instead of feeling excited, I felt hesitant.

Hans-Peter was already in the car and raring to go. He hooted impatiently, interrupting my thoughts. As usual, I controlled my emotions: *Don't think about it, Catherine. Go and join your husband. We'll soon be back....*

That day, as I ran down the stairs saying good-bye to London and all it held of me, I clung to the belief that we would be back as Hans-Peter had promised. I should not feel sorry for myself.

"So, are you coming?"

Hans-Peter's tone of voice was already different, nearly commanding. He was leaving a place that had become irrelevant to him, though he had settled into it with such vitality and conviction. My heart was cold that day. If only Hans-Peter had said, "Don't be sad. We'll soon be back."

But he could not say these words because, I am now convinced, he would have known them to have been a lie.

My heart and soul belonged to London. Leaving it was as if half my life were being torn away from me. But I was a young mother following my husband to the country of his choice for a limited period. There was nothing tragic in that. In fact, I learned to appreciate Germany, to speak its language and understand its ways.

But the harsh truth is that Germany has become the fortress in which my sons are held. And the jailers are those who operate the German legal system.

CHAPTER 5

Endings and Beginnings

We arrived in Frankfurt on December 29, 1985. Hans-Peter unlocked the door, and an empty, unwelcoming apartment stared back at us. We unpacked the cot, and I gently laid Alexander in it. He was fast asleep, and only the flickering of his eyelids indicated that he was dreaming. I could hear Hans-Peter's voice echoing along the empty corridor. He was already on the telephone to his mother, and I couldn't understand what they were talking about.

I felt abandoned and dispirited.

"If you weren't with me, Alexander, I'd be very lonely," I whispered, gently stroking the back of his head. He looked so beautiful and so vulnerable.

Hans-Peter walked into the room, interrupting my thoughts: "My sister and her husband are coming to spend New Year's Eve with us."

"Already?"

"Of course."

Antje and her husband arrived two days later. They were both loud and irrepressible. There was no room for privacy. Antje was quite an overwhelming person. She was six foot one, broad-shouldered, and fair-skinned. Her hair was so very short it looked like a punk haircut.

She was a lawyer, and so was her husband. When they talked with Hans-Peter in the sitting room, it sounded more like an argument than a conversation. I was forgotten, isolated in my new kitchen. From time to time I went to join them. Antje didn't notice me, and although her English was quite good, it was her husband who struggled with polite conversation to include me.

During dinner they continued their incessant conversation while I was serving and clearing away the plates. Antje liked to have the last word, as if she were still contesting a case in court. Even without understanding, I noticed the way she interrupted the others. Hans-Peter was her elder brother, their mother's favorite, and I could sense that their relationship was based on a mixture of rivalry and sibling complicity. Hans-Peter and Antje did not talk but barked at each other, yet if someone intervened to defend one of them, they would both immediately say: "It's none of your business."

I eyed this unfeminine woman with mistrust. Her forceful, abrasive manner seemed so uncompromising that I could not see how our relationship could improve, even with time. She focused her attention exclusively on Hans-Peter, ignoring her husband, who kindly tried to translate when he could and, after the meal, helped me tidy up.

This first reception on New Year's Eve was a foretaste of the future. Antje soon divorced this man (who seemed to me the only considerate person in the clan) to marry another lawyer. Her new husband, Klaus, was a giant. Both he and Antje were eventually to play a decisive role in Hans-Peter's family life and legal crusade. It would be Antje, later employed at the Ministry of Justice in Lower Saxony, who would support Hans-Peter when he abducted our children while Klaus built up the legal case to support it.

I had already met most of the family. Hans-Peter's younger brother, Hans-Jorg, shared a dental practice with their father and would later become politically involved with the CDU (Christian Democratic Union) Party. He, too, later married a lawyer, who practices in Bremen. Gundel, my mother-in-law, also came from a legal family. Her father was a judge who practiced in Hanover during the Second World War and later, I believe, in the small town of Verden, the family stronghold. Gundel's younger brother was the parliamentary spokesman of the CDU Party in Bremen and later its president, while Gundel's sister was married to a famous Bremen lawyer whose family felt it necessary to emigrate to Chile in the aftermath of the war.

The Volkmanns all seemed to make a living as lawyers, judges, or politicians. I had never studied law, and I had no specific political affiliations; the family's political affinities and connections did not worry me at the time.

Unsuspecting, I would visit Wilfred and Ute Monkmann, small landowners living near Verden. Wilfred was, and still is, a local judge who I believe used to practice in the town of Celle. His wife Ute is devoutly religious. Together they were later to aid and abet Hans-Peter in abducting my sons. Thanks to them, Hans-Peter would obtain an absurd psychologist's report to substantiate his claim on our sons in court.

It may sound far-fetched to group all these characters and their motives together, but without understanding the links between them, their respective functions and roles, it would be difficult to imagine how, in our civilized Western society, a mother could have her children stolen from her and be deprived of all human and legal rights to see them, know them, and show her love to them.

·   ·   ·

Life in Frankfurt was rather cheerless—for three months I saw almost no one but Hans-Peter and Alexander. Hans-Peter would set off in my car every morning to Hoechst, and Alexander and I would spend the day together. We could never venture very far, as we were always on foot, but almost every day we took walks in the Palm Garten nearby. Although he was only eight months old, and too young to be real company, seeing Alexander develop was a real joy.

Hans-Peter used to return home early at five-thirty, whistling a tune to announce his arrival, and I would throw myself at him, craving someone to communicate with. But he would usually head straight for Alexander to play with him. Then he would nibble something from the refrigerator and settle down in front of the television. His work remained a mystery. As I had been a businesswoman myself, it would have been interesting to hear about his commercial environment, but he never wanted to discuss it.

Hans-Peter had few relationships in the outside world, besides his elusive work colleagues and the ever-present family. One person outside his family who did call him was the friend with whom he had been on holiday when I met him. They used to spend hours on the telephone, eternally making plans (making plans seemed to be Hans-Peter's constant preoccupation) that were never carried out.

Fortunately, my friends from London kept in regular contact with me. But there was little I could tell them, besides Alexander's developments, and even the most involved mother realizes sooner or later that such information is of limited interest to others. They kept me up-to-date with all the latest events, and Leonard gave me regular rundowns on the market and the office gossip. These short moments soon became the highlight of my day. I missed them all so much, and hearing their voices on the telephone made me question my life with Hans-Peter. I felt a growing sense of unfulfillment, and being away from my environment and friends only emphasized this feeling.

Hans-Peter's mother phoned every day to inquire about her grandson, and soon she paid us a visit. Gundel was not a restrained grandmother. She always knew better than her daughter-in-law and constantly commented on how I fed Alexander, changed him, or acted with him. If Alexander cried, Gundel would order me not to go to him:

"Leave him, he's already too spoiled."

Her tone was so authoritative that I would not dare move. Then she would suddenly get up and rush to him:

"The poor child, he can't be left like that. . . . "

Was she just completely inconsistent, or was it her way of controlling me? I could not tell, and I decided it must be a combination of both.

When Hans-Peter was around, the two of them talked continually, and although I could now recognize a few words of German, I could not make much of their endless conversations. As soon as Alexander woke up from a nap, they rushed over to him. Gundel took the diapers from my hands, and Hans-Peter seized his plate, after double-checking that the food was at the right temperature. Alexander was their precious treasure. He belonged to them. I had given birth to their heir, and this was the extent of my role. I became a mere spectator in their handling of the most important part of my life: my son. Feeling barely tolerated, friendless, and debilitated, I did not know how to deal with this deteriorating situation.

When we went out, in my car, Hans-Peter would drive, Gundel beside him, Alexander and me in the back. We drove where they wanted, stopped where they wanted, and returned home when they decided they had had enough. I could not participate in their conversation, which, in any case, was hard to make out from the backseat. My only consolation was to steal moments with Alexander.

·   ·   ·

One evening in March 1986, Hans-Peter announced that Hoechst was sending us to the States, where he would attend a three-month training program. If he was being sent on such an expensive introductory tour, it obviously meant that his career was taking shape and that his boss appreciated him. This was wonderful. I was very pleased for him and looked forward to an interval away from his family.

It was great to be in New Jersey, in an environment where I could communicate with people. Alexander was still too young to walk, but the two of us used to set off without a care in the world, visiting tourist sights, forests, shopping malls. People were friendly, warm, and welcoming. I was alive again, and summer was coming!

Several weeks after we arrived Hans-Peter was sent across the United States to meet other Hoechst representatives, and Alexander and I accompanied him. The business trip turned out to be more of a holiday tour than a commercial one: three days in San Francisco, a two-day relaxed drive along the coastal road to Los Angeles, three days at Disneyland, five in Disney World, Florida, and two in Philadelphia. Hans-Peter contented himself with a one-day presence in the local offices, and off we went again.

After fifteen days of vacationing (with Alexander ecstatic over the Disney characters), we returned to New Jersey. Hans-Peter unenthusiastically went back to work, coming home at five to head for the tennis courts. I was very worried. I knew little about this industrial sector but couldn't imagine that the rules would be so different from those of the financial world I had known. Hans-Peter had just joined his company, and it seemed to me this was the time when he particularly needed to impress his colleagues. For the first time I realized how unmotivated and unsettled Hans-Peter was. Even if he was not career-oriented, I could not help feeling that he should at least assume the minimum of professional responsibilities for his family's sake.

Life in the United States in general was a breath of fresh air to me. We were on neutral territory, away from the clinging family, with no one to interfere in our lives. The thought of returning to Frankfurt and my in-laws was daunting. What about Hans-Peter pursuing a position in the States? When Alexander was older, I could easily help our finances by returning to work for

E. F. Hutton, which had its head office in New York. I tried out my idea, choosing my words carefully:

"You see, in Germany it would be impossible for me to work. I can't speak the language and haven't any business contacts. Here, there would be no problems."

"You don't need to work!"

"My savings are running out, your salary isn't yet enough for us all, and before we return to London . . . "

Hans-Peter was adamant. We wouldn't stay in the United States. He would miss his family. It was too far from home.

"But I'm away from my family if we live in Frankfurt," I ventured.

"No further than when you were living in London. In fact, France is much more accessible from Germany, as you don't have to cross the Channel. Don't worry, we'll move to Wiesbaden. You'll see, it's much nicer there!"

Hans-Peter no longer wished to discuss the subject.

.   .   .

And so we packed up and left America. As the plane landed in Frankfurt, I was overcome with sadness. I felt as if I were being handcuffed, pulled back into a cage. I walked disconsolately through the airport crowd with Alexander tightly locked in my arms, our cheeks together. I was haunted by the idea that we would never be free from the tight control of our extended family.

We reached our flat, and as soon as I had fed Alexander and put him to bed, I let myself collapse on my bed in despair. I cried tears of frustration, of utter powerlessness. The way Hans-Peter had dismissed all discussion had made me realize his resolve: I would never be allowed to work again. Hans-Peter was, I believe, subconsciously jealous of my achievements, my friends, and my interests.

"Catherine, I love you so much. I need you, and you make me so happy being here."

It was up to me to make him happy. "Just two years. You'll see how quickly the time will go," he had said, holding me in his

arms in the London flat. When we had married, he had known I
had a job and enjoyed my career. He had known London was
my chosen and cherished home. He had led me to understand
that he loved it too. At the time there had never been any indication that he disapproved of me working, or that we would not
live in London.

Hans-Peter was so different from the man I had met in
France. Or perhaps he was just the same and it was I who had
made the mistake in thinking he was someone he wasn't. I
found myself mothering two children—and one of them was
over thirty and suffocating me!

My London friends ventured a comment:

"You're simply unhappy with Hans-Peter. He isn't the man
you thought he was."

They were right, but "unhappiness" can be such a confusing
emotion and often difficult to admit. I blamed my environment,
the cold town, my inability to communicate, Gundel's interfer-
ence, and the social desert in which Hans-Peter was keeping me.
I felt alone and discarded. I began dreaming of freedom: the
freedom to be myself again.

.   .   .

Wiesbaden, to the west of Frankfurt, is a pretty town still carrying the vestiges of its elegant past. I enjoyed walking in its
peaceful streets, admiring the unspoiled houses, and imagining
the splendors of what had once been a fashionable spa. The
Kurpark was beautifully kept and welcoming. A Russian Orthodox church perched on the hilltop above it; I learned, curiously,
that a great-aunt of mine had been married there. The Russian
side of my family had always had a close affinity with Germany,
and several of my great-uncles had studied in its universities.

During my strolls with Alexander, little old ladies would
invitingly smile and talk to us. People seemed kind and friendly
here. It was only when Alexander and I ventured into the commercial center of the town that I realized that these polite ways
did not always prevail. In the 1980s, Wiesbaden still belonged

to the American zone, and there was a large army base outside the town. Some of the local population seemed to resent the fact that foreigners were still "occupying" their homeland.

At that time I mostly spoke in English to Alexander, and when people overheard me, they presumed I was a "Yank." On a few occasions I was taken aback by snide comments made by passers-by. I had never experienced any sort of racial hostility and began to become aware that the implications of the past were far more complex than I had thought. It was as if I were suddenly looking at history through the other end of the telescope, and I realized how narrow my vision had been.

.   .   .

I would have liked to discuss issues such as these, but there was no one to talk to. The elderly ladies I met on my walks were my only source of communication during my days with Alexander, and the only constructive thing I could do was to practice my few words of German and expand my vocabulary.

The days passed with nothing to differentiate one from the next until one morning I discovered I was pregnant again. That evening Hans-Peter welcomed the news, kissing me lavishly.

"Another baby! Maybe this time it'll be a girl."

He was overjoyed and immediately rushed to telephone his mother.

I had not planned this and was rather taken aback. Alexander was only fifteen months old, and the thought of another baby so soon frightened me: two small children, no help, a husband whose future seemed uncertain, and his mother now congratulating him on his achievement.

Hans-Peter was delighted, and in his usual fashion, he grabbed me by the arm to place me next to him and feel the stomach that would again become the object of his devotion. Catherine was once more only the carrier of Hans-Peter's child.

Tenderness, care, and attention are what a pregnant woman most longs for. Instead, Hans-Peter was taking control of me, and I could already hear in my mind Gundel's voice telling him, "I'm coming!"

At four months I almost lost Constantin. We were walking along the street when a sudden acute contraction forced me to sit on a bench. I was as white as a sheet and feeling dizzy. I was rushed to the hospital, the doctors operated immediately, and the baby was just saved.

I was still in the hospital when Gundel arrived, smiling and very happy with herself, Alexander in one hand, Hans-Peter in the other. The doctors had ordered me to stay in bed for the rest of the pregnancy. There was no question of getting a nanny for Alexander; Gundel would take care of him!

My pregnancy was particularly difficult, and I was taken back to the hospital twelve times. The rest of my days were spent lying down. I longed for my mother to come, but with Gundel around, the space was already occupied.

I could no longer be with Alexander. Gundel would bathe him, feed him, take him for walks, and completely monopolize him while the kitchen was mostly left to me. Both mother and son expected me to clear up.

When Gundel finally left, Antje appeared to help out, grudgingly, until I finally called for my mother to rescue me. I never liked to impose on others, nor to complain about my private life, but as far as I was concerned, this was an emergency!

My mother was shocked to see me living under these conditions. Hans-Peter, so used to being waited on, did not change any of his habits in my mother's presence. He would come home, nibble on a sandwich while my mother was still preparing dinner, and leave a trail of crumbs. He would then play with Alexander, overexcite him, and then push him away when he decided he was bored.

My poor mother would run around after him: "Hans-Peter, please, take a plate at least. . . . "

But he simply ignored her entreaties. Hans-Peter had a habit of waving his hand dismissively as if to say, *"Raus*—away with you."

The tension between my mother and Hans-Peter intensified, and I was caught in between: "Catherine, I'm not his maid. Nor are you!"

In the evening it was Hans-Peter who assailed me with complaints: "Your mother's getting on my nerves. She's constantly interfering. When's she leaving?"

I couldn't make him understand that his mother had done the same. In fact, she imposed far more. At least my mother did not take Alexander away for herself but was helping me—she did the shopping, the cooking, and relieved me of household duties.

All I could do was hold on to the new life I could feel growing inside me. Although my pregnancy was difficult, I knew the baby would be fine. It was another boy, and I tried to imagine how he would look—probably very like Alexander. The same cute face with its slanted eyes and sweet nose, and for the moment, no one could take him away from me! He felt more fragile and was much calmer than Alexander had been inside me.

I enjoyed being alone with my unborn child in the hospital. I would spend my days there endlessly talking to him, reading, and studying German out loud.

When it came to giving birth, I was luckier than I had been with Alexander. Hans-Peter was at work, and the doctor who looked after me was a woman. Immediately, she noticed how nervous I was.

"Why don't you have an epidural?" she asked after I explained how painful it had been the first time. "You won't feel a thing, and you'll enjoy the birth."

"My husband doesn't want me to have one. He says it's risky for the baby."

"Nonsense." At once she called an anesthetist.

"But my husband—"

She stayed beside me. Even when Hans-Peter arrived, she took no notice of his outstretched arms and gave the baby to me. Efficient and discerning, she had protected me, and this time I was not denied giving birth the way I wanted. It had lasted only two hours, and I had felt nothing. Instead of suffering, I stayed conscious and enjoyed the ultimate experience of childbirth. Hans-Peter rushed to my side to admire his second son and embrace his wife. This was the picture I had longed for—mother and father united with their newborn baby—and we shared this moment of bliss alone.

Spring had arrived in Wiesbaden, and Constantin was born on a sunny day, on May 17, 1987. He was adorable, much smaller than Alexander had been, and he looked very fragile. I was surprised at how different he was.

The next morning Gundel and Hans-Peter brought Alexander to meet his new brother. I hadn't seen Alexander for two days. Gundel had bought him new clothes. He smelled of her soap. He looked different, as if Gundel had in some way transformed him. I tried not to let myself be irritated by these little details, and I took Alexander in my arms. "So, what do you think?" I asked.

"He's so cute, Mummy."

Alexander was shyly examining tiny Constantin, wide-eyed, with a mixture of disbelief and excitement.

In June Hans-Peter suddenly abandoned his job at Hoechst, announcing that he did not enjoy the pharmaceutical industry after all. He was unemployed, and his proposed solution was to move to Verden, where the four of us would live in one room at his brother's house. As I had no savings left, I also had no independence. Catherine, the self-reliant woman, who once had made a living and owned a flat, had become a helpless wife who was totally dependent on her in-laws, the Volkmanns.

As I try to recount the failure of my marriage and my refusal to acknowledge this fact for a long time, I realize that I was gritting my teeth and clutching onto one last hope: Hans-Peter can't go on relying on other people, especially his mother. After all, he has two children and a wife and must realize that he cannot build his future on capricious whims. One doesn't just leave a job without another one, or at least without having a definite aim! He'll pull himself together and mature. It's just a phase.

CHAPTER 6

God and Verden

The only explanation I managed to extract from Hans-Peter was, "Marketing isn't for me. In any case, I hate flying, and the job would involve too many trips abroad."

I wondered why he hadn't considered this before joining. He went on, "I've decided that I'd actually much rather have a general medical practice."

There was not much I could say. Hans-Peter's mind was made up, and he had already left his job. He had no specific plans, though, and before he could open a practice, he still needed two years' hospital training. Furthermore, opening a practice required a lot of sacrifice and hard work to build up a list of patients. But Hans-Peter talked about it as if everything would just fall from the sky and be brought to him on a silver platter. My own resources had been depleted; the forty thousand pounds that I had when we left London had been the remains of my savings from ten years' work. By now there was practically nothing left.

It was July 1987. Alexander was two years old, Constantin nearly three months. Our furniture went into storage, and with a few suitcases, the four of us set off for the north, along the motorway. The Volkmanns' family home was in Verden, in the center of Lower Saxony. The nearest town was Bremen, from whence came, I once read, the Saxons who invaded England in 449. Verden, on the river Aller, is a small provincial town with a population of about twenty-five thousand. It prides itself on its eighteenth-century cathedral, a large horse auction, a small equestrian museum, and its own law court.

Gundel had arranged for us to live with Hans-Peter's brother Hans-Jorg, who lived alone in what had once been the family home. At the back the house joined onto the dental practice that he shared with his father. The welcome Hans-Jorg gave us was lukewarm, to say the least. But I could understand why—after all, the arrival of his chaotic elder brother, with wife, toddler, and baby in tow, was hardly a pretty sight!

Hans-Jorg decided from the outset that we would not infringe on his life and that he would closely guard his territory. Hans-Peter, the boys, and I were allocated one room on the first floor. The white-walled room was sparsely furnished with two single beds, a small wardrobe, and an old table. Old-fashioned turquoise tiles covered the walls of the shower room, which consisted of a small basin and a plastic shower cubicle. Opposite was Hans-Jorg's bedroom and bathroom. The other two bedrooms were cluttered with old furniture and junk that had accumulated over the years. Downstairs his drawing room, library, and study were kept in the most meticulous order, and it was clear that they were out of bounds to us.

Hans-Peter's thirty-year-old cot was quickly brought down from the attic by Gundel, who had been impatiently waiting for us to arrive. Immediately, she began reminiscing about her first-born:

"You were so cute, so blond, *mein Junge*. Now your son will sleep here!"

It was summer, and I should not have felt so cold. But I shivered as I realized the kind of life that lay ahead of me here: no music, no books, no photographs, no space . . . not even a tiny little corner where I could snuggle and feel comfortable. This was a barren island, firmly under Gundel's control.

It was gray outside and bleak inside. Gundel seemed to fill every room with her presence, attending to the organization of our lives. I could not fight it. There was nothing left for me to fight with, bound to a husband who had willingly imposed us upon his family.

Gundel and her husband lived only ten minutes away, and every morning she would drop in. She usually appeared when I was giving Constantin his bath:

"Catherine, you shouldn't use this soap. *Nein,* don't hold the baby this way. . . . "

Then, taking Alexander by the hand, she would vanish to do her shopping in the town, feed him lunch, and spend most of the afternoon with him.

Hans-Peter's father, who seemed to have an extensive network of contacts, made a phone call to some general and immediately secured a position for his son in the Bundeswehr. It was not long before Hans-Peter was admiring himself in the mirror dressed in his uniform and driving off to the army, leaving his little family anchored safely on his mother's territory.

My life was becoming a series of daily complications and worries. I was at the mercy of others for the simple necessities of daily life. Everything involved difficulties, from the careful bathing of the children in Hans-Jorg's bathroom to running behind Alexander to make sure he did not touch any of his uncle's belongings. Uncle Hans-Jorg was not very tolerant or keen on children, and it was obvious that our presence was as much an ordeal for him as it was for me.

Helpless, I slowly withdrew into a shell. Alexander was continually taken away and hidden from me, and there was nothing I could do to prevent it. My sole consolation was little Constantin, to whom I instinctively turned for affection. He was mine, and no one would ever take him away!

Unlike Alexander, Constantin was a peaceful and easy baby. He would wake up smiling and gurgle happily in his cot until he spotted me, when he would jump and squeal with joy. We would play on my bed and spend most of the mornings alone in our sterile room. I would invent stories for him and talk to him about the happy world we would have when we finally got our own home. . . .

Hans-Peter usually returned well before five, delighted by the lack of demands his job imposed on him. His dream was now to become a colonel. However, Hans-Peter's dream was viewed critically not only by me but also by others. I noticed Hans-Jorg frown as he watched Hans-Peter take books from the shelves without putting them back. Hans-Peter seemed immune to any remarks his brother might make and would merely shrug his shoulders. I also noticed that Hans-Jorg seemed to resent Gundel's blatant preference for Hans-Peter. Even in front of Hans-Jorg, she would slip money into Hans-Peter's trouser pocket, pampering her elder son and pandering to all of his whims.

The months went by. Suddenly, Gundel grew bored with Alexander:

"Catherine, I just can't take him with me every morning!"

I had never asked her to take care of Alexander. I said nothing. There was little point in poisoning our relationship further, and anyway, what mattered most was that I would be able to spend time with Alexander at last.

Life was restrictive and dull. Lunches and dinners with Hans-Jorg, Sundays at Gundel and Hans-Werner's, and constant encounters with the family members who would walk in or out of the house through the communicating doors leading to the practice. I had no privacy and felt as if I were being continuously checked up on.

"Hans-Peter, we just can't go on like this. We can't live in your brother's house, eat at your parents', and be financially dependent on them."

Hans-Peter dismissed the conversation and walked off. I followed him out.

"Why do you want to stay in the army? Is it so important to become a colonel?" I asked.

"If ever there is a war, I won't be sent to the front if I'm a colonel!"

His answer stunned me. Where had the great plans he had talked about in London vanished to? He hadn't liked the pharmaceutical industry, and now he was considering being an army doctor as long as he did not have to be in danger himself.

A short visit from my sister and her family that rainy August depressed me even more. I was an utterly different person from the vivacious, happy London career girl they had known. Here I was kowtowing to Hans-Peter's domineering family. No friends, dependent, with a husband who had no ambition and could not care for his family.

"You can't live like this, Catherine. You must do something. I hardly recognize you!"

I summoned up the courage to speak to Hans-Peter again:

"Okay, I'll look for a hospital job."

Halfheartedly, he started to send a few applications to the hospitals that would not distance him from his mother.

"Hans-Peter, you should apply to big towns: Berlin, Hamburg or Munich."

What I really meant to say was, *a place where we could reestablish a social life and feel free again. Here I can't even telephone my family or my friends without feeling I'm imposing. Hans-Peter, please, I'm suffocating here, alone with your family*—but I did not dare say any of this. I was too intimidated by his moodiness and too weakened by my own depression.

I had been approached by someone I knew in London who wanted to break into the German market with a famous brand of office diaries. Convincing prospective clients to invest in the futures and options markets had been part of my daily routine when I was a broker. Convincing a store to order diaries should not have been insurmountable! Yet my self-confidence had been so crushed that I asked Hans-Peter to go with me, incapable of confronting the store buyer by myself.

Although I was aware of how far I had strayed from the person I once was, I seemed unable to break the rhythm of my decline. I was permanently tired and would wake up in the mornings practically paralyzed at the thought of facing another day. The road that lay ahead seemed dark and unrelenting. I felt a prisoner of my fate, being swept along, powerless to resist.

Hans-Peter had not even noticed, and I myself was unaware that I was going through some sort of depression. The approach of winter did nothing to improve my prospects, and in despair I called for help. But my parents were abroad, and my sister was busy. Had I been allowed to escape for a week or two, maybe our future would have been entirely different.

As it was, I was on a sinking ship with nothing but my two beautiful boys to hang onto. The three of us would retire into a world of fantasy and dreams. By now I spoke mostly in French to them, sometimes in English; even this was a release, as I could express myself without being endlessly corrected. My sons were my only source of hope, but I longed for the company of an adult, a friend, a confidant.

It was on an autumn walk, seeking out the last ray of sunshine, that I met Ute Monkmann in a Verden street. I was pushing Constantin in his pram, holding Alexander by the hand, when a tall, dark woman, in her forties perhaps, came toward me with an engaging smile on her face:

"Are you Catherine, Hans-Peter Volkmann's wife?" she asked. I nodded.

"I'm Ute Monkmann. I heard Hans-Peter got married in England and that you've moved to Verden. And these are your children?"

A smile, a friendly face in this cold town, during these lonely days. . . .

"I don't expect you know anyone. Why don't you come over for tea at my place tomorrow?"

When I got home, I told Hans-Jorg about my chance encounter.

"Oh, yes, Ute Monkmann. She spoke to you?" He nodded approvingly. "They're very proper people. Her husband's a judge, and she is an aristocrat, born a von Klemp."

Obviously, this was some great achievement on my part!

Nobility impressed Hans-Jorg. In fact, he was a passionate, if not obsessed, genealogist, utterly absorbed in people's origins, names, and inheritances. It transpired that the von Klemps were a small, rural noble family. Hans-Jorg did extensive research after I met Ute and proudly announced some days later that thirteen generations ago they had been related!

Hans-Jorg's behavior began to intrigue me. He entertained strange men in his house. They would suddenly appear, greet me politely, and mysteriously disappear with Hans-Jorg. He belonged to a fraternity, and I presumed that his guests were fellow members, but I was never properly introduced to them.

But Hans-Jorg's affected, arrogant demeanor, the rigid, disdainful manner in which he usually addressed me, confining himself to the bare minimum of civilities, were that day transformed into a strange restlessness and excitement. Clearly, I would have to go for tea since it was such an honor to be invited by this family.

I realized that Hans-Jorg was hoping to be introduced to this "proper" couple through me. I learned that Ute's brother-in-law was a school friend of Hans-Peter's sister, Antje, and also a lawyer. More lawyers!

After the invitation to tea, we met again, and once a week Hans-Peter and I would go to dinner. Hans-Peter, too, was very keen on this new association.

The one recurrent theme that emerged from the small talk of our afternoon conversations, in half-broken English and German, were Ute's religious beliefs. Her opinion was always related to God. If I felt lonely, I would find solace in God. If I was unhappy, I should think of God. . . .

"Your belief will save you. God is our savior!"

"Yes, but it is difficult for me to adapt here. I'm used to having a job, living in a town that has lots going on, being surrounded by friends. We had such a different life in London. Here nothing belongs to me, and I don't even have my own home."

"You should pray and think positive thoughts. God will help you. Pray and you will see how your life will transform itself."

I had been baptized Catholic, spent my early school years in a convent, and eventually became Russian Orthodox, like my mother. I was attracted by the more spiritual and less structured dimension of the Orthodox teachings. Alexander and Constantin had also been baptized Russian Orthodox.

"Actually, there's a wonderful pastor in Bremen. He gives private seminars, and I go to them twice a week. Perhaps you'd like to come with me?"

That Ute was pressing me to meet her pastor made me feel uncomfortable. I believe in God, but I had my own religion and certainly could never become a fanatic. Praying was one thing, but I could hardly expect God to reestablish my finances!

Imprisoned in this small town, I began to realize what a ghastly mistake I had made. I should never have sold my flat and got rid of my base in London. Instead, I should have rented it out so that at least my children and I would have had a basic income. Now I could not even take a short break to Paris or London with the boys.

I tried to share some of my feelings with Ute; I thought maybe she would be able to help me regain some self-esteem. However, I soon saw that I was asking too much of her. She had no understanding of my frustrations and would answer any misgivings I had about life in Verden by saying:

"Here, the quality of life is excellent. The area's extremely green, with wonderful forests. There's an excellent market in Verden once a week, meetings at the church, and for the children it's much healthier to live away from towns."

Ute, who presented herself as a friend, as time went on became an intrinsic part of this extraordinary coalition, which would strip me of motherhood. She would protect Hans-Peter, provide the powerful support of her husband, a local judge, and house him and my sons on their remote property. This would become the fortress where Alexander and Constantin were put under "protection."

At the end of December 1987, Hans-Peter finally got a job, and we moved to Hamburg. I had hoped for Berlin, which I found a fascinating place. Berlin was a vibrant metropolis, and the very moment I had set foot in it for the first time I had sensed its energizing qualities. Artistic, intellectually avant-garde, Berlin is a city full of contradictions and has a special grandeur about it. Immersed in Eastern and Western cultures, it was then an island within the DDR (Communist East Germany); one really felt a part of history.

Hamburg, though, seemed a good second choice with its famous port (its "door to the world") and its Anglo-Saxon influence, seen in the white, London-style houses bordering the Alster Lake. Living there would be pleasant, and at last Hans-Peter and I could be on a more neutral territory, out of his family's pocket. I was convinced that there I could breathe again, reestablish a reasonable lifestyle, and teach my sons something more than just the way to Gundel's and Ute's houses.

My vitality returned, and I threw myself into the organization of our move with enthusiasm and determination. Most people in

Germany rent rather than buy, and flats would usually go on the very day the advertisement appeared in the papers. Being nearly two hours away and not knowing the geography of the town made flat hunting difficult. One place was especially nice, but Hans-Peter gave up easily: "There's already an offer on it."

"Well, make another one?"

We had no chance of grabbing it. Hans-Peter lacked the dynamism and the incentive to do so. He stared blankly at me as if I had just asked him to move a mountain.

"But, Hans-Peter, my German isn't really good enough. You must call them back."

For the past six months, we had been without a home and living out of a suitcase. I suddenly stood up and lifted the telephone. However good or bad my German, I was going to persuade the landlord—suddenly it seemed a matter of survival.

.   .   .

January 1988, Hamburg.

At last—our own space and privacy. I had become very active, unpacking, buying the essentials, getting the furniture out of storage—which needed as much dusting as I did! My mother could finally come and visit her daughter and grandsons in their own home. She stayed a couple of weeks, and together we started getting to know the center of Hamburg.

Our flat was in an old building, *Altbau,* in the university area of Hamburg, close to a museum and within walking distance of the center and the banks of the Alster Lake. Alexander first went to a kindergarten close by, and as soon as Constantin was old enough, they both started at the French Lycée. Hans-Peter and I were keen that they should be raised multilingually. They were fortunate to be exposed to three languages, and my mother even taught them a few words of Russian. Alexander and Constantin would be teenagers in the year 2000, and with this background, we hoped the doors of Europe would be open to them.

I had left the deep countryside with enormous relief. In Hamburg I learned to understand and appreciate Germany, and I made friends. I learned to speak German and continued to bring up my children. Paradoxically, as my state of mind improved, I saw my love for Hans-Peter disintegrate further.

January 1988 was a month during which I realized many dreams but destroyed others. Hans-Peter had promised two years in Germany and then we would return to London. Now he was adamant:

"I'll never leave Germany," and, "You shall not work."

Hans-Peter refused to acknowledge our precarious financial situation; as for our responsibility for two growing children and the happiness of his wife, these, in his mind, were even lesser considerations.

When I mustered the courage to point out that his sister Antje worked, although she had children who were even younger than ours, his only answer was, "That's different!"

"Why?"

No reply.

Chapter 7

The Breakup

Hamburg was less than two hours away from Verden, but it was home. Alexander, who was going to be three in May, was overjoyed when he discovered that Constantin and he had their own bedroom. The day we moved in, he ran around the flat, calling out from each room in excitement, and I realized then how he, too, had missed his own private territory where he could be alone with his mummy, his daddy, and his little brother.

We spent over four years in Hamburg. It was where Constantin learned to walk and talk, where Alexander will have his first childhood memories, and where I established our life as a family. The boys and I developed our daily life routine of school, play, and outings with friends. I entertained and soon spoke enough German to get by and allow me to make German friends.

Among these, there were two special ones. Amélie was my bosom friend and confidante. She was exceptionally warm, generous, and loyal. We spent a lot of time together, often with our children, who got on very well.

Joachim was my mentor, and he became nearly as indispensable as Leonard had been in London. Exactly eleven years older than me, Joachim came from an aristocratic family who had fled Prussia when it fell into the hands of the Communists. His life had been particularly difficult. His family had lost everything, and his widowed mother had raised three children on her own. Joachim had also spent most of his childhood days in various hospitals and clinics after he contracted an acute and unusual rheumatoid illness, which had left him slightly handicapped physically. Through the hardships of his illness and the influence of a Prussian education, he had developed strong principles and an iron will. He was now a banker and had never married.

We got on extremely well, and I respected and admired Joachim's intelligence and rational mind. He had a particular quality about him that he shared with Leonard. He was logical and detached, yet at the same time extremely sensitive.

Through him I began to understand Germany and appreciate its history. Joachim would talk about it with love and passion, yet his interpretation was lucid and at times critical. What had confused and sometimes even shocked me in the behavior of Hans-Peter's family became clearer, and I realized that their views were only representative of an isolated minority.

Germany is a young country. It was created only in 1871, when eighteen sovereign states of various sizes, with their mixture of regional characteristics and entirely different forms of domestic policies, were drawn together under one constitution and one foreign policy. But Bismarck's Germany lacked a uniting philosophical framework and the aspirations of a nation-state. Bismarck's concern was above all with the creation and expansion of a greater Prussia. Much of his foreign policy, or "realpolitik," was orchestrated to restrain the latent incompatibilities of the states from erupting into war. For two hundred years Germany had been more the victim than the instigator of the wars in Europe, but after Bismarck, Germany would lack moderation.

The light and dark sides of Bismarck's achievements and the tragic two wars that ensued have deeply marked Germany's short history. The mistakes of the past, aggravated by the destruction of values and traditions in the course of the brutal intellectual *Gleichschaltung* of the Nazi period, left an enormous social void in the aftermath of the Second World War. But because demolition had been so complete, the German people could now begin all over again, while trying to reconcile themselves with a belligerent past.

However, some *Länder,* or states, remained inward-looking and resistant to the new vision of Germany's role in Europe. Lower Saxony (created in November 1946 by the Allies), rural and provincial, was less flexible and adaptable to change, although even within this isolated environment my husband's family did appear especially conservative.

Gundel once showed me a photograph of her standing in a row of hundreds of other teenagers, all wearing white dresses, bows in their hairs and their right arms straight in the air:

"Ah, but those were the good days," she declared and quickly put the picture away. I had been stunned and somewhat frightened by her comment. I asked Joachim how he interpreted it. He sighed regretfully: "Maybe it was just the nostalgia of the youth, as any individual of her age would have."

"What do you make of Gundel's father with a huge scar on the right cheek?" I asked Joachim.

"Oh, that comes from his fraternity days. Fencing was part of the ritual of acceptance as a member of the club. In fact, a scar was a symbol of courage. There are still many fraternities in Germany, but most of them no longer abide by these strict rules. They're similar to those in American universities. The few that keep up the rigid, traditional codes of conduct are considered outdated and are often criticized."

At least Hans-Peter was not an active member of his fraternity, and although he had changed a great deal since we returned to Germany, he had never expressed radical, conservative views.

Meanwhile, he was uninterested in his job, constantly avoided household duties, and couldn't decide on career plans. He would swing between opening a practice, becoming a university professor, and returning to the pharmaceutical industry.

Since we had been living in Hamburg, our financial situation had not improved. Joachim would consistently pick up the tab at the restaurants where we ate together, and my mother chipped in as well. She had been heartbroken when she saw me and offered to pay for a cleaning woman to help in the house once a week. But Hans-Peter continued to accept his mother's handouts, which she discreetly slid into his hand or trouser pocket during the regular, tedious visits we made to Verden on Sundays. He sold my car and bought an old diesel instead, yet he still objected to the idea of my working.

By the autumn of 1991 things were getting worse at home. Hans-Peter complained about his boss, his colleagues, and the nature of his work. More unpaid bills piled up on his desk: he forbade me to touch them, dismissing me and locking the door of the dining room, which he had turned into his study. We even received a summons.

"Hans-Peter, we can't go on this way. We must pay the bills!"

Without Hans-Peter's consent, I finally decided to take a part-time job in an interior design shop. I thought it would restore my self-confidence. The children were now both attending the French Lycée, and I felt I should actively strive to improve our situation, even if Hans-Peter disapproved.

My working full-time was dismissed as "criminal." The boys could not be picked up from school by a babysitter! Instead, Hans-Peter suggested applying to be on the Hamburg list for emergency night call, to improve our income.

A few days later, after a long telephone conversation with his mother, Hans-Peter announced, "I have been selected for the Hamburg area of Saint Georg. There are a lot of drug dealers and sleazy clubs around there, but my mother said I don't have to do the night calls. She'll send me the eight hundred marks instead."

During one of my rare trips to London, I confided in Leonard.

"Help him find a practice in London. It seems the only logical solution for both of you," he said.

But Hans-Peter still refused to leave the fatherland—to him, his "motherland." Joachim, who had observed for months Hans-Peter's untidy ways and lack of discipline, tried to come to my rescue and suggested Berlin. For a moment there was hope, and Joachim drove us to the capital he knew and loved, in search of a suitable practice. Hans-Peter remained undecided. Finally, he declared that he would only consider a practice in Hamburg. Berlin was too far.

Then, in December 1991, Hans-Peter suddenly gave up his job at the hospital. As if a brick had fallen on my head, I woke up to the realization that I no longer respected him. As abruptly as I had fallen in love, I fell out of love.

Hans-Peter's version was that he gave in his notice because he needed a year's experience in a general medical practice before being qualified to open his own.

For a few weeks he looked in vain for a position in Hamburg; then Hans-Peter rushed off to his parents.

This permanent recourse to his family for help exasperated me. Hans-Peter later commented that I was obviously jealous. But how could I tell my husband that as long as his parents gave in to his whims he would never get on?

His father, Hans-Werner, had picked up the phone, and a position was instantly found for his son in a large practice in Verden. Hans-Peter was now back in his mother's nest where he had always belonged. He stayed there during the week and came to us at weekends. With the move from England back to Germany, then from the south to the north, and now back to

Verden, Hans-Peter had finally returned home. Now he only needed to convince us to join him. I knew that sooner or later he would play on my sympathy, and that financial considerations would be part of the justification.

However, I had adapted to life in Hamburg. The children were settled at school and happy. They had friends, and so did I. I had regained my self-confidence, but I worried about my relationship with the man I no longer loved.

How could I make Hans-Peter understand that I had given him all I had, followed him everywhere, accepted all his whims, and that there was nothing left for me to give? Yet I knew now that Hans-Peter could not change, and somewhere inside me, I felt very sad about it—for him, for me, but more for our children.

One evening, as the children slept, I sat at my desk in the silence and put my thoughts on paper. I went back step by step, through the years we had spent together, apologizing and trying to explain why our love had turned to failure. I concluded:

"This is a sad love story. A love story between two people who were probably too different from the start, two people who were in different stages of their development and who had different needs. We never reached an equilibrium, we never lived in peace. I am too tired now—the fight has been too long, too intense. I need peace. . . . "

I did not want to hurt Hans-Peter. I still felt protective toward him. I thought he would understand and forgive me for having failed to love him in the way he wanted. But I should have stayed silent; I should have known that written words remain engraved forever. What I hoped would be the start of a reasoned and adult discussion, Hans-Peter saw as an attack.

Three years earlier we had had a long discussion, but Hans-Peter had dismissed my words, pretending they had never been spoken, closing his eyes to the blunt reality. But this time my decision was made, and it was final. He could no longer appeal to me on grounds of pity.

Hans-Peter arrived for the weekend, and I dragged him out to a restaurant: we needed to talk in peace away from the boys. He kept changing the subject. He was drawing up new plans for our future. I couldn't listen to his endless projects any longer. I had to explain rationally and put emotions aside.

"Hans-Peter, we can't go around in circles anymore. For the past six years you've been trying to settle down in your life and in your job. For the past three years we've talked about it. Yet you still change your mind continually: London, Berlin, Hamburg, and now you're in Verden. It's not right for the children. They need stability, and so do I."

"So, what will you do?"

"I want to separate. I'll probably return to London since I'll have to go back to work. My German is not fluent enough to get a proper position here. Besides, even if I could stay in Germany, I'd have to move to Frankfurt to get a job in my field. The boys can continue their French schooling at the Lycée in London and come to visit you during the holidays."

"Hans-Peter, I won't take the children away from you. You can come to visit them in London, too, if you wish. They are *our* children. They have nothing to do with our personal problems. Our marriage has failed, and it would be useless to go on pretending. You, too, obviously feel uncomfortable in our relationship if you need to ask me all the time whether I still love you. It would be best for all of us, and the children need stability," I tried to reassure him calmly.

Hans-Peter left the next afternoon to go home to his mother, and for two days there was silence. The boys and I returned to our normal daily routine. But by Wednesday, Hans-Peter was back home, as if nothing had happened. We had another long discussion that evening, and I hoped that this time Hans-Peter would understand. The next morning he left early for Verden, and on Friday he phoned to say he would be arriving at six.

"Hans-Peter, I don't really think this is a good idea. Let's just talk on the telephone."

Hans-Peter started pleading with me.

"I need you. You can't leave me. . . . "

I found myself explaining everything all over again, but after an hour of useless talk I finally got off the phone in frustration and anger. For a while I heard nothing more, and I felt relieved.

The boys had been used to Hans-Peter being away during the week and did not query his absence. Our life settled down peacefully. Hans-Peter had never been keen on socializing, but now we invited their friends over in the afternoon, and some evenings I would go out with my friends. I started to enjoy Hamburg. Had it been possible for me to obtain a job in finance, I would have considered staying.

At least, that is, until I received the first call from God. It was Ute, telephoning to offer help and advice. She had heard through Hans-Peter that I wanted to leave him.

"Catherine, I just can't believe it. You're both such kind and wonderful people. You shouldn't make a rushed decision like this. You're probably just going through a phase and should pray for God's guidance. What about going to see this pastor I told you about in Bremen? He would be able to help you both. . . . "

"Ute, this is not a phase. It has been a preoccupation for the last three years. It is not a question relating to believing in God: our personalities are simply incompatible. And do tell Hans-Peter to call me if he wants to talk to me."

"Oh, but Hans-Peter didn't ask me to call you. He doesn't even know about it. I just like you both so much and think it would be such a pity for you to part. I would like to talk to you, as I'm sure I can help in bringing you back together. You know, God . . . "

I began to realize what was happening in Verden. Hans-Peter was looking for help and support. His tough wife, the City "career" woman, was leaving him—a husband who adored her. Ute's beliefs would guide me back on the right road.

"Ute, thank you very much, but this is really not necessary."

A few days later her husband Wilfred was on the telephone, trying to rescue the situation by interfering in our private lives. His approach was more down to earth:

"Catherine, I really understand what you're going through. You're just frustrated. Hans-Peter is still unsettled in his career. I know he is rather young and immature, but this is exactly why you should be reasonable and lenient with him. You know, I also went through a crisis a few years ago when I fell in love with another woman. I even considered leaving Ute, but thank God I didn't. . . . "

"But I'm not in love with anybody else!"

"Yes, of course . . . I only mentioned my experience as an example in the sense that I had thought of breaking up my marriage. Catherine, you must think of Hans-Peter and the children too. . . . "

"Thank you, Wilfred . . . Good-bye."

I had remained polite with these people—too polite, since I felt their intervention was distasteful and obstructive. Hans-Peter had obviously spent his evenings in their house seeking their help. Had he shown them and his family my private letter to him?

Ute did not abandon her rescue mission. She called again. This time she suggested coming to see me in Hamburg. I was angry at Hans-Peter's exposure of my privacy and answered her curtly, "Thank you, but I'd rather be alone. I've made up my mind, and it is really not necessary for you to come to Hamburg."

A week or two of silence followed. I began to draw up my plans for the move to London: I needed to find a job, a flat, and a place at the Lycée for the boys. This was a tall order: we were in the midst of the worst recession since the Big Crash of 1929. E. F. Hutton had been taken over, commodities were no longer the order of the day, and I had not worked for six years. My London friends were skeptical about the possibility of finding a job at the age of thirty-nine, given the current market conditions. But I was determined and had always been very energetic; it had taken me three years to make a decision, and now that I had, nothing would stop me. Since I did not want to leave Hamburg until the end of the school year so that the children would have the least disruption possible, I had more than five months to organize the move. I felt I could do it.

But Hans-Peter allowed me only two and a half weeks during the February school break, and I saw that he would not give me a second opportunity. He came to pick up Alexander and Constantin and take them to his mother in Verden. Walking down the stairs, he sneered at me, "You'll see, your friends won't be there for you after six years. You'll never get a job!"

Hans-Peter was wrong. All my friends rallied around me to help. Even my City contacts went out of their way to arrange interviews and introduce me to companies where there might be openings. It was very heartening. Suddenly I felt strong and self-confident, and I must have radiated this energy, because I managed to get two offers in the bond brokerage business. The only problem was that they wanted me to start immediately, and I was unwilling to move in the middle of the school term. Finally, we agreed: I would start at the end of April. Now I needed a flat and two places at the Lycée. I had less than a week.

By coincidence, I bumped into my old headmaster, who had come by to pick up his mail at half-term. He was delighted to see me after so many years and introduced me to the director of the primary classes. But he was unhelpful, totally unsympathetic to my problems:

"Mrs. Volkmann, do you think I can find a space for your two boys, just like that, in the middle of the school year? Some people would offer me money but even that will not change matters."

"Well, I certainly don't have any money to offer. . . . "

Phone calls to the director of the Hamburg Lycée, mobilization of all concerned—and a place for Alexander was secured at the École Française in Brook Green. More phone calls, more running around, and just two days before I was due back, a flat was found. I had managed! Exhausted, but in seventh heaven, I tried to prepare myself for the next big hurdle.

Hans-Peter and the boys were in the arrival lounge at Hamburg airport. The children rushed to greet me; Hans-Peter stood behind them with an anxious expression. He had hoped to see me return with my tail between my legs, admitting failure. We drove home in silence. After the boys ran off to their bedrooms to open their London presents, he asked in English:

"So, how did it go?"

We were sitting in the kitchen, a very large and beautiful room, with original tiles and an authentic coal oven.

"Well, I found a job."

"What type of job?"

"Bond broker."

"So, it means you'll be working late and the boys will be alone with a sitter."

"Not at all. The boys' school finishes just before four and the bond business works on continental hours. I'll be home by five-thirty."

"But have you got a place at the Lycée?"

"At the French school. It's a small, really cute school—in fact, it will be a much easier transition for Alexander before going to the Lycée."

"And what about Constantin then?"

"They will take him at the Lycée next year, but for this term I've enrolled him in the Knightsbridge Kindergarten."

"But that must be ridiculously expensive."

"I've sold my watch to pay for it."

"And where will you live?"

"I've found a flat within walking distance of the kinder-garten."

"And who'll take care of the children until you get home? She must be German. I want my sons to speak German with some-one."

"I'll find someone, and after the summer holidays I thought Isabella might want to come to London. She's often mentioned wanting to go abroad after her A levels."

"Ah, Isabella," Hans-Peter said pensively.

Isabella was a seventeen-year-old who came to babysit after we had moved to Hamburg. She had known Constantin as a baby. The boys loved her, and she had developed a teenager's crush on Hans-Peter.

Hans-Peter was silent, slowly absorbing this information. His last hope had just been crushed, and he no longer knew how to react. I went on:

"But, Hans-Peter, you have to promise me one thing: we must never, ever fight. That is the most horrible thing about separations. People sometimes become bitter with each other, and it's the children who pay the ultimate price."

"I promise."

I offered him my hand, and we shook on it. Hans-Peter said good-bye to the boys and left for Verden.

.   .   .

A week later everything changed. Hans-Peter phoned. An angry voice dryly announced:

"So, if you've decided to move to London with the boys, we should draw up a contract. I've got a lawyer here in Verden, and I suggest you get yourself one as well."

There was not even the possibility of a conversation. In icy tones Hans-Peter said good-bye and hung up. He had been so bitter that he had not even been interested in hearing about the boys' day. What was he up to? I began to be a little nervous.

Joachim gave me the name of a lawyer, and I went to see him the next day. Eight years of marriage, two children, and I was answering to statistics:

"How much does your husband earn? You cannot be expected to support the children on your own. Your husband must give them and you financial support."

I had found out in the meantime that the practice where Hans-Peter was employed in Verden had offered him a partnership, but he had refused and gone back to work for the Bundeswehr.

My lawyer thought that Hans-Peter could be trying to demonstrate smaller earnings so as to avoid paying alimony. He said, "You came into the marriage with money, a car, you gave up your career, and are now eight years older. We'll have to fight this. I don't like your husband's attitude."

The tone of my lawyer frightened me. I did not want to face Hans-Peter's temper. I wanted everything to remain civilized, as he had promised. Joachim advised me:

"Catherine, don't be an idiot. You've made this mistake once before, after your first marriage. But you were young and fell on your feet. Now you have children and responsibilities toward them."

But as usual in situations like this, I listened to no one—only to my desire to avoid confrontation at all costs. But a letter had already been sent by my lawyer in answer to Hans-Peter's offer of $580 maintenance a month for the two children. The letter stressed the fact that if Hans-Peter earned little, it was only due to his unwillingness to work. He was a qualified doctor, with a Ph.D., and had even had the possibility of well-paid night calls, which he had immediately turned down. The next day Hans-Peter stormed into our Hamburg flat.

"What the hell are you doing to me? You're walking out of my life, taking my children, and now your lawyer is implying I'm lazy and not offering them enough support." He leaned against the oven. His face was red, and his whole body was shaking with rage. I felt frightened. Then he put his hands in his empty trouser pockets, turned them inside out, and yelled:

"Look. *Ich habe kein Geld!* (I have no money!)"

Just at that moment Alexander, who had heard his father's voice down the corridor, walked into the kitchen, followed by Constantin. At the sight of his father standing facing them and screaming furiously, he rushed out like a terrified little dog to seek refuge in his bedroom. Constantin ran behind him. I was horrified—even more horrified when I saw that Hans-Peter hadn't even noticed and continued screaming:

"I'm nothing. I have nothing—nothing."

I was speechless.

Finally, he stormed out, running down the stairs of the building, still screaming that he had no money. His reaction was intimidating, but the anger that was brewing inside me was such that I managed to reply frostily, "Your problem is that you never want to do any work."

This was the last image I have of our life together. The breakdown of eight years of marriage had ended on a bitter note. I had wanted to remain civil—we needed to, for the children's sake. But from that day on Hans-Peter never ceased to be angry.

I tried to soothe the situation and calm his fury by abandoning my lawyer and accepting all his terms. Even surviving with the minimum legal child support was better than venturing into bitter litigation—for the sake of our sons, I wanted a truce. My lawyer told me I was mad. Joachim tried to talk to me:

"Catherine, Hans-Peter is avoiding his responsibilities. If he joined the army rather than accept that offer of a partnership, his reasons are obvious. You have put a lot into this marriage, and you will be coming back to London with nothing and two boys to feed. Think of the future. You're thirty-nine. Don't leave before you settle everything. Be careful. . . . "

"Oh, Hans-Peter won't be able to settle this problem. It's just the way he is. But I can't take it anymore. I've waited too long, and I can't fight against him. I'll be okay with the boys, and hopefully Hans-Peter's anger will calm down in time."

"You're making a mistake, and I'm afraid you may regret it later."

.   .   .

But my judgment had been right: no lawyer, no more screaming. Hans-Peter practically never called. The storm was over. I later came to believe that Hans-Peter, surrounded by his family and the Monkmanns (all lawyers and a judge), was already embarking on his plan, setting legal traps and examining loopholes. Only later would I realize how right Joachim had been.

Two weeks before the children and I were due to leave, Hans-Peter came to pick up the boys and take them to Verden while I organized the two sets of moves, looked for a new tenant for the flat, paid off all the bills, packed his things and mine . . . I had no time to think. Amélie arranged a farewell dinner, and when all was ready, I drove to Verden to pick up the boys. But first, Hans-Peter wanted to meet me at a notary's to sign our contract. My lawyer had seen the initial draft:

"Don't sign it. It's a very bad deal for you, and I can smell a rat," he had told me.

The children were at Gundel and Hans-Werner's, and I knew Hans-Peter would not allow me to take them before we had signed. At 10:00 A.M. I met him in the waiting room. He looked tense and did not look at me when I said hello.

A young man, who said he used to be at school with Hans-Peter, admitted us to his office. We sat down, and he proceeded to read through a long document in German. He spoke slowly so that I could understand. However, German legal language is very complicated, and there were many words that were unknown to me. But the crucial paragraph was there, and I felt I could relax:

> The custody of the mutual children . . . shall be transferred to Ms. Volkmann. Dr. Volkmann expressly declares his consent to Ms. Volkmann moving with the mutual children to London, England, to take up residence there. . . . Until a court ruling on custody of the mutual children, Dr. Volkmann provides Ms. Volkmann with authorization to represent the children in legal relations, in legal transactions of daily life, and in other transactions. . . . The parties agree that the children shall live with their father for at least two months (per annum).

The later part dealt with the maintenance Hans-Peter and I had agreed on. The young man asked us to sign and date the last page. We shook hands and left.

Hans-Peter and I drove to his parents' house. He sat in silence, staring straight ahead of him. His bitterness was so intense that I could feel the vibrations emanating from his body.

The children were ready to go.

"I'll see you in two and a half months," Gundel said, kissing Alexander, and the three of us drove off waving good-bye.

"That's it. I'll never have to set foot in Verden again." I was so happy, I felt overjoyed. However, I had a strange feeling. Hans-Peter's tense attitude at the notary's office and his mother's ironic expression when we parted were rather disturbing. *Oh, well, in time Hans-Peter will quiet down,* I thought. He was bitter now and in shock, and this was in keeping with his personality. But he loved his boys, and for their sake would soon reestablish a civil relationship with me.

Next morning we were en route to our new lives—and freedom. I had finally freed myself from the Volkmanns' domination.

Freedom tasted so sweet. . . .

CHAPTER 8

The Conspiracy

The contract I had signed before leaving was notarized several days after I left Verden. When I received my copy a few weeks after my arrival in London, I simply put it in a drawer. It was only two years later when I took it out and carefully deciphered it with the help of a dictionary that I got a surprise. The contract stated that our "first place of habitual residence was in the Federal Republic of Germany"—not only did we first live in London, but Alexander was born here! I had not noticed this when the contract was read aloud in the notary's office in April 1992; it is surprising that I hadn't, as this was stated in simple German.

But when I received the contract, it never occurred to me that I should check it for legal catches. In any event, at that time I had other things on my mind.

Alexander, now seven, was falling behind at school. The academic level in the French school in London was much higher than at the Hamburg school, and he needed to catch up to be admitted into the next grade. Constantin, on the other hand, had adapted well at the English kindergarten. Language was not a barrier for him. This was the way I, too, had learned French. My mother had spoken only Russian to me in my childhood, but within a few months at a French school I was fluent. Most children have this amazing ability. Hans-Peter used to say that in order to speak a language without an accent it should be learned before the age of seven, when the vocal muscles are formed to produce only specific tones. I was so glad both boys would have the opportunity to be fluent in three important European languages.

What was amazing was to watch how Alexander immediately started talking in English while Constantin refused to say a word for several months—at least in front of me! Constantin did not like to fail. He needed to feel he had mastered the language before he would speak in it. It became our little joke, and I would tease him about it, until one day he forgot, and I overheard him playing with his English friend:

"Don't touch this. It belongs to my brother."

I peeped through the door of his bedroom and smiled. Constantin looked back at me with a mischievous expression in his eyes. He was very sweet—but I knew proud Constantin wouldn't appreciate me kissing him then. He and I had a special code—we understood each other completely. A look was enough. We accepted and respected each other and were particularly close. Constantin and I belonged to each other, and we had a harmonious relationship. For him, living in London meant having Mummy more to himself, and he never questioned the separation.

Alexander, however, seemed more concerned, and while he did not mention it at first, on his return from the first summer holiday with his father he asked me: "Mummy, tell me. Why doesn't Daddy live with us in London?"

I explained as simply as I could that grown-ups sometimes decide that they want to live separately, but it certainly never changes their love for their children.

"Mummy and Daddy will always love you." He trotted off and didn't ask much more for a while.

From time to time, Hans-Peter would phone to talk to the boys. He always addressed me in German. This had been a new development; it began about a year before, when Hans-Peter started to speak to me systematically in German and demanded that I answer in it. This deeply frustrated me since I was unable to express myself properly and often made grammatical mistakes (I never had time to study the language except for introductory self-teaching), and Hans-Peter would constantly correct me. But, as if he had put a barrier between us, he would speak English only when the conversation concerned us personally— which had been more and more rarely.

My new life in London, however, had brought me different challenges, which were of more concern to me now. During my six years of absence the City had changed dramatically: Big Bang, the Crash, takeovers, mergers, faxes, computers, "global" markets . . . I felt as if I had landed in a totally different world to which I had to readapt quickly, and at my age it was tough. But what was tougher still was the new character of the financial world. Traders were rude, and often aggressive—survival was the name of the game, and money its only aim.

My boss was not much more than half my age, and in this environment no one was anxious to help me out. I was no longer the little queen with a private assistant. Generalists were out and private clients' business practically extinguished. The new era consisted of specialists and computers, and I had no idea how to use one.

I had to learn fast. For me, too, it was a question of survival. Not in order to make big money as fast as possible, but to survive within my new life: to see to the children's needs, give them a happy home, ensure their good results at school, and satisfy the au pairs. Otherwise, I knew I would be in danger.

Brigit, our German au pair girl, would take the boys to school in the mornings, pick them up in the afternoons, and play with them until I returned home. Tini was always the first one to greet me. He would run up the stairs of our basement flat with squeaks of joy; Alexander would follow, and the two of them would start talking at once, each telling me enthusiastically about his day. The arrangements worked well, although it was quite exhausting!

The bond markets opened very early in the morning, which meant waking up before dawn. Trading was draining, and I had to learn the discipline of working again. Sunday mornings were often dedicated to supermarket shopping and the rest of the weekends to the children, who were still young and needed to be constantly entertained.

But in the circumstances, we managed well. The children liked Brigit, and I got on well with her, too. As any working mother knows, however, dealings with au pairs are often difficult, as they are neither guests nor staff. I was sad when Brigit eventually left. The children, however, were overjoyed that Isabella would come and live with us after their first summer holiday in Verden.

Isabella arrived in London in September 1992 for the start of the new term. Our arrangement was different. She was not employed as an au pair. In fact, this made matters much more difficult for me since she was, like Hans-Peter, extremely disorderly, and I would spend most of my time tidying after her and the children to keep our cramped flat in a livable condition. With the children, however, Isabella was wonderful, and the three of them would play joyfully and laugh as I was tidying up. They loved being together, and it was a pleasure to see the children so happy.

Isabella walked them to the Lycée (they both attended now), which was ten minutes away, and picked them up at 3:45 P.M.

She would then supervise Alexander's homework, and I checked it on my return from the office. She spoke French fluently and so was able to help him. My philosophy was that he should learn to manage as much as he could on his own. But unlike Constantin, Alexander was not very studious, and like most boys of his age, he preferred to play. His early results showed that he needed to work harder, and unfortunately, Isabella was a little too young and slack to discipline him.

Isabella seemed to suffer from the same symptoms as Hans-Peter. She was constantly tired and unprepared to help with the housework, and that first year was very trying for me. My financial situation was also difficult. The rent was very high in relation to my income, but the flat was close to the school and had a wonderful communal garden where the children could play with their friends.

After six months Isabella became bored. She was now eighteen and had decided that London offered many better distractions than Alexander and Constantin. She started complaining about her monotonous day and wanted to find a job to occupy her while the boys were at school. I approached a friend and eventually convinced him to employ her part-time in the City.

Soon Isabella's life became very busy as she started going out in the evening with the young men she had met in the office. I had to organize my outings according to her schedule. She was very attractive, so at her age this was probably inevitable. However, my mother was not of the same opinion. She had recently come to stay with friends in London and warned me: "Katia, I don't like your Isabella. She only plays with the children, goes out, never helps you, and expects you to care for her. She's too young, too self-centered, and I find her rather false. I wouldn't trust her if I were you."

My mother was always intuitive, and I should have acted on her advice on the day when I came home earlier than expected and found Isabella on the phone to Hans-Peter. She was happily talking to him in German as if she were mistress of the house.

She continued her conversation oblivious to my presence, then hung up.

"Was that Hans-Peter?" I asked, surprised.

"*Ja.* I was just telling him about the boys. He says hello."

I later found they used to talk to each other regularly—Isabella was Hans-Peter's London agent. There was nothing specific for me to hide, but Hans-Peter was inquiring about the school, his sons' well-being, my work, and my social life. Isabella had always been in awe of Hans-Peter, and I now believe that he took advantage of this to collect any useful information that might later help him devise his supreme plan in case I did not return to Germany. Hans-Peter was still holding on to a vague hope that I might fail in London and come back to him.

However, none of these details raised my suspicions then. I simply found it irritating that Isabella should be talking about my private life behind my back. But when she began to invite her friends around in the evening, I became annoyed. She had begun to treat the apartment as her own, as if I had no say in the matter. Then one day her best friend appeared from Germany—Isabella having told her that, since the children were away on their holiday, she could stay here. I finally reacted:

"Isabella, don't you think you could ask me first? After all, this is my flat, and I think it is just normal courtesy to ask."

Unknown to me, this eighteen-year-old would provide Hans-Peter with the testimony he had longed for. "Catherine was only interested in her work and keeping the flat tidy. . . . She was never there for Alexander's homework, and I had to do it with him. . . . She regularly went out in the evenings."

In the meantime, Hans-Peter had come to London for a weekend in May 1993 with his friend, Judge Monkmann. When I returned home from work, the two of them were in my sitting room drinking tea with Isabella, and I had a most awkward feeling—as if they had come for an official examination and I was the visitor in my own flat. Hans-Peter made a few phone calls, Isabella poured more tea, and they left.

"Katia, I don't like the smell of this. Why is Hans-Peter coming with a judge? You have to get divorced and protect yourself."

Mother was always too suspicious. Hans-Peter still seemed antagonistic toward me, and I didn't feel this was the right moment to anger him further. In a few months he might find a new girlfriend and become better disposed to the final legal break.

.　　.　　.

Alexander was eight years old and Constantin six when the new nanny started with us. Isabella remained in London and was still employed at my friend's office, but she contacted me on only a few occasions.

Masha was Russian, from a small town east of Moscow. She was the antithesis of Isabella: forty-seven years old, unmarried, austere. After my experience of the previous year, I had decided I wanted someone to help me with the organization of the house rather than with the children. Masha would only take them to school and pick them up; I would supervise their homework. The boys were now more responsible and no longer required full attention, only the presence of an adult. They usually played in their bedrooms or in the garden with our new neighbor.

I had recently been offered a good job at an excellent German bank and bought a three-bedroom flat with direct access to a large communal garden. Masha had her own room and shower. Most of the rooms were spacious, and the boys could run in the corridor to their hearts' content.

The 1993 school year had started on a very happy note. The boys had their friends, and Constantin was particularly pleased because his best friend lived in the house opposite ours. Alexander's school reports had improved amazingly, and he had a new friend in the boy who lived in the flat above ours.

I was still under pressure with my busy days, but since Masha took care of the washing, cooking, and cleaning, I was entirely free for my boys from the moment I came home. We usually sat in our large kitchen to do the homework. Constantin was a terribly keen student, and as soon as I opened the entrance door, he would come with his satchel:

"Mummy, let's do the homework."

Sometimes he even did it on his own before my return, to surprise me. Alexander, on the other hand, was irregular, and it all depended on his mood of the day. Our weekends were usually full of activity: movies, roller-blading, swimming, entertaining their friends, visiting them. . . . If the first year was a little unsettled, adapting to a new environment and living in a flat that was too small for four people, the boys had now established themselves in their new London life—as twenty-four witnesses would later testify!

Constantin would return from his holidays in Germany (about every six weeks) excited to find his room, return to school, and see his friends. Alexander, however, found the transition more difficult. He preferred being on holiday and was less enthusiastic to return to school, and I noticed that when he was with his father for a longer period of time, he needed a few days to readjust.

Masha adapted amazingly quickly to life in the West. Within five months she started asking for a raise. Her change of attitude was quick and drastic. When she first arrived, she was grateful for my invitation to London. She cleaned the house and attended to her duties so well that I suggested, "Masha, you really do not need to clean the kitchen on your hands and knees. Why don't you use the mop?"

I did not want a slave, and her subservience was embarrassing. I suggested she called me Katia rather than Madam.

Masha, like many who come from the Communist bloc, had soon discovered the magic of capitalism and decided that she should have an affluent life. I tried to explain that unfortunately money had to be earned and that in the West no one had a guaranteed job. But this did not convince her, lost as she was in her fantasies of the glamour of capitalism and its buying power.

Her visa was due to expire in May. On April 1, I had to announce to her that it was impossible to renew it from England.

"No, I won't return to Russia. I want to stay another year in London."

"But that's impossible. I talked to the Immigration Department yesterday."

"Well, then I'll find another job. But I will not return to Russia."

Without a visa, her attempts to find another position were totally unproductive. Masha's harsh and inflexible ways did not impress even those who had been prepared to employ someone without a permit. I had no intention of keeping her, and my boys did not like her much anyway. She "got on their nerves," they said. I started to look for someone else and tried to break the news as gently as possible.

"Masha, you really will have to go by the end of the month. I can't keep you without a visa, so I must employ someone else."

A few weeks after this conversation, Hans-Peter unexpectedly came to London for the weekend, and I could not fail to notice his bitterness at the obvious signs of our comfortable life without him. The flat was attractive, the boys were very happy and had excellent results at school, and my career had been reestablished. The signs of our successful reintegration into London were clear. In his usual way, Hans-Peter had failed to face the truth, clinging to the belief that our life here was temporary. But on this visit he could no longer escape the fact that we had managed well, even though he was giving me the minimum legal child support allowance. With hindsight, I feel that this was the turning point for Hans-Peter. He had sown the seeds earlier on, but now, unknown to me, he would finally reap the ultimate revenge.

In the past Hans-Peter had complained to me about Masha over the telephone.

"Catherine, why have you got a Russian woman? She sounds terrible and is always moody with me when I call."

Suddenly, though, after this visit and the discovery that I had dismissed Masha, Hans-Peter would phone before 5:30 P.M. to talk exclusively to her. I learned this through Alexander, who had been surprised that his daddy did not bother to talk to him. I found this extremely odd but consoled Alexander:

"Oh, don't worry, you'll see Daddy next week. It's almost Easter."

The first real warning sign became apparent on the children's return from their Easter holiday in Verden on April 24, 1994. I was in Heathrow's Terminal One waiting for their plane to land. The stewardess came out first, and Constantin rushed toward me and jumped into my arms:

"Mummy!"

Alexander stood still as if refusing to move. I was shocked. I walked toward him and kneeled down.

"Alexander?"

He didn't answer and looked terribly grim. Then really quickly he said: "I am German, and I want to go to a German school!"

"What are you talking about, Alexander?"

"I am German."

"Don't you even say hello to your mummy?"

He kissed me but remained silent. As we walked toward the car, Constantin was jumping with excitement and telling me about his holiday. Alexander, on the other hand, was staring into space, and his movements seemed strangely rigid.

Constantin, as usual, sat behind me in the car. He locked his arms around my neck, put his cheek against mine, and started talking exuberantly. Was his friend back from holiday? Could he see him later? Tini was excited, and he was impatient to reach home. Alexander remained motionless and silent. He looked peevish. Constantin went on:

"Do we have school tomorrow?"

"No, tomorrow's free. School starts the day after."

Tini was just about to suggest an exciting outing, when, in a hardly audible voice, I caught Alexander saying:

"I want to go to the German school."

The tone of his voice was flat—lifeless. I was amazed.

"Alexander? What's the matter, my angel? Aren't you happy to be back home?"

"I want to go to the German school."

Tini had stopped talking and stared at him for a second. Then, as children do when they have a thought in their mind, he went on unperturbed: "Mummy, can we go to Battersea Park tomorrow?"

I looked in the mirror. Alexander sat still, with a tense expression on his face. He did not listen to Constantin; he didn't even look out of the window. It was as if he were paralyzed. I became impatient with the traffic. I wanted to be home and to take Alexander in my arms. What was happening? I had never experienced him like this and was worried.

When we finally got home, Alexander stepped out of the car and stood still while Constantin hurriedly jumped out, took his bag, and ran to the front door.

"Mummy, come on."

I took their suitcase, and Alexander walked beside me. As I opened the door, Tini rushed to the bedroom and I kneeled down to comfort Alexander.

"What's the matter?" He did not answer.

"What's this talk about your wanting to go to the German school?"

"I just do! I am German!"

"But, Alexander, the Lycée is very nice."

"The German school is better."

"But you've never been to a German school before."

"I just know it's better!"

"How?"

"Because . . . because it finishes at midday."

"But you often have sports or outings in the afternoons."

"That's not true!"

Alexander had answered me as if I were a liar. He had never talked to me in this tone before, and I was profoundly shocked. What had Hans-Peter done to him? For the past half-hour

Alexander had been pulling a face, saying the same sentence endlessly.

Constantin, who had come out into the hall, interrupted my thoughts:

"Oh, stop it! You're boring with your 'I'm German, I want to go to a German school!' all the time." He had imitated his brother's voice with a twinge of irony that made Alexander smile. Tini went on: "Look, Alexander, this is your present," and he handed him the parcel I had prepared for him. They trotted off into their bedroom. I brought in their suitcases and started unpacking while my two little boys were happily playing beside me.

Tini was in a particularly chirpy mood. As I ran their bath and called them, he rushed in with more Ninja Turtles than he could carry, threw them in the water, and got into the bath.

"Alexander, are you coming?"

I called several times. Finally, Alexander appeared, empty-handed. Tini was splashing, talking, laughing, while his brother remained impassive. I had never seen Alexander this way.

"What is it, my angel?"

"Don't call me that, it's stupid."

I was taken aback, hardly knowing how to react.

"Alexander, why are you pulling a face like this? What's the matter?"

"I am German!"

"Well, of course you are. But you are also French and English. You know you are lucky—you belong to several countries, not just one."

"I want to go to a German school. In any case, when I'm nine, I can decide."

"Decide what? What are you talking about?"

"I can tell a court that I am German and want to go to a German school."

I was dumbfounded—courts, Alexander deciding, being German . . . what had my son been told?

"Who told you all this?"

"I'm not saying!"

Constantin interrupted his brother:

"Will you stop this 'I am German'? It's boring, isn't it, Mummy? Besides, we are here now. Have you called Karim, Mummy? Can I see him tomorrow?"

Tini was getting out of the bath, and I helped Alexander, dried him, and held him in my arms. He was still my baby, and I could feel how comforted he was. He did not move, his body wrapped in the towel, close to mine. I felt so sorry for him, realizing what had been done to him. Tini came running back with another question, and Alexander followed him into the bedroom, a child again.

The next day, as I was sitting at my office desk, the department manager called me to meet him upstairs in a conference room.

"We've decided that we won't extend your probation period, which falls due at the end of the month," he said.

As if the sky had fallen on my head, I was unable to speak.

"Well, I'm terribly sorry. This wasn't my decision, but I can't help you."

"But . . . why? There must be a reason."

There was none, but I was to leave the premises within the hour. The personnel assistant manager, whom I went to see later on, did not know either. There was nothing negative in my file, no problems of performance . . . she was sorry. I called home to tell Masha I would be late, and Alexander answered. As soon as he heard it was me, he coldly stated, "I'm German!"

I had lost my job, on no grounds, my son didn't even say hello to me and was repeating the same sentence like an old record . . . I collapsed in tears.

I returned home, but, thank God, Alexander had forgotten his repetitive sentence. Next day school started, and he was soon back to his usual life, with his changeable moods—but they related only, as they always had, to his friends, football, and homework. Germany was forgotten.

On April 27, Isabella, who had not called in months, decided she wanted to come and see the children. Alexander, though, was at a friend's house that evening, and I thought it odd that she had surfaced and affected a sudden and pressing interest in the boys.

Since my dismissal, Masha had become ill-tempered and sulky. She had been used to having the flat to herself, and my presence irritated her, she told me. The boys found her infuriating: she nagged them all the time, and I hoped she would leave quickly. Her visa had expired by now, but she was determined to stay in the West and urged me to give her a few weeks' grace to find another job.

Meanwhile, Hans-Peter never seemed to call to talk to the boys anymore until one morning Masha announced that he was in London for a few days and that she had met him for tea. I was startled and felt terribly uneasy, wondering why Masha (who had never liked Hans-Peter) should meet and talk to him behind my back. The explanation she gave me was that she needed some spare plugs from Germany for a friend in Russia. I suspected she was not telling the truth and had an ill-defined suspicion that they were conspiring. She had become insolent, but I was more absorbed with the immediate problem of how I would support the boys without a job. I confided in her later that I ought to talk to Hans-Peter.

Masha must have conveyed my message to Hans-Peter, as she told me he would come to see me the next day. It was May, ten days before Alexander's ninth birthday. Hans-Peter arrived, looking tense and nervous. He shook my hand without glancing at me and blasted into the kitchen, a hateful expression on his face. He knew I was under pressure, and I could detect scorn in his voice:

"So, I hear you lost your job?"

"Yes, I did, and I'm really worried. This is why I thought we ought to talk. The bills are mounting, and I don't know how I'm going to be able to carry on if I don't find something quickly."

"Well, don't count on me. I've no money!"

Remembering the scene in Hamburg when he had turned his pockets inside out screaming, I immediately abandoned the subject. I imagined that all his travel expenses and visits to London shops had been financed by his mother.

"I could take the boys to Germany if you can't manage."

"Well . . . I don't know. This would be a rather difficult solution. The point is that we must think of them first. I don't know. . . . Yet, if I don't get a job quickly, how am I going to care for them? We must think of a solution."

Nearly a month had gone by since I had been dismissed from the German bank and I didn't have a single lead. The recession in England was still hard and jobs were scarce. My situation was alarming, and I had believed Hans-Peter would cast aside his resentment and consider the boys' stability. I wished that, as a father, he would say, "Catherine, I'll help you out for a couple of months, give you time to sort things out."

But this was another man I was dreaming of. Instead of sharing the responsibility for our sons, Hans-Peter had put a different plan into action.

The phone rang. A headhunter had arranged an interview for me with a bank. Hans-Peter became agitated and in a hurry. He stood up.

"So, it's settled! I'll take the boys," he said.

"Wait, wait . . . ," I quickly scribbled the address for my interview and hung up.

"No, Hans-Peter, we have to think."

It was always the same with Hans-Peter—he would settle matters the way he intended, disregarding my views. The man-child who needed his mummy was a bully who would not allow you to talk, would pull you by the arm: "I want, I want. . . . "

Peter-Pan Hans-Peter, who had seemed wonderfully attentive and caring at first, was motivated only by his feeling of dependency. I had been attracted by this clever, good-hearted, and funny man, and it had escaped me that he had no idea how to build a real, adult life. He made unwise decisions about his

career, acted irresponsibly, and behind all this youthful charm
had been quite lost. He had clung to me, depended on my organization, drawing on my feelings of guilt and compassion until
he had suffocated me; jealous of my friends and my outside
interests, he had wanted to possess me until I finally freed myself
by walking out on him.

Today he saw me weak and stressed, and this was his chosen
moment to take his revenge and secure his ambition. We parted,
both tense.

The next day I made an appointment to see the new director
of the Lycée:

"Both your sons are doing well at school, and it would be disruptive for them to go to Germany, even for one term. If your
husband continues to pay the school fees, you'll be able to survive with unemployment benefit, and if he refuses to pay, you
could request a grant. I'll help you."

In fact, it was still Hans-Peter's mother who settled the school
fees, and his Bundeswehr salary was presumably his pocket
money while he lived with his parents. Hans-Peter still intended
to open a practice, and Alexander had told me he had found one
in Bremen. Ute was redecorating it for him. He had also just
moved onto Wilfred and Ute's property, renting their old house
while Ute and her family moved to the larger one, fifty yards
away, after her mother-in-law had died.

May 1993 was the month Hans-Peter had been waiting for.
Unknown to me, the field was now ready for his last move.

Feeling ill at ease, disquieted by Hans-Peter's animosity and
Masha's suspicious behavior, I made an appointment with a
new lawyer specializing in family law. That morning I woke up
feeling terrible and in excruciating pain, but I still managed to
make my way to the law firm. I was pale and felt dizzy. The
solicitor started to take a few preliminary details, but I could
not go on and rushed to the bathroom, where I was so sick that
a taxi was called to take me back home. Masha had cooked a
Russian dish especially for me the previous evening, and I won-

dered what had gone into it. I was ill for a couple of days and never tried to see the solicitor again.

A week after the meeting with Hans-Peter, I was offered a job as a senior account executive in an Italian bank. That same evening I telephoned Hans-Peter:

"I've got a job. We don't need to worry anymore. All's well. I start on June 28, and the hours will be much more flexible. I'm so relieved. Besides, I've been to see the schoolmaster, and he said it would not have been good for the boys to miss a term."

Hans-Peter was silent. Then:

"I've already talked to the school here."

"What do you mean? You only went back to Verden a few days ago, and we didn't agree on anything!"

"Well, I'll get my lawyer to write to yours."

In the meantime, Masha still had not found a job and refused to go. The boys kept complaining about her bickering, and I was tired of her constant moaning. I wanted to be alone with my sons and enjoy my free days with them. Finally, I had to send her off, ticket in hand. She was bitter and turned on the doorstep to snap, "In any case, I wrote to your husband!"

Little did I imagine then that in September I would find her in Verden! Hans-Peter had obviously helped her obtain a visa for Germany for the extended stay in the West she had yearned for. She would later testify against me.

"A mother who works ... Alexander was unhappy. He wanted to go to the German school, and she wouldn't listen to him. ..."

Now, though, she was gone, and this was a relief to both the children and me. I felt I had ridden the storm and would finally be able to relax. The boys' holiday would give me time to settle into my new job and reconcile myself with these strenuous years. By the time my angels returned after the summer, all would be at its best, ready for them.

I had also taken the precaution of asking my regular lawyer to obtain legal confirmation of the children's return on August

28, 1994. However, the additional sentence that Hans-Peter's lawyer had added in his reply should have made me more wary:

"Dr. Volkmann regrets your client's change of mind in relation to the children going to live with him in Germany for at least a year . . . and he hopes that, notwithstanding her new job, she will be able to give them all the time and attention they need."

My lawyer answered, "I must inform you that there is no question that my client has not been able to give the children all the time and attention they need, she has always done so, and will continue to do so."

We had never mentioned a year, just a term. I had naively thought these words were unimportant, reflecting only Hans-Peter's acrimony, and that I was legally protected.

I had, of course, heard about child abduction, but this concerned faraway lands with different customs and religions from our own. I had custody, and the children's place of residence was London. Hans-Peter was not living in a country where women had no rights. We were in Europe.

CHAPTER 9

The Nightmare Begins

The very day I had been dismissed from the German bank at the end of April, Hans-Peter had called to talk to me. His voice was tense.

"What have you done to Alexander?" I asked. "He came back repeating like a robot that he wants to be a German."

"This has nothing to do with me," Hans-Peter answered dryly.

"Well, *someone* obviously told Alexander to say this! No child could come out with such a ridiculous statement on his own! Alexander is not even nine. How could he understand what nationality means?"

"It's not me. It's him! He wants to go to a German school."

"Alexander has never been to a German school. How could he know?"

"Maybe he talked to Ute's children. . . . It has nothing to do with me."

"Come on. It's Ute's children who told him that at the age of nine he can decide? Since when do children know about the law?"

"I don't know. It's not me!" Hans-Peter's voice was trembling, and he was now shouting down the telephone. I was furious but composed.

"Look. You have no right to use Alexander like this. He is a child. This cannot go on. I am wondering if I should even send the boys to you this summer."

"No. No. You have to send them." His tone was that of panic. "I must see them. They're my sons, too."

"I know they are, and this is why I never turned them against you. But you must do the same and not play with Alexander's emotions."

Hans-Peter continued for a good ten minutes, defending himself as a child would. It wasn't him—he had done and said nothing, he insisted.

This telephone conversation and our meeting a few weeks later when Hans-Peter announced he could take the children to Verden unsettled me. Alarm bells were ringing loudly. But I had not realized that Hans-Peter's feeling of revenge against the woman who had left him had become obsessive. I had not imagined that breaking our agreement, defying the law, and punishing our children would not stop him from achieving what I later came to believe he had been carefully planning for two and a half years. He only needed to be sure that I would send the boys to Verden. From then on—as I was to learn, too late—he would be protected. A lawyer's confirmation that the boys would be returned to London on August 28 would become irrelevant in his home territory.

I knew nothing about German family law, the nonharmonization of European laws, the Hague Convention ... and how unprotected one is. I honored the agreement that the boys should go to Germany and assumed his lawyer's letter would protect me legally should Hans-Peter continue to act irrationally.

Furthermore, Alexander had long forgotten about his declaration. Within days of his return from the Easter holidays, he was happily reintegrated in his London life. His school, his friends, his orderly room, all were here. He loved our evenings and weekends together: being valuable and needed in his role of man in the house, protective of Constantin and his mummy. Sometimes Alexander would surprise me on Sunday mornings by laying the breakfast table. When we needed to go shopping, he often rushed to the kitchen, pencil and paper in hand, to start making a list:

"Constantin, which yogurts do you want? Mummy, can you check if we have enough corn flakes?"

"Mummy, what else do we need?"

By nature, Alexander was easily influenced, and his father played on this:

"Poor Daddy, he feels lonely," he had once reported after his holiday in Verden.

I resented Hans-Peter for playing on his son's emotions, but I knew this was also part of Alexander's character. Consequently, his "German" statements had not alarmed me as much as they should have. Alexander was sensitive and mercurial. For example, one day Sean was his best friend, the next he didn't like him anymore, and the third he wanted to invite him to stay for the weekend. Constantin and I were accustomed to Alexander's changes of moods and opinions, and we treated them lightheartedly, knowing them to be temporary.

My boys were so different, and it was exactly from these differences that each drew his strength. To Constantin, life was straightforward. To Alexander, it was complicated and every day would bring new challenges. Alexander's desk and toys had their specific order, but like most boys his age, he would come home disheveled, his favorite T-shirt sticking out of his trousers, bruises on his knees, happy one day, grumpy the next. Constantin, on the other hand, would carefully pick out the right-colored T-shirt to go with his trousers and neatly pull it out of the wardrobe without disturbing the others, then later come home still well combed, impeccably tidy.

He would do his homework immediately, while Alexander would find excuses to do it later. Even their taste in food was different. Constantin loved well-prepared dishes and salty things; Alexander preferred kids' food and chocolates.

Constantin was afraid of nothing and knew how to gain respect. All the girls at the primary school knew him, and I would be amused to hear them call, "Constantin," when school was out, and see how my self-assured little son would wave his hand with a smile but continue toward our car. Constantin was in control, and he knew it, but he instinctively realized that showing off was not "cool." When I read his last school report with an "A" and "excellent" in all subjects, I turned and said, "Tini, that's amazing! You didn't tell me you were first in your class." Quietly he answered, "But, Mummy, I didn't know I was good at school." I could not refrain from smiling proudly—Constantin was definitely "cool"!

Alexander suffered a little from Constantin's excellence at school, his popularity, and his self-assurance. Having a sister who was always first in her class, I was particularly conscious that it had to be difficult for Alexander to have a sibling who had so many talents. So, I compensated by overpraising him—which was possibly a little unfair to Constantin. But I felt Alexander needed support and approval to build up his self-confidence. Too often he would let himself be dominated or influenced by others.

Physically, it was Alexander who was solidly built, while Tini was thin and fragile—but it was Constantin who would roller-blade, swim, and ski fearlessly while Alexander would be cautious and sometimes anxious. It was Constantin who was the leader in his group of friends, sometimes even bossing them around, while Alexander was more compliant and attentive to their wishes. Alexander was considerate and kind to others. If we walked past a homeless person, he would always ask me to give him money. Constantin was fun, imaginative, and self-reliant.

Alexander was extremely proud and protective of his younger brother. He would always defend him if he felt someone was unfair to him. Once an older boy started a fight with Constantin on the playground. Alexander saw this, and he immediately ran over to defend his brother. Constantin, on the other hand, would never ask for his help, but he would constantly talk to his friends about his elder brother and he would never allow them to touch Alexander's things when they played at home.

Odd and even—these were my two sons. One dark and one blond. One resembling his father, the other his mother.

.   .   .

From mid-May until the end of June 1994, I was with my boys all the time. It was heaven. We did everything together, and no one else was there demanding my attention. Grumpy Masha who interfered with our dinner conversations and evening games, jealously interrupting to talk about herself, had left.

Isabella had restricted me to clearing up. Masha had expected to share my company. Finally, we had our privacy and our time belonged to us. I never enjoyed my sons' company so much, and the three of us had a fun time, laughing and cuddling as if we needed to have extra rations before the summer break. These six weeks were the last memory they would have of their mummy. Apprehensive as I was following the strange conversation with Hans-Peter, now I was relaxed and confident about the future. My new job would give me more flexible hours; past experience had made me more careful in choosing the next au pair and setting her specific duties; the flat was comfortable; and my boys were turning out to be great little guys. I had weathered the storm, and there was nothing to be worried about anymore. . . .

Until that last free conversation I had with the boys. It was in August 1994, and it will remain engraved in my memory as long as I live. Alexander came to the telephone first. He sounded happy and was enjoying his holidays, but with his usual concern he went on:

"Mummy, have you bought the schoolbooks I need for the beginning of the term? You haven't forgotten our Legos?"

Then Constantin came on, and his conversation worried me:

"Mummy, where are you?"

"In our flat, Tini."

"Yes, but tell me where, in which room?"

"I'm in the drawing room, sitting on the green sofa and looking out on to the garden as I'm talking to you."

"Ah. And is your hair long? You didn't cut it again, did you?"

"No, Tini. You'll see by the time you come back it will be just the length you like."

There was a pause, as if Constantin were trying to visualize the room and me.

"Why, Tini, are you bored?"

"Yes, Verden is boring. When are we coming back home, Mummy?"

"In three weeks. But you're going to the seaside tomorrow with Daddy and your grandparents."

"Yes, but where are *we* going on our holiday with you?"

"I won't tell you, it's a surprise, remember?"

We blew kisses over the telephone. I told him how much I loved him, and these were our last words. I hung up and remained seated. Something indefinable worried me. Constantin's voice had been different from his chirpy self. He had sounded sad and worried. It was unlike him.

I usually called the boys once a week, sometimes less. I did not want to disturb their holidays and thought that it would be unsettling for them if I was constantly on the telephone to them. This was Constantin's motto as well: either he was in Germany or he was in London, and he didn't like to mix the two. When I telephoned Verden, he would usually tell me briefly what he was up to and rush off to continue his activities. Never before had he sounded so disinterested in his holiday, never before had he needed to build himself a picture of London.

That night I could not sleep, hearing his voice over and over again.

The next evening I telephoned, but Hans-Werner told me they were still at the beach. The time after that he told me they were asleep, and the next time that they had gone out with Gundel and Hans-Peter. But he assured me they were well and happy.

I began to panic. Hans-Werner never used to answer the telephone, yet now it was only he who picked up the receiver. Why did they not allow me to speak to my sons? Where were they? Fourteen days . . . fourteen interminable days before I would be able to kiss my sons again. I thought of nothing else. I continued to telephone without success. The boys were due to spend a few days in Verden before returning to London. Hans-Peter's number did not answer, and when I tried his parents' house, Hans-Werner answered, giving me another excuse. A horrible feeling came over me. I knew there was something wrong, but I was not capable of thinking about what it could mean. Instead, I concentrated on my boys' return to London.

Would Alexander come back in the same state as he had after his Easter break? He had sounded so happy to return home when I last spoke to him. But that was over two weeks ago; what had been said to him since? Alexander was like blotting paper, absorbing everything around him. He had always been this way. As a little baby, he needed to be held tight, talked to, and comforted with words of love. I often felt inadequate to Alexander's anxious nature, wishing I could climb into his body and extract what made him unsure. In so many ways Alexander was like his father, while Constantin was more an extension of me. I never needed to make an effort to understand him—it was simply as if I were looking at myself in the mirror, except that he was much more self-confident, intelligent, and gifted than I was! I never worried about my Tini. I always worried about my

Alexander. Now I wondered what Hans-Peter was imposing on him. My poor, poor kind and loving boy was being made guilty about his father's emotional inadequacies.

Hans-Peter had kept me for six years through pity and guilt. Now he was trying to possess his nine-year-old son:

"I am so sad. . . . Daddy needs you. He needs to be loved. Alexander, do you love Daddy? Are you happy here? You shouldn't leave me on my own."

I had overheard Hans-Peter talk this way in the past. I had seen some of his postcards. I was realizing that during these two weeks of silence Hans-Peter was begging for our child's love instead of offering him his unconditional love. During the Easter holiday Hans-Peter had already added a new idea: "I am German."

I tossed and turned at night, was unsettled during the day, and still could not get through to my sons on the telephone.

On August 24, four days before my children were due back, I opened the door of my flat at six o'clock in the evening and found a large DHL envelope on the floor. I picked it up, and as I started to tear it open, the phone rang. It was John, a friend of mine. We started talking as I took out a twenty-one-page letter, starting "Dear Catherine" in Hans-Peter's handwriting. I was surprised and felt uneasy. I hung up quickly and started reading: "I find it very difficult to write this letter to you today . . . however, as a father . . . "

I started to shake as I began scanning the paragraphs, trying to understand what Hans-Peter was leading up to. Twenty-one pages, in English—this meant Hans-Peter wanted to make sure I understood. This meant it concerned a personal matter between him and me.

> . . . I know it is my duty to speak and let you know the following. . . . Since you left me two years ago and since you took the boys with you to England . . . the boys have repeatedly, and especially Alexander, expressed that they would

rather live and go to school in Germany ... that Germany was their home and that it was German that they wanted to speak rather than English. You know as well as me that especially Alexander has over the last months become increasingly depressed, and you have yourself told me ... that you had to accept the fact that he felt at home in Germany rather than in England. ...

Since they returned in July Alexander's (and Constantin's!) views about where they want to be have not changed. ... They both vehemently express their strong wish to live and go to school in Germany. ... I have now said to them ... if you want to live and go to school here you can. ...

As a father who loves his boys, I knew and know that I had and have to be honest with them. ... Knowing that something can be done about it, I feel (and know) that something had to be said ... and it is my duty as their father. ... In order to make sure that something will be arranged which I clearly see is in the best interest of the children I have last week contacted the Youth Authority here who will now interview the boys about what they want and where they want to be. In order for you not to think that I act illegally in any way I have ... applied for the right to keep the children here. ... Please know and please understand that this is by no means an act of aggression vis-à-vis you but something which I feel *must* be done for the boys' sake.

I have always expected you ... not to let me see them anymore. And I can assure you that I would never think of anything like this myself. I know that the boys love you as much as they love me, and I also know that you love them as much as I love them. ... I feel rather depressed, as I am not sure whether or not you understand why I act now. But I desperately hope that you understand that all I do is for the boys, and that you understand that as their father ... I have no choice but to speak up in a way which I feel is my duty vis-à-vis them.

Please understand, I do not want to act against you, and
I do not want to sabotage your relationship with the boys.
. . . I have also told them that should they, after all, change
their mind and prefer to live in London, there would be no
problem . . . and . . . that in that case I certainly would not
be upset.

This is a very long letter, but I do hope you see I try to act
in the best interest of the boys. . . . I am giving you such
short notice . . . simply because until now I still hoped that
their or especially Alexander's sadness would stop. . . . I sin-
cerely hope and pray that you understand why I am doing
this . . . and you should see them now: they both are very,
very happy that we have spoken about the situation . . .
and I hope you understand why and for whom I have done
this. . . .

I was shaking like a leaf, in a cold sweat, in total panic. Automatically, I called John, the last person I had spoken to. Then I
picked up the phone again and called Leonard at his office. My
voice was trembling, and I only remember repeating, "Hans-
Peter isn't sending the children back. I've just received a twenty-
one-page letter telling me he isn't sending the children back."

Leonard and John were both on their way from the City. I did
not move. I reread the letter, this time carefully, stopping at
every word, going over each sentence. I felt as if I were suffocating and all the blood had left my body.

Hans-Peter had nothing to do with this, he wrote, and hoped
I would understand! Just as in April, when he had never told
Alexander to say he was German? He was blaming the children
for his actions, quoting Alexander, and Constantin only in
brackets, mentioning "they" when he meant "him," underlining
Constantin's name to convince me that even he had expressed
his "will" to remain in Germany.

I know my children: they were inside me before anyone else
had seen them. I knew that Alexander could easily be influenced, but I also knew Tini could not. Hans-Peter was playing

with words, trying to tell me Alexander thought we had come to London on holidays, that he had felt homesick and wanted to go to a German school. Was Alexander mentally retarded? Would it take him two and a half years of schooling in London to realize this was not a holiday? How could he feel homesick for Verden when he did not remember living there and it represented holidays for him? How could he and Constantin feel so unhappy about returning to London when their mummy, their friends, and all their toys were there? When a few weeks ago they had told me the exact opposite? And when had I ever said that they felt at home in Germany rather than England?

I was scared. My sons were in danger. In a sudden flash, I saw that Hans-Peter had been planning this for months, and all the ideas he had been planting in Alexander's head resounded in my mind: "I am German, and I want to go to a German school"; "In Germany school finishes at lunchtime"; "Daddy is moving into Ute's old house. I'll have my own room there." There was Masha's parting comment: "I've written to your husband," and Hans-Peter's "I can take them to Germany if you can't manage." But it was not until later that I understood the significance of Hans-Peter's wording "in the interests of the children" and according to "the wishes of the children." I did not know about German family law—these two sentences were the basis of his legal case.

As I picked up the telephone in anger, Hans-Peter was already calling me:

"Did you get my letter?"

"Yes, I've just finished reading it," I said, and before I had time to say more, Hans-Peter continued in a trembling voice, "It's not me. It's Alexander. And Constantin, too. They want to stay here."

He was shouting, as I had never heard anyone shout before. The more he raised his voice, the calmer mine became. I felt that I was faced with a mental patient and that I had to talk in a certain way:

"Then, can I talk to Alexander, please?"

"No, you can't. He's sleeping, and I'm not going to wake him up."

"It's seven-thirty in Germany! Hans-Peter, please let me talk to him. . . . "

"Well, he's not coming back. There's no point in you talking to him. They both want to go to school here."

"Hans-Peter, you know perfectly well this does not make sense. Why would they suddenly want to go to German schools? They don't know anything about German schools. They've always been at French schools. How can you even suggest this? It would be too unsettling for Alexander to change. . . . "

"It's not my fault. It's him."

"How can you ask a nine-year-old which school he wants to go to? Verden is holiday times for Alexander: of course he would choose to stay there. Most children would say the same. Shouldn't you be more interested about what's right for him, instead of cornering him in a situation he can't understand?"

"Well, it's not me. It's him. He wants to go to school here. I've already told you—I am not sending them back." His voice suddenly changed to a commanding one. "In any case, Alexander wants to be German."

"What are you talking about? No child has any idea what a nationality means. It's not an innate feeling. Besides, our children have always been raised in multicultural environments. . . . "

There was a bleep—then silence. Hans-Peter had hung up. I was still holding the receiver, hearing the echo of his hysterical voice. People say women are hysterical, yet I had never heard a woman talk this way. I sat staring into emptiness until the doorbell rang. It was Leonard.

I handed him the letter. Leonard read through it slowly. I could see the expression on his face become bleaker and bleaker. Finally, he finished and stared at me in silence for a moment. His face was pale:

"Catherine, this is terrible. I can't believe it."

He was still trying to absorb the content of the letter.

"Hans-Peter sounds completely hysterical," he went on. "He repeats himself all the time, and he's hiding behind Alexander as if he had nothing to do with this decision—asking you to forgive his actions!"

Leonard was picking out sentences:

"'I had no other choice. . . . Please know and please understand . . . this is something which I feel must be done for the boys' sake. . . .' *He* feels depressed, as he is not sure you will understand. *He* will not feel sad if the boys one day decide to return to you! Catherine, this is ghastly! Hans-Peter is refusing to return the children, and he wants you to understand and forgive his actions! He doesn't want to 'sabotage your relationship with the boys,' and yet he presents you with a fait accompli!"

We were still debating the letter when John arrived. John was an old friend of mine with whom I had got back in contact when I returned to London. He had never met Hans-Peter but knew my boys a little. John was fifty-four, and an extremely successful banker in the City, on the board of several companies. He was bright, matter-of-fact, and had read law at Cambridge.

He read the letter carefully as if it were a business contract.

"This letter is incredibly manipulative and frightening. Catherine, this is very serious. You must get yourself a lawyer tomorrow. One who specializes in child abduction."

"Child abduction?" I murmured.

"Yes, this is what it amounts to. You have legal custody, your children are resident in London, and his refusal to return them is therefore a criminal action. Your lawyer will have to make an injunction and place your children under English court protection."

I was speechless. My babies were supposed to be back in four days, and John was talking about legal action and courts. I had read Hans-Peter's letter over and over. It was explicit. But I still had not grasped what it implied: my sons were not coming back.

As if in a trance, I could no longer think straight. Leonard took over.

"John, do you know a good lawyer for Catherine?"

"Yes, there is an excellent firm I know. I'll call them tomorrow and introduce Catherine. They specialize in cases like this."

Leonard and John continued talking, but I caught only the drift of their conversation. I was in a state of shock.

"Do you know Hans-Peter well?"

"Yes, I know him well. He is totally immature and irresponsible. But that he would actually do a thing like this . . . ," I heard Leonard explain. "I know Catherine's boys very well. I'm Alexander's godfather, and they often came to visit us in the country. They are great children, full of life and well behaved. Both Alexander and Constantin were happy, well-adapted boys. In fact, I saw them the day before they left on their holidays. Constantin wasn't even looking forward to going, and Alexander was asking me when he could come to the country again. . . . I cannot believe that Hans-Peter would do this."

"Did you notice this sentence in his letter: '. . . and maybe Catherine could come to Verden and stay in Ute's house for the weekend?' It sounds to me as if her husband is trying to use the children to manipulate her back to him."

"Well, Hans-Peter was always very possessive of Catherine, and knowing him as I do, he could never accept her leaving him. . . . "

They talked further, then John stood up:

"Catherine, I'll call the lawyer first thing tomorrow morning. You'll have to act immediately. This is very serious."

He took my arm and squeezed it in a comforting gesture, bid good-bye to Leonard, and left. *Thank God, I have such friends,* I thought.

Leonard stayed a while longer. As soon as he left, I rushed to my bedroom and threw myself onto the bed, face down in my pillow, my clothes still on, and I began to weep. The tears began to flow gently. But soon, as if I were grasping the full horror of what was happening to me, they exploded into a gushing, uncontrollable flood. I was shaking, unable to contain the fountain of my despair. I must have wept for an hour, maybe longer, simply letting my body rid itself of its pain. The tears poured until there were none left to shed, until my body became drained at its source. Then suddenly, all was silence. Exhausted, my head still buried in my pillow, my mind was numbed. Sometime during the night I called my mother. Somehow, the next morning, I managed to get myself to the office.

As soon as I walked out of the lift into the trading room, my colleague rushed up to me:

"Catherine, what's the matter?"

My face must have given me away.

"My boys . . . my boys . . . they're not coming back!"

She immediately called my friend Nicolette, who worked on the first floor. Nicolette came up at once, took me by the arm into a conference room, and closed the door. My whole body was trembling, and I could only utter the same words over and over:

"My angels, my angels. . . . " Nicolette held me tightly in her arms. I could not stop crying.

Nicolette was a senior manager at the bank. She had had some legal dealings in the past that might prove relevant. Once I calmed down a little, she took me down to her office, and we started to assess the situation. John had left a message with the name of the lawyer and an appointment time. I had brought all the papers that John had said I would need. Two hours later I was sitting in the office of my new lawyer, Jane Keir. An assistant was also present to take notes.

Jane looked at the documentation and read Hans-Peter's letter:

"This is a very manipulative letter. Tell me about your husband."

I explained as much as I could, between sobs.

"This is illegal retention. We'll have to go to the High Court of Justice and make an application for a resident order and a wardship order. We'll also make an injunction under the Hague Convention for the immediate return of the children to this jurisdiction."

I had no idea what she was talking about. Wardship, Hague Convention . . . I could only think of my boys. Where were they now? What was being said to them? Was Tini asking how many more days were left before he would be coming home to Mummy? It wasn't really happening. This was only a bad dream. Soon I'd wake up and my boys would be here. . . .

"Can we send Hans-Peter a fax first?" I asked. "Maybe he'll change his mind and send the boys back."

"I very much doubt it. His letter is pretty explicit. He's already taken legal steps, and I must tell you that he knew what he was doing well in advance. He's also trying to trick you into going to Germany. You must not go. If you do, it will mean that you have accepted the situation. He also mentions the local Youth Authority. Do you realize that he's trying to get their support? I believe that in Germany they play a major role in child custody battles. Your husband knows exactly what he's doing, and from the connections you tell me he has in his town, he's in an excellent position. . . . But if you wish I'll still send him a fax."

Everyone around me kept repeating how serious it was. They were talking about abduction, legal actions, English and international law, but I was incapable of grasping the reality of the situation. Hans-Peter was only acting irrationally. He wasn't serious. The boys would be back in three days. This was only a bad dream . . . and all would be sorted out soon. The boys would be back. . . .

I couldn't remember how I reached the office, how I got home—I was moving like an automaton. I needed to talk to Hans-Peter and make him return to his senses.

There was an answering machine at his practice, no answer at his house. I called again, and again and again. No answer. A girlfriend came to see me with a take-out dinner. I had no appetite: all I could think of was frantically fast-dialing Hans-Peter's home number. Finally, at 11:00 P.M., Hans-Peter answered.

"Hans-Peter . . . ," As soon as he heard my voice, he hung up. I called again. The telephone was busy. He had taken it off the hook. I could no longer get through. I did not sleep.

The next day, August 26, a fax was sent to Hans-Peter's practice in Bremen, with a copy to his London lawyer:

> We have been shown a letter written by you on August 22 which categorically states that you do not intend to return the boys as agreed. We consider this to be child abduction. Our client has instructed us to commence proceedings through the English and German Courts . . . but she very much hopes that the matter will not go to a full-blown hearing and that you will agree to return the children on the agreed flight of Sunday August 28.

My parents and my friends rallied about me, calling me, offering their help and support. I do not think I could have survived those early days had they not surrounded me with their love and care. Hans-Peter was still unreachable, and I did not know where my boys were. My world had collapsed, and I was in a constant panic.

A few days later the director of the bank I was working for called me in. He was Italian and very understanding:

"Catherine, what's happening to you is absolutely horrific. The bank is behind you. Don't worry, we'll support you in any way we can."

Thank God, I had friends and was working in an Italian bank. How awkward it would have been if I had still been employed at the German one! I had been at my new job only two months and was still on probation. Luckily, I had started with such energy and determination that my results were excellent—at least the bank knew I could be productive.

Finally, I managed to get through to Hans-Peter's parents.

"Gundel, where are my sons? I would like to talk to them."

"I don't know!"

"Please. I haven't talked to them for nearly three weeks. . . . "

"I don't know where they are. I won't tell you!"

"But I'm their mother! You can't hide them from me. I need to talk to them. . . . "

"Okay, Okay, I'll tell Hans-Peter to have them call you."

"So, you know where they are. Please tell me."

"No. I promised Hans-Peter I wouldn't say."

"But, Gundel . . . what sort of people are you? You're a mother, too. How can you. . . . "

"You're the one who left my son!"

And she hung up.

So there it was. My children had been kept to punish me, as it was I who had left Hans-Peter.

The next morning Hans-Peter called me at the office:

"I'll fetch the boys, and in half an hour you can call me at the practice and you'll be able to talk to them."

"But why can't I talk to them now? Where are they?"

"They are in Bremen. At my aunt's house."

"Well, can you give me her number? I'll call them there."

"No, I want to be present when you talk to them. Call back at the practice."

Half an hour of hell. I was glued to my watch, shaking and scared. My little boys were not even allowed to talk to their mother.

"Hello, Alexander? How are you, my darling?"

"Hello." His voice was cold, toneless. I was frightened.

"I'm German, and I want to go to a German school!"

"But, Alexander . . . what about our holidays together? Remember, this was a surprise. All your toys are here, your friends, your mummy. . . . "

There was silence. Then Hans-Peter's voice shouting down the telephone:

"Stop it! Don't talk to Alexander this way. Now you've upset him, he's crying!"

Constantin came on the line. A tiny peevish voice that I could hardly recognize:

"Mummy?" I felt he was about to cry.

"Yes, Tini." I was nearly crying, too, but I went on in a gentle voice: "How are you?"

He was silent. "Mummy loves you. . . . "

"I know. (pause) But I have to go to a German school, I have to . . . "

He didn't finish his sentence. His voice was small, and he sounded scared.

"Tini, I . . . "

"I have to go now and . . . "

He never finished. My little Tini . . . his voice had sounded so sad, so lost . . . I could see his little face: he was probably biting his lower lip to control his tears, probably looking down to escape his father's directives. I could see Alexander's expression, his eyebrows knitted, tensed up in repressed pain.

Hans-Peter was acting like a madman. He was acting like a kidnapper—controlling the conversation, making the children repeat sentences. They sounded rehearsed, forced. I ran down to Nicolette's office, barely able to control my tears. I was petrified. My poor little vulnerable boys, held hostage . . . August 9, 1994, had been the last time I had a free conversation with my own children. They were now kept behind a wall, forbidden all contact with their mummy in the hope that they would grow to hate and resent her.

That evening, I received an envelope from the Verden court. It was a court decision, dated August 22, 1994. I was horrified: Hans-Peter had applied for a transfer of custody, and I had known nothing about it. In Germany—probably the only country in Europe with this legal arrangement—it is possible to make court applications and obtain court decisions on issues as important as child custody, without one party ever being informed! As a result, there have been several cases in which a German parent, living abroad, has returned to Germany with the children ostensibly on a short visit and has succeeded in gaining custody in a German court without the other parent's knowledge. The custody decision then becomes the basis for the

German parent to inform the non-German parent that the children are not returning home. The non-German parent soon discovers that because of the change in custody, he or she can make no headway in the German courts. It is also possible for a German parent to change a child's surname without the approval of the other parent.

Sometime in July Hans-Peter had asked for custody to be transferred to him. He had waited for the decision, hoping it would be in his favor. But on August 22 he had been informed that Judge Moritz rejected his application on the grounds that the children "should remain with their mother and in England where they had already been living for two and a half years." Irrespective of this, Hans-Peter had decided to retain the children. He wrote the letter on the day of the decision.

Hans-Peter had defied both the English and the German law.

CHAPTER 10

The Legal Maze

The next day I awoke to the realization that my solicitor had been right: Hans-Peter knew what he was doing and he *was* serious.

Now I had the proof: when I had last spoken to the children on August 9, 1994, Hans-Peter had already applied to have the custody transferred to him. Alexander had asked me whether I had bought his schoolbooks, and Tini had told me he was bored in Verden. This was why the Volkmanns wouldn't let me talk to the boys anymore. Hans-Peter was establishing his legal argument based on the "will of the children" (which, as I would later discover, is very effective under German law) in case his demand was rejected—he could hardly jeopardize his defense by allowing the children to express an opposite opinion on the telephone!

Why had I let the boys go to Germany? I thought of them all alone, unprotected, with a father who was betraying them, betraying their mother, and pushing her out of their lives. What he had done was horrifying, and it terrified me. How was it possible? How could German law admit ex parte demands for such crucial issues as custody? Had Hans-Peter obtained a decision in his favor, I would have been removed from my sons' lives there and then and would have had little legal recourse.

I tried to calm myself. The judge *had* rejected Hans-Peter's conspiring maneuver. The law was on my side in both countries, and justice would protect the children. Yet I could not suppress my alarm. Hans-Peter was surrounded by lawyers and a judge, and his father was very powerful in the small town of Verden. The boys were under their control, and I could not even reach them by telephone.

My nights were sleepless, and my days full of panic. On the morning of Sunday, August 28, I rose at dawn. Maybe Hans-Peter would change his mind, maybe he would send the boys back today. After all, why would anyone want to embark on a bitter legal battle? I had never obstructed his contacts with the children, never complained about him to them, never been unreasonable. . . . Why should he want to provoke arguments and drag his sons into it?

By ten o'clock I was frantic. Instinctively, I knew Hans-Peter would not call, but I tried to hold on to the only notion that gave me a glimpse of hope: logic. I sat on my green sofa, the phone in front of me, praying it would ring. We were due to drive to Alton Towers the next day, then up north to see my friend Valérie and her boys. Alexander and Tini had asked so often whether we could visit them again. Their presents were lying on their bunk beds, ready to open, their schoolbooks and new pencil cases beside them. . . .

Everything was ready for their return—but they never would return. An hour later I dialed Hans-Peter's home number. No answer. Finally at noon: "I've told you. The boys are not coming back!"

"But, Hans-Peter, I'd planned a holiday with them, school's starting in three weeks. . . . "

"Well, too bad. The boys are staying here," and he hung up.

I called back. An answering machine was on. Hans-Peter had obviously just installed it to screen the calls. I tried Ute's number. Wilfred, the judge, answered, and he allowed me to speak to my sons, who were in his house.

Both said little, answering only yes or no; Alexander sounded stressed, and Tini's frightened little voice startled me again. My self-confident Constantin sounded intimidated and perplexed. What were they being told? I was devastated.

My sons' lives were being dismantled, never to be serene again. They were being held prisoner, spirited away from their mother, and prevented from talking to her. I was not allowed to speak to them again until October, except for one evening on September 8.

Between tears, I managed to talk to my mother, then, once I had regained control, to my solicitor, who had given me her home number. Monday was a bank holiday, but first thing on Tuesday morning we would apply for the emergency orders at the High Court of Justice. We were to meet at her office at 10:00 A.M.

The hours passed interminably, alternating sickeningly between moments of rational reflection and gushes of emotion. I imagined my boys lost in the dense woods, walking hand in hand, their rucksacks on their backs, crying for me. . . .

On Tuesday, September 30, my solicitor, her assistant, and I went to the High Court of Justice, where we met our barrister. He had received preliminary reports from Jane, but there were details he needed from me. He took a few notes, Jane presented him with the papers she had prepared, and we sat waiting for the judge to call us in. I had never been inside a courtroom in my life and felt nervous. My sons, my flesh and blood, were reduced to names in a file, to another routine case to be argued.

A man whom I had never met would speak on my behalf, and a judge would decide our destiny.

Hans-Peter had cast me out of my sons' lives, and now barristers and solicitors controlled our future. I didn't even hear the voice calling us through the loudspeaker.

"Let's go in," the solicitor said.

We walked into the impressive wood-paneled room. Our barrister sat in the front row. Jane, her assistant, and I sat in the one behind. The judge walked in wearing a wig and a black robe, and we all stood up. We sat again, and the hearing began. Our barrister spoke, but with all the legal language and the various articles, I understood very little. I was numb.

Jane woke me from my stupor with a nudge:

"Great," she whispered, "we've got an injunction under article 3 of the Hague Convention."

I had no idea what she was talking about but could see that the verdict was good and that we had surmounted the first hurdle.

Jane was pleased, and so was the barrister. Justice Ward's decision would soon restore my children to me in London. It was not as though they were in Iran or Yemen. Germany was a signatory to the Hague Convention on child abduction.

I was relieved but not convinced. My boys were far away and in Verden. In Verden the rules were different: the Volkmanns and the Monkmanns were in control.

"Hans-Peter lives on a judge's property, his father knows everyone in town, his sister is a lawyer, so is his brother-in-law. His uncle is a politician in Bremen. . . . "

"Don't worry, the German central authorities will look after things. I'll inform the Child Abduction Unit of our Lord Chancellor's Office immediately of the court decision."

Perhaps Jane thought I was overdramatizing and under emotional stress. She tried politely to take leave and hailed a taxi.

"And you'll need to get yourself a German lawyer as soon as possible," she advised.

"I don't know any German lawyers."

"I'll try and find one for you. I'll call you later," and she was off.

I went back to the office and tried to concentrate on business—there was nothing else I could do now. Like a robot, I talked to my clients and bought, sold, wrote confirmations. Only one thought was in my mind: my children.

Jane called me with the name of a lawyer from Munich who specialized in child abduction cases. I called him immediately and left my office and home numbers on his answering machine. Nicolette accompanied me home, and I spent all evening on the telephone, between my parents and my friends, still unable to reach the children: Gundel's number was not answering, and Hans-Peter's new device recorded my eternal unanswered messages.

Two days later I finally reached his aunt in Bremen, who held me on the telephone for ages, playing innocent, until she admitted everyone was away but she couldn't tell me where. I was beginning seriously to panic. Where on earth did they disappear to? School holidays were ending in a week's time in England. In Germany school had started two weeks ago—soon the children would be missing class here.

The Munich lawyer, Dr. Kram, finally called.

"Mrs. Laylle? I received a fax from Jane yesterday. So your children have been abducted? Well, I'm familiar with the procedure—I've dealt with many such cases. I'll put the necessary papers through to Berlin first thing tomorrow. Then I'll be away for a few days. In the meantime, would you send me one thousand marks."

Dr. Kram had spoken in English to me. His voice was strict. He had run through my case. I hung up and felt uncomfortable. He sounded as if he knew what to do and that he would act fast, but he had not seemed interested in listening to my concerns about the boys. However, what choice did I have? Jane had told me he was a reputable lawyer, and though my world had fallen apart, it was just a routine job for him. So many things separated me from my sons now.

Soon my days became a maze of legal terms, phone calls, faxes, photocopies, and my regular office job. My evenings were consumed by further phone calls between helpful friends who had just heard the news, my parents, my sister Véronique, Leonard, Nicolette—and Hans-Peter's answering machine. At night I could not sleep until finally, too exhausted to think further, I would doze off and be transported into a maelstrom of nightmares. Some were so harrowing that I became afraid of going to sleep.

My boys were calling me, I could hear their cries of help, see the frightened expressions on their little faces—but I could never reach them. Either Hans-Peter came running up, grabbing each child under the arm and vanishing into the darkness, or I would find myself suddenly lost in the dense forest, unable to find them again . . . but still hearing their cries.

I tried Dr. Kram on Wednesday, but he was not yet back. By Friday I began to panic again. I called Jane. She couldn't help me further. No one had his home number. I arrived at my empty flat that evening and found another letter from the Verden court. My heart started beating fast: what now?

A short note on recycled paper said something about a hearing time of 2:00 P.M. on Tuesday, September 20, 1994. I called Véronique, whose German was fluent, and faxed her the note. A few minutes later she was on the telephone:

"Catherine, this is a hearing for custody. Hans-Peter has lodged an appeal against the decision of August 22 refusing him custody."

"But that's impossible. There's been an injunction from the English court ordering the return of the children to England under the Hague Convention. This has priority. The Verden court can't decide on custody. It will be determined here in this jurisdiction."

"Well, call your German lawyer immediately on Monday. Monday is already the twelfth!"

"I can't get hold of him."

Everyone got on the telephone. No one knew of a German lawyer who specialized in abductions and Hague Convention cases. Only Joachim had a friend who was a commercial lawyer, a partner in a large law firm in Munich. Maybe he would be able to help.

"Yes, yes, I've heard about the Hague Convention. I've never dealt with these cases before, but Joachim tells me you urgently need help."

"Thank you." His voice sounded soft and considerate. He spoke almost no English, and dealing with legal terminology in German would be impossible for me, but at least Véronique would be able to help.

I had managed to reach Ute a few days before. Her voice was chilling:

"Catherine, you don't want to understand, do you? Your sons want to live in Germany, and you had better get used to the idea. Behave as a mother, respect their will, and stop trying to call them."

"But I *am* the mother. They are my sons. Please tell me where they are. What Hans-Peter is doing is illegal."

"Don't talk to me about the law. Just leave your children alone."

"I need to know where they are."

"I've promised Hans-Peter I won't tell you. But don't worry, they'll be back in two weeks' time. I'll ask Hans-Peter to call you then."

"Back in two weeks!? From where?"

"That's all I'm going to say. Be satisfied with that. I can't say more."

Ute, with her forbidding hostility, would not even tell me where my children were and in her self-righteous tone had told me I should content myself with talking to them in two weeks' time. Were these people human?

The next day I called the Child Abduction Unit. They faxed Berlin and found that the police had instigated a search.

The director of the French Lycée was on the telephone.

"Madame Laylle, I have just received a fax from your husband stating that the children will no longer be attending the Lycée since they 'have moved back to Germany after the last school term.' Had you not told me about your story, their places would have been given away. You know how long the waiting list is. But of course, I'm keeping them open." I was horrified. Hans-Peter's planning went so far! Had Mr. Cock been less attentive, there would have been no places at the boys' London school; another positive legal argument for Hans-Peter.

Nicola and Franz, two of my office colleagues, were helping me with a flood of calls. Nicolette lunched with me to talk things over. Véronique deciphered my German lawyer's court applications, my friends rallied around me in the evening, and my parents were devastated . . . but the German police were still unable to locate the children.

I was beside myself. Finally, I called the local police in Verden. A constable answered:

"Oh, *ja*. We received a fax from Berlin two days ago. *Ja, ja,* I'll check their house tomorrow."

"But that's the point. They're not there! I'm worried. . . . "

"We'll look into it. Tell me, are you married to Hans-Peter or Hans-Jorg?"

The police knew them by their first names. They had not even started their search!

On Thursday, September 8, Gundel finally picked up the telephone.

"*Nein*, I don't know where your children are."

"But, Gundel. . . . " She was nervous. Her voice was insecure, and mistakenly she let slip that they were in southern Germany, in Freiburg.

"Can I have Antje's number?"

Annoyed with herself that she had given out this information, she resentfully gave me the number of Hans-Peter's sister. I dialed at once. It was engaged—Gundel had obviously got through first, not needing the international prefix, to warn her daughter that I would be calling.

When the line was finally free, a disconcerted au pair answered:

"*Nein,* I don't know where your children are." But during the conversation she revealed that Hans-Peter would be back later. At that moment Antje grabbed the phone. Her voice was spiteful:

"Catherine, they're not here. The children don't want to talk to you."

"Antje, please . . . this isn't credible. Why should my children suddenly not want to talk to their own mother?"

"Your children want to live in Germany."

"Well, this is what you're telling me. But even if so, why should they be barred from talking to me? I would like to speak to my sons. I haven't spoken to them since the twenty-eighth of August. You have no right to forbid my children to talk to me."

Antje was becoming extremely aggressive. She was shouting down the phone, interrupting me, and throwing legal terminology into the conversation. I got scared. She was a lawyer, and I had better get off the phone.

But Antje went on:

"You should have come to Verden as Hans-Peter suggested in his letter!"

"But I couldn't. My lawyer told me not to go. It was a legal trick."

"What trick? It's you who left Hans-Peter, isn't it? You aren't interested in your children. You didn't take care of them. You worked."

"But, Antje, you work, too, and left your first husband when your son was still a toddler."

"That's entirely different!"

That evening I phoned about ten times. Finally, I managed to talk to my boys, who "had just come in with Hans-Peter from an outing in the woods." It was ten o'clock at night!

Hans-Peter came on the phone first:

"And you accuse me of being a kidnapper! You're mad, mad." He was hysterical, and I was terrified. "Alexander, tell your mother—" and he passed the phone over to our son, who sounded petrified.

"Mummy?"

"How are you, my love? I've been trying to call you every day. . . . " I heard Hans-Peter's voice in the background: "Tell her, tell her!" Alexander was hesitant. I could sense his disorientation and nervousness:

"I am German, and I want to go to a German school," he said in French.

"Are you going to school?"

"No."

"But school started a month ago."

"Constantin and I are going to the kindergarten with Antje's son."

My nine-year-old son was going to kindergarten, in southern Germany, when Hans-Peter had a medical practice in Bremen, some four hundred miles away?

"Doesn't Daddy go to work?"

"Yes, he goes to the practice."

"But when he's not with you, who's taking care of you?"

"The babysitter."

Again Hans-Peter barked in the background. His voice was shaking: "That's not true. Tell her it's not true."

Alexander's voice was unsteady. I could feel he was about to cry. In a faint tone he asked me whether I wanted to speak to Tini, and a little desperate thread of a voice came on:

"Hello."

"Tini? Mummy loves you. I've been trying to call you. I didn't know where you were."

I was shaken. I tried to choose my words carefully so as not to upset the children, yet I suspected this might be the last opportunity I would have to talk to them and find out what was going on.

"And are you with Alexander all day?"

"Yes, but, Mummy . . . ," and in a tearful voice he added quickly, "I've got to go now."

Hans-Peter's voice came on:

"Now they're upset. What you're doing is horrible. I don't want you to speak to them anymore!" he yelled and put down the phone. My boys had been standing there throughout Hans-Peter's threats and shouting.

I fell to pieces, unable to manage my emotions anymore. The pain was so acute that it had become physical. I was crying, shaking, everything inside me was aching. My sons . . . my mind was in total turmoil, and I was frightened as I had never been in my life: Hans-Peter was acting like a madman, and there was nothing, nothing I could do to rescue my children.

How was all this possible? How could nothing be done to protect two innocent children? Didn't the lawyers, the bureaucrats at the Lord Chancellor's Office and in Berlin, realize that this was urgent?

The following day Jane sent me a fax she had received from Hans-Peter's English lawyer, dated September 8, 1994, the same day I talked to the boys in Freiburg:

"The children are with my client at his home address in Verden. The children are well and happy, and there is no reason why your client should not telephone them on his home number."

A fax from Berlin dated that same day stated, "The police investigations have not been successful yet"; and on September 9, "The police investigations have revealed that the respondent and the children are in Freiburg until the end of this weekend. Then they will come back to Verden." But they were not, and on September 12 Berlin advised us that they had "again requested the police in Verden to look for Dr. Volkmann and the children."

I never managed to speak to the children again. Antje's number was switched onto an answering machine, as was Hans-Peter's number in Verden. Gundel did not answer. Hans-Peter's English lawyer and the police were misinformed. The children were not in Verden, and they did not return on September 12. I would find out later that, on that weekend, my sons had been taken on a six-hundred-mile drive to a small North Sea island to spend ten days at a psychologist's private home.

My new lawyer, recommended by Joachim, called me on September 16:

"Everything's fine. The judge in Verden has been informed about the Hague injunction. He will only deal with the custody after he has heard the Hague Convention case."

"What do you mean?"—my voice was trembling—"deal with the custody? My sons were illegally retained and under article 3 of the Hague Convention they have to be returned to England immediately. This is what the Hague Convention is about—to protect children against abduction and illegal retention."

"Yes, but your husband might argue that their return to England would cause them psychological damage."

"What?" Alexander's "I'm German, I want to go to a German school" was resounding in my mind.

"There is an exception under which children need not be ordered back. I can imagine your husband will use it to defend his case."

"But how could a return to England cause psychological damage to my sons? England is a civilized country. We have no famine, nor are we in a state of war!"

"I know, but I am just preparing you for the eventuality."

"But the Verden court cannot discuss custody in any case. My sons are wards of court; they are under the protection of the High Court of England and Wales."

"Well, we'll just see what happens."

I hung up and ran downstairs to see Nicolette, in a panic. Why was my lawyer being negative and dispassionate?

"Most lawyers are the same. But your case is black and white, I shouldn't worry."

But I did. With the support that Hans-Peter had in Verden, anything was possible.

On Monday, September 19, I took the plane to Hamburg. Véronique's flight from Paris arrived twenty minutes later. Joachim met us at the airport, and the three of us drove to his flat, where the lawyer was to join us later. This was our first meeting. His colleague who specialized in family law would arrive the next day.

Véronique and I were very nervous. Joachim's friend was a gentleman who seemed detached and unaware of the seriousness of the case. At 6:00 P.M. Joachim's fax machine rang. The Munich office was sending us a copy of Hans-Peter's court deposition, which they had just received. My sister and I were perplexed: in Germany was evidence brought in at the last minute admissible?

Reels of paper were coming out. Joachim gave Véronique some pages and both started reading. There was silence, and I saw my sister's face fill with consternation:

"What's the matter?"

"I think it's better if you don't look at it. I can't believe what I'm reading. I'll just tell you in brief. There are testimonies from two of these au pair girls you had. One from Isabella and one from Masha. What they basically say is that you're a bad mother. You worked all day and did not take care of the children. They claim they had to attend to the boys."

"But that's ridiculous. And Masha never took care of the boys. They didn't even like her. . . . "

"Yes, but the fact is that they have made their statements, and with a hearing tomorrow you'll not have time to provide evidence against them."

"And, Véronique, look at this!" Joachim interrupted in a grim voice.

Véronique started reading, and her face became even more somber.

"What is it?"

"It's a report from a child psychologist."

"What child psychologist?" I asked in a panic.

"Someone who lives in Norderney, an island in the North Sea."

"What? My children were taken to a psychologist? But that's horrible. . . . "

"Well, you had better not see that report."

Joachim and Véronique were shielding me from the information.

"Catherine, you have to be strong. You'll need to sleep tonight."

"Let me see that report," said Dr. Schirker, the lawyer. "Ah, yes, as I thought—your husband is arguing that it would be psychologically harmful for the children to be returned to England."

"But how could the judge accept a report made by a psychologist whom Hans-Peter appointed? The mother was not even present when the children were examined, and the psychologist doesn't mention this rather crucial point," Joachim interjected.

"Well, we'll see," the lawyer concluded.

Véronique and I looked at each other in horror.

CHAPTER 11
Verden Closes Ranks

Joachim had booked us into a small hotel nearby. Before going to sleep, Véronique tried to reassure me as best she could. Véronique, the intellectual, was a professor at "Le Grand Palais" University in Paris and a lateral thinker. She gave me gentle advice, but I could not fail to notice how worried and nervous she was herself. She had been to Verden once, in the summer of 1987, and had observed the prejudiced and insular atmosphere of Hans-Peter's entourage; she knew that tomorrow would be trying.

The next morning Joachim and the lawyer, Dr. Schirker, came to fetch us. We picked up the second lawyer at the airport, and all five of us set off for Verden. The second lawyer seemed very young, and I was surprised by how little English he spoke, considering they were both working for an international law firm.

Finally, we reached Verden. Everyone was silent.

"Gosh, it's even smaller than I imagined," exclaimed Joachim's friend, Dr. Schirker.

I directed Joachim to the court, "Amtsgericht—Verden," Hans-Peter's pride.

Everything was deserted and gray. I was filled with angst.

The small building seemed empty. There was one courtroom. In front of it was a large hall with several chairs and to the left another small waiting area; to the right was a corridor with several doors. A small notice on the side of the courtroom read, "12:00 A.M. Volkmann vs. Volkmann."

I gulped. We sat and waited. The loudspeaker called, "Volkmanns, please come forward."

The five of us walked into a white-walled modern room. A blonde woman sat on a bench to the left, the judge on a platform on the right. On either side of the room were four wooden chairs and a table:

"*Nein, nein.* Only the client and her lawyers, please. The other two will have to wait outside," the judge announced.

Véronique and Joachim looked at me and left. My lawyers, with me between them, sat to the left of the judge. I wondered who this blonde woman was, but from the way she had looked at me I felt she was there to testify against me. The minutes passed.

The judge leaned down toward the speaker on his desk and called, "Herr Volkmann, *bitte.*"

Still nothing. My mind was racing. It was 12:07 already. Was he not going to show up?

Suddenly, the door flew open. Hans-Peter's brother-in-law Klaus, who is six foot three, a short blond man, and Hans-Peter frantically rushed in and took their seats opposite us. Hans-Peter looked flustered: his eyes were glazed, staring into the distance. I shivered.

The judge began in German. He spoke slowly and clearly. I managed to understand most of what he said.

Dr. Schirker stood up and, from what I could make of it, explained how Hans-Peter had failed to return the children, breaching our agreement . . . how settled and happy the children were in London. Hans-Peter's expression did not change. His eyes stared at the white wall behind me. He didn't look at me once.

Klaus interrupted my lawyer in an arrogant tone and began a long speech. He was slouched in his chair and spoke so fast that I did not understand a word. But what was being said was obviously against me.

The judge agreed to whatever demand Klaus had just made, and the blonde woman started talking, spitefully glancing at me from time to time:

"I have talked to Alexander and Constantin. They both expressed their strong will to remain in Germany. They do love their mother but felt unhappy in England. They did not like their school. They endured Nazi taunts. They said their mother works and is not around for them. There is a very nice school next to where they live now. . . . "

I could not believe my ears. What was this woman saying? My sons, teased at school for being Nazis? This was insane. And what had this to do with a court case about abduction? I stared at her, stared in front of me, stared at the judge. I was horrified.

"What's this talk of Nazis? This is 1994!" I asked my lawyer.

"Don't worry. Keep calm. This woman is a social worker, from the Verden Youth Authority. Let the judge make up his own mind."

The judge then asked me to present my case, which I managed to do with deadly calm. This was very serious. It concerned my sons, and I knew I had to be composed.

Hans-Peter then spoke: the children felt German, wanted to go to a German school. . . . He still stared at the wall, his lip trembling, and his voice, too.

I felt as if I were part of a war movie, brought before the court on a nationality trial.

A discussion followed as to whether the children should be brought in. The judge spoke into the loudspeaker: "Volkmann children, please come forward."

Suddenly, the little blond man, the local lawyer, stood up and shot out of the room. Dr. Schirker exclaimed, "But this is totally irregular. You cannot just leave the courtroom in the middle of a hearing. . . . " The man had already disappeared.

Five minutes later he was back. The judge asked for an explanation: the children were not in the building but in Café Jens downtown.

The judge called for a recess. Hans-Peter and his two lawyers loudly stormed out of the room, followed by the blonde woman.

As my two lawyers and I walked out into the hallway, we saw a crowd of people belonging to Hans-Peter's party standing opposite. We dashed to join Véronique and Joachim, who had waited in the small area on the right. They both looked pale and worried:

"Katia, do you know who's here? Masha!"

"Masha!"

"Yes! And I wonder how Hans-Peter got her a visa."

We quickly recounted the hearing.

"But the children should have been in the building. This is completely irregular," Joachim interjected.

Joachim was deliberating on strategies when we heard the judge's voice calling us back in. Both Véronique and Joachim squeezed my arm:

"Courage, Catherine!"

We went in first and sat down. I looked at Hans-Peter walking in; his movements were uncoordinated, his expression bitter. This was the man I had married, with whom I had had two sons, and now he had declared war.

The judge said something and started reading his decision. My mind was too paralyzed to focus on any discernible words I might recognize. Then: "The respondent, Dr. Volkmann, is ordered to surrender to the petitioner the two children of the marriage to enable their immediate return to the United Kingdom. The court orders the immediate execution of the ruling. The obligation to surrender the children may be enforced with the aid of a court bailiff. The court bailiff is empowered to enlist police support where necessary. The order for surrender may where necessary be enforced by the application of physical force."

My sons were coming back! We would be reunited at last! The nightmare would end, yet I could not rejoice: something inside me could not believe it. Hans-Peter's face had disintegrated into the most hateful expression. His lip was shaking. His eyes were glazed. Klaus and the other lawyer said something to each other, then:

"Dr. Volkmann would like half an hour to bring the children," and before I had time to react to the meaning of the request, Dr. Schirker answered, "Of course, I am sure I can trust my colleagues. Police enforcement will not be necessary. Half an hour to bring the children to the court building. . . . "

I stared at him with horror, but Hans-Peter, his two lawyers, and the social worker had already charged out of the courtroom.

We packed our papers, thanked the judge, and walked out; the corridor was deserted. Only Véronique and Joachim stood by the door. We kissed and sighed with relief.

"But why did they all gallop downstairs? We saw Hans-Peter run out of the courtroom, his party behind him, and in a flash they'd disappeared. There's something fishy about this," Joachim interrupted. "Catherine, where's this Café Jens? I think we should go there immediately. You stay here with the lawyer, in case the children are brought back. Véronique, Dr. Schirker, and I will go and see what's going on."

The three of them left. It was 1:30 P.M.; the building was deserted. The atmosphere felt ominous. I knew something was desperately wrong. Why had my lawyer allowed this half-hour? Dr. Schirker was an honorable man and probably couldn't imagine that a forty-year-old doctor would behave irresponsibly. Had Joachim been in court, this would never have happened. He knew Hans-Peter's capricious and obstinate character. He knew how his family would bend to all his demands and how Hans-Peter saw the boys as his possessions.

We waited. I sat down, weak and unnerved. The minutes dragged on, and the tension became insufferable. I lit a cigarette.

We heard hurried footsteps. Véronique, Joachim, and Dr. Schirker came rushing toward us breathless. Joachim reported:

"We walked into the coffee shop, and Véronique heard children's voices coming up the basement stairs. She turned around and saw Alexander and Hans-Peter. Constantin and Antje were behind them. Véronique hardly had time to say, 'Bonjour, Alexandre,' when Hans-Peter grabbed him by the hand. Antje grabbed Constantin, and they ran out of the café. For a second we stood there stupefied, then we started running after them along the pedestrian walkway. I shouted: 'Stop,' but they didn't. Passersby were staring. Antje turned and yelled at Dr. Schirker: 'You criminal. We'll never return the children.' Then Hans-Peter and Antje threw the children into the backseat of a car, slammed the doors, and accelerated away. Antje was at the wheel. As she drove past us, she opened her window and yelled, 'In any case, we're off to Celle,' and their car vanished around the corner. It was incredible. She and Hans-Peter looked as if they were mad, nearly possessed."

"And Antje is a lawyer!" Dr. Schirker exclaimed in disbelief. "She could be debarred for this."

I was speechless. For some unknown reason, Dr. Schirker had taken his heavy briefcase with him. I could just imagine the scene: my polite and subdued lawyer carrying a load of files, my sister overwhelmed—only Joachim would have had the quickness of mind to grasp the situation, but he was unable to run owing to his physical disability.

Dr. Schirker muttered, "We need to get the court order and present it to Hans-Peter's local lawyer," and he set off down the corridor. Fifteen minutes later he was back.

"I can't believe it. There's no one around. The judge has gone home. We seem to be the only people in this desolate building. But I finally managed to find a secretary. She'll type the order."

We waited. My sister and I lit more cigarettes.

The secretary was ready, and Dr. Schirker went off to deliver the order. He came back, beside himself:

"Do you know what's happened? Hans-Peter's Verden lawyer has closed his office. There's no one there. They've all walked out and simply shut down for the day! I couldn't serve the court order."

Joachim was the only one who still had his wits about him.

"We'll have to find a bailiff. Is there a phone anywhere?" he asked.

We found a small room with a telephone equipped for local calls only. Court order in hand, Dr. Schirker began dialing the numbers on the list the secretary had given him. But Verden was closing its ranks and its doors to outsiders. No bailiffs were available. One was out to lunch, another was off duty, a third otherwise engaged.

"Phone Hans-Peter's father, maybe he'll see sense," Joachim suggested.

"Dr. Volkmann? This is Dr. Schirker, I am your daughter-in-law's lawyer. Your son is acting irresponsibly. . . . "

"My son isn't here. I don't know where he is."

"Dr. Volkmann, this isn't a game. This is extremely serious. Please tell us where your son is. He has abducted the children and defied a court order. Are you aware that he's risking a jail sentence? You must be sensible and realize that this behavior is in neither your son's nor your grandsons' interest. I urge you to cooperate—for everyone's sake."

"It's none of my business. Nor is the court's decision!"

The conversation was hopeless. Dr. Schirker hung up, furious, and disappeared out of the room. There was still no one to be found.

"Where are we? I've never seen a place like this!"

It was four o'clock. The children should have been returned by two.

The door of our room opened, and a smiling man walked in.

"I hear you're in a spot of trouble. Tell me," he said.

Dr. Schirker explained the situation and said that we could not locate a bailiff.

"Ah, *ja*. I know Hans-Peter Volkmann. A very prominent family in Verden. Dr. Hans-Werner Volkmann is a member of the Rotary Club. . . . I was never admitted as a member."

Joachim immediately caught on and joined in the conversation, understanding that we might have discovered an ally. Indeed, within half an hour, two court bailiffs were waiting downstairs for us.

They were both very young and looked hesitant.

"Hmm . . . Judge Monkmann? We have to go to Judge Monkmann's property?"

They got into their car with the young lawyer and led the way out of Verden and down a country lane. It was about five o'clock when we turned off onto the forest track leading to Wilfred's and Hans-Peter's houses.

We proceeded along the muddy track, across the abandoned railway line, and onto private property. All was uncannily quiet and eerie. We stopped the cars between the two houses. The court bailiffs and Dr. Schirker got out. Ute's daughters came out of their house on the left and walked toward them. The eldest said hello, while her twelve-year-old younger sister stood behind her with such an expression of hatred that I shivered. One of the bailiffs asked the fourteen-year-old where the children were.

"No one's here," she answered, "and I don't know where they are. Good-bye," and both girls retreated into the house. My sister, Joachim, and I had stayed in the car, frozen by the chilly atmosphere of this desolate place. Even Joachim's zeal had evaporated.

I looked at Hans-Peter's house. Could my sons be hidden there? I got out of the car and asked my lawyer whether we could look inside.

"There's no one here, I'm certain!"

We drove away and tried Hans-Jorg's house back in Verden. The bailiff timidly rang the doorbell. He was extremely ill at ease. He knew the Volkmanns and dreaded his present duty. Hans-Jorg opened the door. His expression was worse than I had anticipated. Arrogant, spiteful, his lip curled up, he dismissed us as if we were beggars seeking a handout:

"Neither my brother nor the children are here. I don't know where they are. Good-bye, gentlemen," and he closed the door without having said hello or looked at my sister or me.

Dr. Schirker was horrified. He turned to his friend, Joachim:

"My God, he was just incredible! I thought the sister was arrogant and rude, but this one!"

Our next stop was Hans-Werner and Gundel. My sister and I got out of the car as if we were living through a bad dream.

No answer. The bailiff rang again.

Finally, Gundel opened the door. Hans-Werner, standing behind her, looked old and tired. As usual, Gundel took over.

"*Nein,* the children aren't here, and I don't know where they are."

I moved forward.

"Gundel, please," I said. "Tell me where my sons are. I'm their mother. . . . " I had tears in my eyes, and although I knew the appeal would prove useless, I still hoped.

"You think I'm hiding them? Please search the house!"

The bailiff was getting very embarrassed.

"Catherine, I do not know where your children are, and I don't want to know. This has nothing to do with us. I've always been a good grandmother to them," and she shut the door on us.

We returned to our cars. The bailiffs quickly took their leave, relieved their job was over. I had no tears left. My mind was empty, and my body drained.

"I'm leaving," the young lawyer announced. "Tomorrow I have an early meeting at the office. Could you drop me at the train station in Bremen?"

I had lost my *sons.* Two small boys had been spirited away from their mother in a most horrific conspiratorial way. Justice was on my side, Hans-Peter was acting like a criminal—but my lawyer had another meeting to attend.

Only Joachim seemed to care.

"But what about Celle? Isn't that where the higher court is? It's only forty minutes away. I think we ought to drive there first."

"Well, I don't know. Let's wait till tomorrow," suggested Dr. Schirker. My sister and I were too overwhelmed by our day to add anything.

After we dropped the lawyer off, we found a hotel in Verden for a sleepless night. The next morning the four of us met the bailiff in front of the court building as arranged.

Dr. Schirker dropped the court order into Hans-Peter's lawyer's office just opposite. Then we set off on our vain search. Our last stop was Gundel's house. She still claimed not to know the whereabouts of the children. As we were about to drive off to the police station to report Hans-Peter, we saw Klaus walking toward the house, carrying a bag from the bakery. It must have contained more than a dozen buns. Dr. Schirker jumped out of the car. The two of them stood in the street, talking for what seemed to be a very long time.

"But the children must be in the house!" I exclaimed.

"Klaus has certainly brought enough buns for an army," mused Joachim.

"Well, why can't we go in and have the order executed?"

"Calm down. Dr. Schirker must be dealing with this," my sister answered.

We waited. Dr. Schirker finally came to the car.

"Well, we may be getting somewhere. Klaus wants to meet me at eleven at a coffeehouse to discuss handing over the children, but let's go to the police station and report Hans-Peter first."

I was worried. Dr. Schirker seemed to be overcome by what had happened. He had never come across such difficult people in his customary commercial litigation. I feared he was being naive.

I could not blame Joachim's friend. Joachim was a very loyal person. Criticizing his friend would be unkind, especially when he had been so helpful and supportive.

And at that time I did not know about German law or its application. But instinctively I realized we were being too "civilized," especially as it was my sons' futures at stake.

I conferred with my sister in Russian. She felt Dr. Schirker was a lawyer and no doubt knew how to deal with the situation.

I fell silent. We reached the police station. A constable calmly led us into his office and began taking long notes about our case, which he then dictated to a secretary. He wanted us to stay until she finished typing it to check if all was correct. Why did he need a full report? I wondered. We had the court decision in hand, ordering the immediate return of the children to England—with the help of the police force, if necessary. I had expected him to launch a police search. I remembered how, the year before, a Frenchman who had abducted his son had been chased by the French police and sent to jail for seven years. But here in Verden the police saw Hans-Peter as their next-door neighbor and a pal, court order or not.

Time was speeding by. It was five minutes to eleven. Dr. Schirker was getting impatient. Finally, the policeman was satisfied with his well-written report and let us go. We rushed back to the car.

"Joachim, you'd better go to the court building with Véronique and Catherine and get an Interpol alert while I go and meet Klaus. We have to make sure Hans-Peter doesn't leave the country."

Leave the country? I thought. Hans-Peter wouldn't leave the country—where else could he be better protected than in Verden!

Véronique, Joachim, and I walked into the red brick modern block. Today there seemed to be people around, but none were ready to help:

"*Nein,* it's the other office, down the corridor."

"Oh, they must have made a mistake, I don't deal with these matters. Try the second office on your left."

"Sorry, he's out on his coffee break."

Joachim was furious. I could see the veins on his forehead dilating. A woman approached us.

"What can I do for you?" she asked in a severe, unsympathetic voice. Joachim explained.

"Let me see the court decision." Véronique handed it to her.

"Well, I see . . . ," and she went on without my being able to understand. Then she pointed toward another office door and turned to leave.

"Véronique, the papers?"

The woman was holding them tightly to her chest as if she wanted to keep them.

"Oh, yes, of course," and she handed them back.

We knocked on the door, and a voice called, "Come in."

Joachim walked in first. I followed him and turned toward my sister in horror: "It's Wilfred Monkmann's sister!" I exclaimed in Russian. We looked at each other as if we had just seen a ghost.

"Hello, Catherine."

"Hello, Sophie."

Joachim started to explain what we needed, completely unaware of the situation.

"Well, I'm sorry. I can't do anything for you."

"And why not?" Joachim's voice was trembling with anger, but he remained courteous.

"Because your lawyer is not here."

"This is completely irrelevant. Here is the court order—"

She looked at it.

"No, I'm sorry. I can't help you." She stood up and led us back to the door. Then she turned toward me:

"Yes, and how are you, Catherine?"

I do not know what came over me, but I smiled and answered her politely. I had been so affected by the daunting events of the past two days that I was too frightened to reply otherwise.

We walked toward the Café Jens on Verden's main street. My thoughts were in a blur, I felt strange, the blood was streaming away from my head, and suddenly everything went blank. . . . When I opened my eyes, Joachim and Véronique were leaning over me, trying to help me up from the footpath.

"Catherine, we'd better go and eat something. Are you all right? How's your head? You fell backward, straight onto the ground. Are you sure your head is okay?" Véronique held me by one arm, Joachim by the other, until we reached the coffeehouse.

My head did not hurt—but everything else did. We ordered some food and waited. It was three o'clock when Dr. Schirker finally appeared.

"I had a long conversation with Klaus. In principle, they agreed to return the children by five o'clock. . . . " Then he hesitated, as if realizing for the first time the meaning of what he was about to say, "but Klaus mentioned something about the Celle court. I'd better call the court." He left to telephone.

The children back? At five o'clock? I so desperately wanted it to be true—but I couldn't believe it. Dr. Schirker came back:

"I've just talked to the judge in Celle. He said Dr. Volkmann has lodged an appeal against yesterday's decision. The judge accepted it and ruled that until the case is heard, Hans-Peter should keep the children because you might try to hide them in England if they are given back to you."

"What? What do you mean, accepted the appeal?"

"Well, Celle is the higher court, and appeals can be lodged there."

"But that's impossible! How could the judge accept an appeal when Hans-Peter was in contempt of court, when he was reported to the police? How could he accept an appeal without even informing us and letting us defend ourselves? How can the children not be returned to England when the judge in Verden ordered their return?" I was beside myself. "I guess Judge Monkmann accompanied Hans-Peter to Celle. We were tricked, and Celle is supporting Hans-Peter's illegal actions!"

Véronique took me in her arms:

"Calm down. All is not lost. Hans-Peter can't get away with this!"

"But the boys! Where are my boys? I want to see my boys. They've been tricked, too, by their own father. Imagine what they must have been told when they were running out of the café! What lies are they being fed? And what were my boys doing at a psychologist's house for ten days? My poor, poor boys." I was sobbing, my head in my hands. Joachim and Véronique were silent, absorbing the full tragedy of the situation.

Dr. Schirker spoke first. "Well, there's nothing more I can do for the moment. I'd better return to Munich. I think I can catch a plane from Bremen in an hour. As for you, there's little point in staying here now, you had all better go home, too."

The three of us drove back to Hamburg. I sat in the back of the car, resigned and depressed, looking blankly at the fields streaming past. My children were hidden away somewhere and held prisoners, their little minds tortured. . . . Joachim saw my blank expression in the car mirror.

"Catherine. Don't worry so much. We'll win in Celle! I know how you feel, but try to look at it just as a snag, not the final outcome. Hans-Peter won't be able to defy the law forever. Our only problem will be that here family law is different from England and France. In Germany, the 'will' of a child is taken into account—even at Alexander's age. This is what Hans-Peter is basing his case on, and he'll continue to influence the boys into saying they want to remain in Germany. However, the judges in Celle will be aware of this and will have to consider Hans-Peter's illegal behavior. They'll also have to examine the evidence. Your boys were excellent at school, and everyone knows how indicative this is of a child's mental stability and home environment. What you must do is get your friends who know Alexander and Constantin to give their testimony. Catherine, I know how much Alexander and Constantin love you. Hans-Peter won't be able to destroy that—at least not in the long term."

The three of us parted, sad and exhausted. I felt lost, betrayed, and frightened and could not stop worrying for my boys. There was something so threatening about the Monkmann property lost in the woods, the abandoned railroad track, the mist hanging over the long muddy road, and the two lone houses, cut off from the world. It reminded me of the scary fairy tale "Hansel and Gretel." My sons were out there, lost in the forest without my arms to protect them. Verden, the social worker, the drawn curtains, and closed doors belonged more to a horror movie than to reality. I was overwhelmed by an awful sense of fear.

But this was only the beginning of the terrifying nightmare my sons and I now live.

CHAPTER 12

The Abyss

The evil of modern society isn't that it creates
racism but that it creates conditions in which
people who don't suffer from injustice seem
incapable of caring about people who do.

—LOUIS MANAND

I returned to my empty London home. The presents were still lying on the beds with the schoolbooks. The Lego knights and pirate boats were still neatly arranged in the wardrobe, the cars lined up on the windowsill, the big American flag hung on the yellow wall of my babies' room. All was still.

I closed their bedroom door. The entrance hall grew dark, no longer lit by the sun shining through their window. I opened the door again and tried to find solace in Joachim's words:

"Think of it just as a snag. Your children will be back!"

But everything was worrying: "In Germany, a child's wishes are taken into account." I felt sure their wishes were being manipulated. This would be the only way of conditioning children to reject their own mother, and I knew now that Hans-Peter was capable of even that.

On Friday, September 23, surprisingly, I reached Hans-Peter at home:

"Hello, Hans-Peter? It's me."

"What do you want?"

"Well, I'd like to talk to the children." I heard Hans-Peter's voice: "Alexander. Tell her!" Alexander came to the telephone.

"Hello."

"Hello, Alexander. It's Mummy."

Silence.

"Alexander, I was in Verden two days ago. I wanted to see you, but I didn't know where you were."

"I won't tell you!" His voice was aggressive, shut off, and distant. He had obviously been told that he was being hidden from me—the enemy! Alexander was repeating coldly a series of ready-made sentences conveyed to him by adults.

"Alexander, aren't you going to school? School started six weeks ago."

"That's not true! You're lying!"

"Of course I'm not lying. Why should I lie? I've never lied to you."

"Yes, you lie. And the judge lied, too. He's an idiot!"

Alexander had never spoken in this way. Even his voice was different: cold and bitter, similar to his father's. I was horrified at what my son was saying and how alien he was to the boy who had left London three months ago. I tried to change the subject, but there were few avenues open. I found out that Masha was still there, and how nice she was!

"But you never liked Masha. She was too strict and grumpy. Don't you remember how you and Constantin used to imitate her nagging? And we were so pleased when she finally left."

"That's not true. She was strict because you forced her to be strict."

"Do you want to speak with Constantin?" And Alexander passed the phone over without saying good-bye. Tini was different. There was no bitterness or aggression in his voice. He did not retire into self-defensive coldness. On the contrary, a thin little whine of a voice came on:

"Mummy?"

"Yes, darling. How are you?"

"Okay," he said in a weak and unconvincing tone. I felt so sorry for him.

"Tini?"

"Yes . . . "

I felt he wanted to say something but was scared to.

"Tell me, Tini?"

"No . . . I have to go now, Mummy. Bye."

I pictured them—Constantin abandoned and distressed, Alexander overburdened and angry. I imagined how Hans-Peter and Antje had panicked after seeing Véronique, Joachim, and the lawyer in the café. How hysterically they had executed their next move, insulting Dr. Schirker and the judge, screaming at the children, and defaming their mother. Maybe Tini had asked, "But why are we running away from my mummy?" and had been scolded.

Alexander was probably terrorized by his father's aggression and single-mindedness. Cornered, under his control, he had no choice but to conform. Yet the upheaval in his mind was such that it had made him angry and aggressive.

I agonized about my sons' well-being, grieved at their loss, and was tortured by the thought of what was being done to them. As their mother, I could sense how deeply unsettled Alexander was, and I could hear Constantin calling for me in his dreams. How did Hans-Peter respond to their fears? What was he doing to control them? Thinking about what they were undergoing made me shudder.

I was also increasingly alarmed by the legal development of the case—justice was on my side, yet the courts' decisions had not been enforced. My sons were still unreachable, and the way Hans-Peter had obtained a stay of execution on Celle boded ill.

On September 20, 1994, a further summons had been issued by the High Court of Justice under article 8 of the Child Abduction and Custody Act of 1985 and article 15 of the Hague Convention with an order for it to be disclosed in the proceedings in Celle. The Verden decision had also been explicit: "The retention of the children is unlawful. . . . The children are only seven and nine years old, and in the view of the court there can thus be no question of considerable intent on the part of the children. . . . The expert opinion obtained by the father is to be viewed with reservations. It has been obtained for the sole purpose of supporting his view. . . . "

A consultant physician at a prominent London teaching hospital and senior lecturer in medicine at London University, with professional experience of children, read the report and wrote:

It is not clear to me why the children had to travel to this island to see this particular doctor. My information is that Dr. Schoen is not a leading expert in child psychology and that other experts could have been more easily contacted (closer to Verden). It would be important to determine why Dr. Schoen was specifically requested to issue this report. . . . It is extremely important to note that the report was prepared following interviews with Hans-Peter Volkmann and the children but in the absence of the mother. . . . This failure to interview independently all the parties involved, indeed, even to comment on this failure, seriously prejudices the professional integrity of the report. Dr. Schoen identifies a number of disturbing factors: discontinuity of care, that the mother is not around, the nervous symptoms of the boys, the angst displayed by Constantin, the aggression of Alexander toward his mother, the sense that the children are being verbally manipulated. . . . While these symptoms are presented as evidence that there is a poor relationship between the mother and the children, alternative interpretations of these symptoms should have been considered. At the time of the interview the children had not seen their mother for three months. It is quite extraordinary that an expert in child behavior would not take account of this important issue. . . . An alternative interpretation is that the children's behavior at the time of the interview reflected the problems encountered since their abduction ... [and] the effects on children in a disrupted environment who have been under the care of one parent who is aggressive toward the other parent. . . . Dr. Schoen's professional independence is in conflict with his interpretation of much of the data presented. He has concluded that the children's return to London would cause severe psychological damage. This is a most serious allegation, yet his professional judgment must be questioned. In summary, I found this report fundamentally flawed. It has a biased interpretation of the observations.

In the meantime, Dr. Schirker was still unable to obtain a date for the Celle hearing—he would be advised in due course. By the end of the first week of October I was frantic, realizing that the longer the children were under Hans-Peter's influence, the more rehearsed they would become. I implored Dr. Schirker to inquire further. The judge could not be reached for two days. Two days later he was celebrating his birthday with the staff and could not be disturbed. We had to wait—but how can a mother wait patiently when she believes her children are in danger?

Finally, a date for the hearing was set: October 20—just within the one-month limit. The director of the Lycée, teachers, and friends provided me with detailed statements. The teachers praised the boys' academic results; the director testified how well integrated and popular with their classmates they were; parents confirmed how polite, gentle, and happy they were; my friends (most of whom have known me for over twenty years) testified how devoted a mother I was; and my past and present employers attested that I was a responsible individual. Everyone told me not to worry, that justice would prevail, the law was on my side, all the evidence was in the court. Leonard, Alexander's godfather, would accompany me as a witness and for moral support.

I hesitated about which lawyer to use. Dr. Kram, the Munich lawyer, had reappeared and was willing to take the case back.

He was a specialist in Hague Convention cases. Dr. Schirker was not. I conferred with my parents, my sister, and my close friends until we reached a unanimous consensus: stay with Dr. Schirker. He would surely be less trusting now that he knew what we were dealing with.

On October 19, 1994, Leonard and I flew to Hanover, where we met Joachim, my sister, and the two lawyers, and we drove to Celle that evening. I felt nervous and unsettled. How would my sons react to me? They had not seen me for four and a half months, had hardly been allowed to speak on the telephone, and I assumed Hans-Peter had indoctrinated them further, perhaps taking them to his psychologist again.

The atmosphere in Celle was very different to that of Verden with its quaint streets and picturesque houses. The High Court of Lower Saxony, situated in this town of fifty thousand inhabitants, was in an old building in the town center. Winter had arrived.

The court building was deserted, and we waited apprehensively in the cold corridor.

At five minutes to two, the two lawyers and I went to sit in the empty courtroom, leaving Véronique, Joachim, and Leonard outside. We waited in silence. At ten minutes past two, a crowd of people arrived. Hans-Peter, Klaus, two other lawyers, Judge Monkmann, Frau Kranitz (the social worker), and my two little boys walked straight into the courtroom while the rest of their party remained outside in the small anteroom. They had an aura of hysteria about them. I could see Ute, Antje, and two men I did not know standing outside. Hans-Peter and his lawyers went to sit in their allocated places opposite the judges' tribune, to our right. The rest sat on a bench behind us, my sons next to Wilfred Monkmann. At that moment the three judges, in black robes, walked through the door opposite us. It seemed they had arrived with the others.

My boys . . . I left my seat and hurriedly approached them. I kneeled on the floor to kiss them. Alexander's face was hardly recognizable—angry and tense. I bent forward.

"Hello, Alexander," I said in French.

He did not look at me and started to hit me with his arms and legs. I was flabbergasted, shocked, staggered. Wilfred stared at him fixedly. What had they done to my children? I turned to Constantin, tears in my eyes:

"Tini?"

He turned his head to the side to avoid looking at me. My God, what have they done to the poor boys! I ran out of the courtroom, sobbing. My friends surrounded me, but I felt alone in my agony. Anyone could hate me, but being rejected by one's own children is beyond human endurance. Dr. Schirker came over quickly:

"Don't worry, the judges must have realized how manipulated your sons are. No child would react so to his mother. Just stay calm." I wiped away my tears and went back into the courtroom in a complete daze. Nothing could have hit harder, no emotion could have been deeper.

I looked at Hans-Peter, surrounded by his lawyers. He was staring at the top of the wall opposite, his hands joined together as though in prayer. I shivered.

The judge started talking in German legal language, and the boys were led out by Wilfred, who then returned to his seat behind me. My second lawyer stood up to speak his only sentence during the whole hearing:

"We would like to ask the court whether court bailiffs could be provided, as we would not like to see a repetition of last month's events."

He sat down, and the main judge proceeded. He talked at length while his two colleagues looked straight ahead.

I did not understand a word the judge said, nor any of the long statements made by Hans-Peter's lawyers. Finally, the three judges stood up and took off their black robes. My lawyer whispered to me, "They're going to interview the children now."

"But they've been brainwashed for months. You saw how Alexander reacted! This is awful . . . and awful for them." I was saying the words but was incapable of thinking straight, over-powered by events, unable to understand the procedures, dependent on my lawyers.

Hans-Peter's party rushed out of the courtroom into the small anteroom immediately outside, and Hans-Peter led Alexander into another room for his private interview with the judges. We joined my party; they had been waiting in the larger waiting area leading off the anteroom. All three had a quiet, doom-laden expression. Leonard and I decided to go back to the ante-room. Little Constantin was sitting on Hans-Peter's lap, shielded by a group of tall adults. As we walked in, Hans-Peter turned Constantin around on his lap so that his back was to us. His party was sitting all around the room: however, one chair in the far corner was free, so Leonard and I sat down, sharing it. Leonard said hello to both Hans-Peter and Constantin but was completely ignored. He persevered with Constantin, asking him how he was, but he would neither answer nor look at Leonard; his head was still turned away. I tried as well, softly calling his name. He moved his head, but he would not answer. Hans-Peter kept distracting him with little toys and some sweets that were lying on the table. As both Leonard and I periodically tried to talk to Constantin, Hans-Peter readjusted him on his lap to face the opposite way from us while Ute, Antje, the social worker, and Klaus were actively talking to each other in excessively loud voices—as if to muffle mine.

Constantin's unease was obvious, and I detected an expres-sion of irony on his face—as if this were part of a game he had to perform. He sat still and let himself be handled. This was so unlike the little boy he used to be, independent, full of energy and endless talk. Leonard and I were so struck by it that we sat silent for a while.

A man came up and barked at us: "Get up, I want to sit here!" Leonard's basic German was enough for him to under-stand what the man had said. We looked at each other, shocked by his rudeness, and ignored his request.

This was Dr. Schoen, the psychologist. I felt frightened. Constantin turned his head toward me as I tried to say a few words. I sensed he wanted to tell me something, but Hans-Peter immediately turned him and took out a book to show Constantin. The book had a strange picture in it; a black background with a ghostlike shape similar to a cross. I turned around and noticed that Dr. Schoen had remained standing behind me, his eyes fixed on Constantin. Automatically, I jumped up to stand between them to block Dr. Schoen's field of vision and shield my son.

At this point the door on the side of the room opened and Alexander walked out. His face was pale, his hair disheveled; he looked tormented. Hans-Peter hurried toward him:

"So, what did you say?" he asked. Taking him by the hand, he rushed out of the anteroom through the waiting area and into the corridor. Constantin was led by Ute through the door for his private interview. The psychologist, Ute, Antje, Klaus, Wilfred, the social worker, and the other man (another social worker, apparently) hurriedly left to join Hans-Peter and surround Alexander.

Véronique, Joachim, and the two lawyers stood at the other end of the waiting area. Véronique and Joachim were still distraught and shocked by the hysterical behavior and belligerence of Hans-Peter's party. While I was in the courtroom, Véronique and Joachim had tried to say hello to Ute and Antje but had been ignored. Ute's fiercely hostile expression had paralyzed them. My lawyers had an unmistakable air of defeat about them. Only Leonard had any strength left and could think coherently.

"Let's try to talk to Alexander," he suggested.

We walked down the corridor, Leonard leading the way. As soon as Hans-Peter saw us, he grabbed Alexander by the hand and directed him toward the men's room.

"Leave him alone!" Hans-Peter screamed at me. Leonard and I stood still. Finally, they came out. Leonard walked forward:

"Hello, Alexander. How nice it is to see you."

"You can keep your money and your chocolates and go away," Alexander shouted aggressively as he was whisked away toward Ute and the psychologist.

Leonard was speechless. Alexander used to love his godfather, whom he saw often. They had a running joke about their mutual love of chocolates, and when Leonard telephoned, Alexander would rush to talk to him first—about chocolates! For Christmas and for his birthday, Alexander would receive some money. This was his favorite treat, and he would proudly put it in his own bank account.

When Constantin emerged from his fifteen-minute talk with the judges, there was a slight ebb in the hysterical behavior of Hans-Peter's party. The judges called us back into the courtroom. Hans-Peter, his three lawyers, the social worker, Judge Monkmann, my two lawyers, and I went in; the rest stayed outside.

The senior judge spoke, but the only moment I was able to follow what was being said was when Frau Kranitz spoke. The Verden Social Services had themselves appealed against the decision of September 20. I never understood how this was possible. Neither Frau Kranitz nor anyone in her department had ever talked to me or to the boys' schoolteachers and no inquiry about the children's lives in London, their school results, or our social conditions was ever made. I wondered how their testimony, which represented one side, could be acceptable.

Frau Kranitz used exactly the same words she had used the month before in Verden, and again mentioned the word *Nazi*. I turned to Dr. Schirker and muttered that he should intervene. He held my hand still:

"No. Let the judges decide. They have the information we've sent them, and they know. Stay calm, don't worry." But I worried like mad and felt uncomfortable and helpless. The court recessed for a second time—the judges were to make their decision.

Before the first recess, Leonard had managed to approach the children as we were in court. As he recounted in his later report:

Following the children's interview, I sensed a slight lifting in the constant shielding and escorting of the two boys by members of Hans-Peter's party. . . . I entered the anteroom and found the children sitting with Hans-Peter's sister, Ute and Dr. Schoen. I said hello and sat down with them and was, as before, completely ignored. They continued to talk among themselves in German as if I were not there. . . . After ten minutes Dr. Schoen was called out. . . . There followed a silence, so I turned to Antje and asked her how she was. She seemed startled, but she did reply. I was so encouraged by the first civil interchange that I had had with any member of the Volkmann party that I continued to talk about my children and asked her about hers. . . . The door leading to the waiting area opened behind me, and the boys looked over and ran out. I did not see who beckoned them out. . . . I then suggested to Antje that we go out to the waiting area to find something to drink. The two boys were sitting at a table fiddling with some playing cards. I walked over and sat with them. Antje followed me and sat opposite me. I suggested playing cards. To my surprise, Alexander (who had still not spoken to me except for the one hostile remark) began to deal the cards. . . . Constantin began to laugh and joke with me—for those few minutes he was the jolly little boy I know. Alexander was more guarded, asking Antje where his father and Ute were. However, he also began to loosen up. . . . Catherine appeared from the courtroom, and I called her to come over. She pulled up a chair and joined us while we played the game. This continued for a few minutes, till I saw Hans-Peter appear in the distance. He saw us and immediately gesticulated to Alexander to come. Alexander put his cards down on the table at once and ran to him. Constantin followed behind him. We never finished the game.

I had no further chance of direct contact with the children again, as they spent the remainder of the time sitting in the small anteroom surrounded by members of Hans-Peter's party.

Leonard and I tried to approach the children, but again it was impossible. Ute held Constantin in her arms facing the window, the psychologist standing next to her and other members of Hans-Peter's party surrounding them. Alexander had disappeared with Hans-Peter. We had no choice but to wait and worry in silence while Joachim and Véronique were talking about the members of Hans-Peter's group, trying to work out what could link them together.

We were called back. This time Véronique also sat at the back, as we had decided that since Judge Monkmann had been present during the whole proceedings, there should be no reason why members of my party could not listen in. The tension was high, but I felt resigned. The same judge, sitting in the middle, spoke and started reading out the decision. He glanced at me above his glasses while reading. I knew then what the outcome would be, but I hung onto the rational notion that the law was on my side:

"We declare that the children, and particularly Alexander, have expressed a strong desire to remain in Germany. . . . The appeals of the father and the Youth Welfare Officer are upheld. . . . The [return of the children] is rejected pursuant to article 13 of the Hague Convention, since the children have decisively opposed such return. . . . "

I burst out, "But I'm their mother! You haven't even heard me." Silence.

I collapsed in tears. Hans-Peter, Klaus, Wilfred, and the social worker hurried out to the anteroom to join Ute, Antje, Dr. Schoen, and the other man, who were all standing at the door. There was uproar followed by delirious whoops of joy. I heard voices shouting several times: *"Wir haben gewonnen! Wir haben gewonnen!"*—We won! They laughed and kissed each other noisily, jumping and punching the air as if they had just won a football match. Alexander participated in this unbridled joy. Constantin looked puzzled and uneasy.

I was still crying and completely ignored by them all, when I saw Alexander marching into the courtroom, as if he were a little soldier in Red Square, up the steps of the tribune to shake the judge's hand. I was wide-eyed, horrified, and destroyed.

Still shrieking with joy, they began to lead the children away. I stood up and rushed behind them trying to say good-bye to my children as they left. My attempt was quickly rebuffed by Hans-Peter, who shouted at me in German, "Go away!" As my boys were led quickly away, surrounded by the large group, including the social worker and the psychologist, Constantin turned around to look at me, a deeply sad expression in his beautiful blue eyes, as if to say, "Mummy, help!" But Antje pulled him away, and I only saw my little Tini being dragged by the hand, his head still turned toward me.

The crowd disappeared, and silence fell on us. I slumped on a chair, my head between my knees. My lawyers were discussing the proceedings with Joachim, who was desperately trying to find a way in which we could save the situation. For a moment I felt antagonistic toward these professionals who had been so passive and intimidated. They would be returning to their families now, having simply lost one case among many others, and their lives would go on undisturbed. I had lost my sons.

We left, and once the lawyers had gone, Véronique, Joachim, Leonard, and I went over the details of the day and the attitude of Hans-Peter's group. What had been the most shocking and traumatic was their hysterical behavior and the jubilant cheering that followed the decision. They had vociferously celebrated their triumph—the separation of children from their mother—before the very victims whose lives they had destroyed.

As Leonard wrote:

There was continual shadowing and shielding of the children not only by their father, his sister, and his neighbors, but also by the professional experts brought into the case by Hans-Peter—the social worker and psychologist. The latter, Dr. Schoen, was particularly pervasive, constantly talking to the children, following them about or staring at them.

... The aggression and hostility of Alexander toward his mother and me was particularly shocking. This is a boy whom I have always known to be a well-balanced, well-behaved, and gentle child. Catherine could not go near him (or Hans-Peter) without being shouted at with great hostility. Constantin's docile, blank, and puzzled expression, his passive avoidance of both his mother and myself, was so sad to see in a little boy who I again know to be so full of life, as well as of spontaneous affection toward his mother. These were simply not the happy, well-balanced children who had left for their summer holiday to Germany four months ago. Only for those few minutes, during our card game, did they begin to resemble the children I know.

I had asked Leonard to write a report on what he had witnessed: "But can you do it soon, while all the details are fresh in your memory?"

"Catherine, I could write as detailed a report in ten years' time! I will never forget what I saw today. It was a ghastly, unspeakable nightmare that will remain with me forever. Those poor, poor children—what has been done to them?"

My parents were—thank goodness—in London for my return, sharing the tragedy and trying to comfort me. I sobbed through the night, unable to rest or calm myself. Nothing and no one could console me anymore, and my agony was uncontrollable. I was in a horrendous nightmare. Justice had betrayed my sons and deprived them of their birthright: their own mother.

My friends and my parents were outraged and heartbroken. They rallied around me with warmth and determination. Some wrote letters to the central authorities, others gathered legal information, and two girlfriends secretly set off to raise money to help me with the legal bills. Charlotte, a Greek woman whom I had met only a few times, contributed two thousand pounds to my cause, as did a Danish friend; a man whom I had never met chipped in as well; all in all, over twenty thousand pounds was raised. The unstinting support of my friends and their profound generosity touched me deeply. Without their loving care, I would have probably sunk then. They kept my belief going, and with it my life.

A few weeks after the Celle hearing, I received the court decision. It was faxed to me in the office. I sat in the conference room and read through the twelve pages:

> Following the hearing of the children, the court is also persuaded that they have attained an age and maturity in view of which it appears appropriate to take their opinion into account ... [since] a seven-year-old child faced with the decision to join either the judo or football club generally knows which decision to make. . . . Alexander buried his head in his arms on the table and remained sobbing. . . . Alexander justifies his decision ... not on grounds of the personal characteristics of one or the other parent, but primarily with the statement that he is German. In response to the simple inquiry as to whether the English are "different," he was unable to explain. . . . He confirmed that he has no friends at school, apart from his brother, as he is the only German there and is teased and called a "Nazi." ... In Hamburg he did not apparently feel restricted in terms of the available facilities for play since the French Lycée in Hamburg is attended by many German children. . . . The mother always bought only the most expensive clothes for herself, while buying clothes from cheap shops for the children. . . . The mother was never there. . . . Weekends [were] spent in polite walks through Hyde Park. . . . Alexander's entire environment is based on a foreign language, since German is not spoken either at school or at home. . . . The court is persuaded that the boy is undergoing considerable suffering and is convinced that his mother "simply took" his brother and him away with her. He thus feels even more abandoned in what he regards as an alien environment. . . .

In view of the other social and cultural differences, in particular the apparently demanding school tuition . . . Alexander's refusal to return to his mother is perfectly understandable. . . . The members of the court are also not lacking in appropriate personal experience, in that they are all fathers and grandfathers. . . . [and in less than a page] Constantin also conveys his own opinion, rather than one externally imposed on him. . . . He felt out of place at the school and had no friends, and the older children were always teasing him. . . . His opinion is also not based on a childish whim but on careful consideration. . . . The severe psychological strain is revealed by a manifest physical restlessness which is no longer appropriate for his age. . . . His brother was the most important person . . . as he was the only person with whom he could speak German. . . .

Hans-Peter had flagrantly violated the law. I had abided by it—yet the court was penalizing me and rewarding him, using nationalistic references as the ground for their decisions.

None of my witnesses had been called, and I, the mother, had not been heard by the judges. Yet after interviewing my sons for thirty and fifteen minutes, respectively, children who had been under the influence of their father and a psychologist, the judges concluded that it was the boys' "own" will to remain in Germany. And while the Verden judge had estimated that the children were too young for their view to be taken into account, now Constantin was deemed mature enough at seven to decide on his whole future! Yet Alexander, at nine, constantly changed his mind about whether he preferred rugby or football!

I was shaking like a leaf. The Celle court overruled two previous decisions that had ordered the "immediate" return of the children to England under an international convention because they decided that my sons had been "suffering" in an alien environment and because "German was not spoken at home or at school." Although my sons were trinational and trilingual, to the Celle judges they were not French, not English, not European; they were solely German—and this overrode everything else.

The judges felt it was better for children to be raised as Germans and considered that my boys should play only with German children. Pupils at the French Lycée represent sixty different nationalities, and in both Alexander's and Constantin's classes there were half-German boys like them. The judges considered that the English were "different" and referred to Alexander having stated that he "communicates in English to his school friends" when French, his maternal language, was spoken at the French Lycée. "Alexander obviously thinks in German and is obliged to translate in order to communicate" when no child has a capacity of "translating." I, their mother, a foreigner, was of no consequence. Not speaking German amounted to the infliction of psychological harm. Being denied a mother did not!

A German lawyer I met read the decision:

"This is a historical piece!" he exclaimed. "It could have been dated fifty-five years ago! It only has one aim—the glorification of one nationality. As far as the boys are concerned, it is inconceivable that in the space of such a short interview their psychological state could be established—especially when judges are not qualified child psychologists."

I took the decision to show it to my friends; I faxed it to the central authorities, to the Foreign Office, convinced that someone would take action. No one did. The Lord Chancellor's Office wrote me letters, saying that under the provision of article 13, children could not be returned. My member of Parliament said there was nothing he could do, and the German Central Authority in Berlin stated that the Celle order "is not appealable—unless the decision violates constitutional law. However, they would like to point out that the acceptance of a complaint through the Federal Constitutional Court in Karlsruhe really is an exception." In fact, over 95 percent of applications are rejected. "However, Ms. Laylle can apply for custody of her children at the Family Court in Verden at any time."

Under the international Hague Convention, the children should have been returned to England and final decisions on custody taken by the authorities of the children's habitual residence—England. By not returning the children, the Celle court therefore extended the meaning of the convention by giving an artificial jurisdiction on custody decisions to its own courts.

Not only had Hans-Peter managed to have all his illegalities sanctioned, but he now held an additional advantage, since it was he who had chosen the forum in which custody was to be decided—a forum favorable to him: the Lower Saxony courts.

I had trusted the judicial system, yet my boys and I were betrayed by the very institution that should have protected us. Ever since Hans-Peter had realized that our life in London was a success and that I would not be returning to him, he had embarked on his premeditated and unscrupulous plan. I had not noticed because I had been too busy with survival. Now the law was his accomplice in the ultimate revenge: to strip me of my sons forever, regardless of their suffering.

Every night I dreamed the same dream: Alexander in a dark cloud, tense and tormented, Constantin scared and distraught, calling out, "Mummy, help, help . . . ," and I would wake up with a start, sweat pouring from my face. When I had no more tears left, I would fall back to sleep, but the dream never left me. In the office I would try to switch my mind off—if only for an hour, if only for minutes. But the nightmare of my days was no better, divided between panic and despair.

Hans-Peter had proudly married a foreigner. He had consciously raised his children to be international. But he was incapable of handling his own fragile insecurities. So, he had run back to mother, family, and friends—pulling up the drawbridge against the outside world and holding our sons behind a wall, in its way as fortified as a medieval castle.

CHAPTER 13
Behind the Wall

Dr. Kram contacted me immediately after the Celle hearing, and my parents, my sister, my friends, and I decided I should switch to him. After all, he was an expert in the field. Dr. Kram decided he should meet me, and he flew to London the next morning.

Although I was one thousand pounds poorer, I felt Dr. Kram could redress the situation. He presented himself as determined and knowledgeable. In his opinion, the Celle decision, though legally watertight, was "particularly unusual," and so was the role of the Verden Youth Authority. But the Celle decision was restricted to the "nonreturn" of the children under the terms of the Hague Convention. It had not changed the custody provision or the children's legal place of residence—which was still in England.

Dr. Kram stressed that we should move fast, as time was working against us. With the children under Hans-Peter's control and influence, Klaus, Hans-Peter's lawyer, would soon benefit from an additional legal argument, namely, that the children were now settled in their new environment and that it would be against their "interest" to send them back to England. "In custody cases, possession is nine-tenths of the law," he added.

Since Hans-Peter refused me any form of visitation, Dr. Kram proposed that we file an urgent application for an access order. But our request was immediately rejected. The reason given to us was that Judge Moritz had just left, on October 22, for a three-week holiday and that the replacement judge could not make a decision. He had not yet received the case files from Celle, and anyway, he could not see the "urgency of the matter."

"But I haven't seen my sons for months. I don't understand. Why should the judge not allow me to see my own children, files or no files? When Hans-Peter went to Celle, the day after the Verden decision, the judges had no files, yet they stayed the execution of a *court order*. I am only applying to see my children."

"Don't worry, we'll make another court application."

We made several applications—all were rejected. The court now required a report from the Verden Youth Authority before it could make a decision on whether a mother could be with her children. I was incensed:

"This is crazy! We know in advance what Frau Kranitz will write in her report. She's testified against me twice without even having met me, and she was part of the 'victory celebration' by Hans-Peter and his family in Celle!"

"Well, let's first wait for the report, then we'll attack it. Frau Kranitz will no doubt contact you," said Dr. Kram.

But I did not hear from Frau Kranitz. Accordingly, no report was being prepared for the court. On November 29 Dr. Kram decided to telephone the director of the Youth Authority. An hour later he rang me back:

"I have just had the most outrageous conversation with Herr Lecker, the director of the Youth Authority. He told me that Frau Kranitz has no free time available for you! The earliest she could talk to you would be in two weeks—but only if you come to Verden. Telephone or written contacts are out of the question. . . . He also advises you to accept the Celle decision and leave your children alone. The quicker you withdraw your demand for custody in the Verden court, the better."

Dr. Kram was fuming. He told me he would send Herr Lecker a fax. For the record, he wanted to confirm this conversation. He also stressed how beyond belief it was for Herr Lecker to take such a position when he had never met the children, never spoken to the mother, and never inquired about our lives in England. Dr. Kram concluded that "in his twenty years' experience in family legal matters he had never come across such biased attitudes from the Social Services."

I was up against an insurmountable wall. Even telephone contact was impossible. The few conversations I managed to have with my sons were monitored—Alexander would echo his same repetitive sentences; Constantin would answer with a tense yes or no. I recorded two of these desperate conversations. But the sound of Alexander's blank and robotic words was too depressing and frightening for me to listen to again.

The boys' friends were also upset, particularly Sean. Alexander had given him his phone number in Verden before he had left on holiday. He wanted to invite him to come to Germany for a week during the summer. Sean—also aged nine—had tried to call Alexander, but Hans-Peter wouldn't let him speak to his friend. He had not heard from Alexander since his return to London either. Sean called me, tearful. Where was his best friend? For six months he kept the desk next to his free, believing Alexander would come back to school. The boy upstairs reacted in the same way. He would come down every day, then once a week, to ask whether I had heard anything. Then he would walk into the boys' bedroom, sad and petulant:

"I miss them so much. When will Alexander and Constantin be back?"

I would look at this nine-year-old grieving for his friends. Hans-Peter was breaking the hearts of so many people. I wondered if my eighty-two-year-old father would see his grandchildren before he died.

At the beginning of November, I sent Hans-Peter a fax urging a meeting, whenever he wanted, wherever he wanted, with the help of a mediator. Two weeks later I received a letter from his lawyer, written in German, explaining that no such meetings could take place and accusing me of being a bad mother—I should leave the children alone, stop trying to phone, and comply with their wish to remain in Germany.

Two weeks after that I telephoned again and had my last conversation ever with Hans-Peter. He literally yelled. He was making no sense and interrupted all my sentences. Throughout our conversation, he was shouting "I forbid you."

It started with:

"Hello, Hans-Peter."

"What do you want?"

"I would like to talk to my sons."

"Well, they don't want to talk to you. They are afraid that you want to take them away."

"Over the telephone?"

"The children are scared." His voice was trembling.

"Why should my children be scared of their own mother? It is—"

"You accused me of being a kidnapper! You are lying. You lied before the court in England. You made your friends lie."

"I made my friends lie?"

"Well, I don't want to talk to you on those terms."

"Which terms?"

"I want you to stop making the children's friends phone them, especially when I'm not here. You force their friends to phone them. I forbid you to make their friends phone them. Why don't you forbid their friends from calling? I want them to stop."

"How could I force their friends? I thought you said in court they have no friends. . . . "

He hung up. I dialed again.

.   .   .

"Why did you hang up?"

"I didn't hang up. What do you want? I haven't time to talk to you. I'm busy."

"I would like to talk to the boys. You can't throw me away. I'm their mother. You must realize what harm you're doing the children."

"I know you're their mother! But what's the point? What do you mean by that?" His voice was quavering even more.

"I think that a mother should be able to speak to her sons when—"

"Well, you can. I'll tell them to call you on Friday."

"Why should I make appointments to talk to my—"

"On this basis, I don't want to talk to you. If you insist on making their friends call, I will leave the answering machine on. Especially when I'm not here."

"But . . . "

"Look, I have no time, I don't want to talk to you. You can send me a fax. I don't want to discuss anything with you on the telephone."

"Well, I'm their mother . . . "

"What do you mean by that?"

"I think that maybe a mother and a father could—"

"Send me a fax in the office. I don't want to talk to you like this. I don't have time."

"Do you think your children will be proud of the way you speak to their mother?"

He hung up.

.   .   .

Five court demands had now been rejected. I had not spent any time with my sons for six months, and the central authorities were avoiding the issue. I knew I had to seek other avenues.

Just after we met and before Hans-Peter moved in with me; taken in front of my London flat in 1982.

Alexander and Mummy on the couch in Frankfurt in 1986.

Alexander at the playground in Wiesbaden, 1987. His face behind bars seems to me a premonition of what was to come.

Constantin eating porridge when Mummy is not looking, Hamburg, 1990.

Constantin's third birthday, May 1991.

Constantin playing cowboy in our kitchen in Hamburg, May 1991.

A happy family moment in 1990.

A family still united; summer holidays in Austria, 1990.

Christmas holidays in Paris, 1992. Alexander shares a joyful moment with his grandfather.

Alexander and his grandmother as King and Queen in Megeve, 1992.

Constantin, summer, 1992.

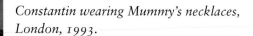

Constantin wearing Mummy's necklaces, London, 1993.

One of my favorite photographs: Constantin wearing a Russian hat, London, 1993.

Isn't it fun to have a bath together? London, 1993.

*It's much warmer in Mummy's bed,
London, 1993.*

*The last photograph taken of Alexander,
just before setting off to Germany for the
summer holidays, London, 1994.*

The public path leading to the Volkmann's house is blocked off, November 1996.

French parents of abducted children and politicians supporting our cause in front of the German embassy in Paris, December 1996.

Desperation gave me strength. In consultation with friends and after hours of discussion, we decided there was only one alternative left: the media.

I telephoned Dominic Lawson, at that time editor of the *Spectator,* for an appointment. My friends had agreed with my suggestion. The magazine, with a circulation of around sixty thousand, is a high-caliber and serious weekly and read by people in the government. Approaching the *Spectator* was a cry for help; publishing my story in a tabloid might have been interpreted as a call for scandal, which I wanted to avoid.

On December 2, 1994, that week's edition came out. I rushed to the newsagent's. My heart was beating fast as I picked up a copy and saw that my story had hit the front page. The article written by Alisdair Palmer, "Is This What We Mean by European Union?" was the main feature on three pages. It was powerful and extremely well written. Surely something would happen now to help my sons and restore them legally to me.

That very day the *Daily Mail,* the *Mail on Sunday,* and two other major newspapers phoned the *Spectator* wanting the story. I felt unsure and decided to go on hiding, but the *Mail* published our story the next day, based on the *Spectator* article: "Germany Defies High Court in Tug of Love Case."

For months I had fought with my lawyers, written innumerable letters, gathered evidence—all without results. I had become thinner, poorer, my sons were still unreachable, yet no one could help! Suddenly, doors opened following the article. My member of Parliament agreed to meet me, and the authorities in England reacted. I had heard criticism of the press often, but I certainly cannot share this view: without its help and support, my sons and I would have remained in oblivion, and the issue of child abductions would never have been brought to the public's attention.

In the meantime, a friend wrote to Peter Hartmann, at the time German ambassador, to bring the article in the *Spectator* to his attention. The ambassador sent a curt note back.

The following week the *Spectator* published a letter the embassy had sent the magazine in response to the article. It was signed by the legal counselor to the German embassy and read:

> I refer to your article dealing with a German court's decision concerning the place of residence of two minors. Verdicts in family affairs involving children always have high emotional content—especially for the unsuccessful party. . . . If one reads the eleven-page judgment in full, every unbiased reader will understand that the judges took great care to ensure the well-being of the two minors—as stipulated by the pertinent Hague Convention of 1980. One would learn that the two children requested rather forcefully to stay in Germany because they were tired of frequently being victims of taunts, such as "Nazi." This—by the way—is, unfortunately, an experience they share with many children in the German community of this country.

The German embassy's letter, of course, got it wrong from the start by asserting that the matter before the German courts was concerning the boys' place of residence. In reality, the issue was one of illegal retention. I was so incensed by this, and by the tone and substance of the rest of the letter, that I spent the weekend preparing a point-by-point rebuttal to send to the *Spectator*. In the event, this was not published because it was too long.

Instead, a letter appeared in the January 7 issue, written by the father of Alexander's best friend in London. Because of its brevity, I had to admit that it dealt more effectively with the German embassy's assertions, and I quote it in full:

> I happen to be the father of one of the children's best friends who often came to our house. I checked with my son, and there has never been any Nazi taunting at school. If Mr. Trautwein wants to defend his country's legal system, which in the circumstances has behaved weirdly to say the least, he

should not use blatant falsehoods which play on the cheap emotional issue of Nazi taunting. He might be drawn into dangerous territory, as the way these children have been snatched away from their mother bears a frighteningly close resemblance to what happened in his country not so long ago.

.   .   .

The distance separating my sons from me was increasing day by day. Germany was pushing me aside. Most of my letters were unanswered. To the first English intervention, the German authorities had brusquely answered that once upon a time three children had been abducted by an English mother and had not been returned to Germany!

Since the beginning of this nightmare, I had spent every free minute of my day writing letters, telephoning, and trying to gather support. Two innocent boys were paying the price of Hans-Peter's devious moves, and now, as far as I was concerned, the German embassy was backing his illegalities, heedless of the barbaric treatment of the children and their mother. And as far as I was concerned, this lack of sympathy and narrow-minded attitude was a blind attack on everything I had been led to believe Germany was striving for: Europe. For one, my children did not belong to the German community. They lived with me, and I am not German. Nor, for that matter, did we belong to any specific national community—we belonged to our friends, irrespective of their nationalities.

A rare point of light in the unrelieved gloom was the sympathy and help shown by the French embassy in London. Thanks to their Consul Philippe Perrier, the French government was alerted:

"You haven't seen your sons for six months? But that's outrageous! I'll tell the ambassador immediately. . . . We'll have to do something to help you." Two days later the consulate was on the telephone with an appointment.

It was Mr. Perrier, who rounded up the support and attention of the French authorities. He had nothing to gain from helping me, only an increase in his workload. Mr. Perrier was there simply because he was a kind and caring human being who was concerned about children and human rights.

In the meantime, Dr. Kram was getting nowhere with the Verden court, nor with Herr Lecker. The latest court refusal stated that I might abduct my sons if a visit were granted!

But the local Youth Authority finally succumbed to the pressure of the press (the *Daily Mail* had gone to Verden) and the supportive intervention of the British consulate and conceded a two-hour meeting with my children. However, the brief meeting was to be held in the Youth Authority buildings, under the supervision of the social worker.

"What do you mean? In the presence of Frau Kranitz—but that's crazy! Can't I see my own sons alone?" I exclaimed to Dr. Kram over the telephone.

"I understand, Catherine, but you have no choice. They will not let you see the children otherwise. Frau Kranitz told me she will have a meeting with you first. At least the report the court needs will finally be written."

I was traumatized and knew this was yet another setup. I telephoned the British consul in Hamburg.

"Mr. Sullivan, I can't go to this meeting on my own. I need an independent witness to be present—otherwise, Frau Kranitz will write a report to suit their ends, irrespective of our conversation."

Mr. Sullivan kindly agreed to a consular representative accompanying me. The consulate then telephoned the director of the social services, Herr Lecker, to confirm the arrangements for the children's visit and politely requested whether a consular representative could attend the meeting between Frau Kranitz and me.

"Why don't you just bring a whole British delegation while you are at it?"

What aggressiveness and insolence to show to an official representative of the British government!

We had little choice, but realizing the strain I was under, Mr. Sullivan suggested that his chauffeur Alan take us to Verden. The representative of the consulate would still accompany us and wait outside the building during the meeting. Nicolette, my London friend, who knew how distressed I was, kindly offered to join our party, which also included Dr. Kram. We left Hamburg early on a Monday morning. I was extremely nervous. I had been through so many emotions during the past months, and now finally I would be able to see my children. Yet the thought of the antagonism of Verden and Frau Kranitz's biased attitude frightened me.

My meeting with Frau Kranitz lasted an hour. She greeted me politely, and I began, in my inadequate German, to explain the children's lives in London and our relationship. Frau Kranitz took no notes. If, as Hans-Peter (and she) insisted, it was the children's "will" to remain in Germany, why had he not discussed it with me first? Or even, why hadn't his lawyer applied to the English courts for a change in the custody provisions? And why had he taken the children to a psychologist? How could a professional psychologist recommend blocking all forms of contact between us? And how was it that the children looked so happy in London? To illustrate my point, I showed her a picture of the boys before their summer holidays. She looked at the photograph of little Constantin, blond and blue-eyed amid his dark-haired French schoolmates, and exclaimed: "Goodness, there are so many foreigners in his class!"

I did not comment.

"Well, Mrs. Laylle, you have to understand that your children are scared. Their father thinks you will kidnap them."

"But it is he who abducted them! When the boys were living in London, Hans-Peter could see our sons whenever he wanted."

"Well, maybe. But that's the past. The current situation is that he is scared. In fact, the children are not coming to meet you here later. Dr. Volkmann has changed his mind. He will not bring the children. He has only agreed to your seeing them in his house."

"But that's impossible. It has been agreed, and confirmed with the British consulate. I am scared to go to Hans-Peter's house, and I would like to see my sons on neutral ground."

"Well, I'm sorry. I was unable to convince Dr. Volkmann. If you want to see your children, you have to accept his terms. I'll meet you back here at three." We parted.

After lunch we dropped the consular representative at the railway station, met Frau Kranitz as agreed, and set off in two cars. It was a cold December day. There was snow on the ground. I was shivering. Would Hans-Peter be waiting at the door? How would the children react? So long without their mummy, prisoners in this fortress, and subjected to Hans-Peter's manipulations! Six and a half months at their age would have been an eternity—comparable to years at my age.

We drove in silence into the dense forest, along the misty driveway. A mother was simply going to see her own children, yet this was more like an official visit: a consular car and the protection of Dr. Kram and Nicolette. As we reached the end of the long beaten track, both cars turned right and parked in front of Hans-Peter's house. Frau Kranitz and I got out and walked toward it. The other three remained outside in the freezing cold. My heart was pounding, but I knew that nothing could prevent me now from marching forward to see my boys.

Hans-Peter was standing in the large entrance hall with Judge Monkmann; both were wearing gray Bavarian jackets; both stood straight and impassive. They greeted Frau Kranitz and shook my hand with contempt. Impatient to see my boys, I walked straight through into the drawing room ahead. It was sparsely furnished and cold. Frau Kranitz followed me. A very tall woman was sitting in an armchair in the left-hand corner of the room. My boys were standing still, facing the door. They did not move as I walked in, and although I had expected this—in intimidating circumstances, observed, and under control—the sight of my children, usually full of life and mischief, threw me into dismay.

Constantin did not move, let alone jump into my arms as he had always done. His body was frozen. Yet I could see an excited gleam in his eyes. Immediately, I knew that notwithstanding what he had been through, he was happy to see his mummy, maybe hoping that she could change the course of his existence.

Alexander, on the other hand, seemed distant and his gaze was empty. His eyes, which had always sparkled with life, were dead. The Alexander I knew, naughty, restless, and emotional, had become a shadow of the child he had been. My boy of nine looked old, as if he had been through too much and was resigned to the cruelty of his existence. My heart sank. The great excitement of seeing my boys had changed to utter helplessness. The two women remained in the room, watching over us.

My sons ... no child reacts as they did, passive and controlled, unless he is scared. If only I could take them into my arms, cuddle and comfort them. . . . I knew that with gentle words and warmth we would be able to find each other again. Instead, two women were monitoring every move, following Hans-Peter's wish for there to be no privacy between mother and sons, hoping to cut the instinctive bond that ties them together.

Aware of their stress, I retired calmly and sat on the sofa. Constantin walked toward me, but he did not dare sit. I asked him what he had been building, pointing at the Lego box on the floor. His movements were slow and inhibited. He answered my questions in an even, flat voice. Despondently, I remembered how ebullient their voices once were; how, like all children, their enthusiasm would make them unable to sit still.

I had the impression I was sharing the world of two tiny prisoners. Both were pale, drawn, and obviously too frightened by the circumstances of this visit to relate to their mother.

They quietly led me upstairs to show me their bedrooms. To my amazement, I saw that the walls of what had been Ute's house had been knocked down, leaving one room to the left, one to the right, and a large open space in between where Hans-Peter's mattress lay on the floor. It was as if he were guarding them even through the night!

The bedrooms were small, uninviting, and cold. There were hardly any toys, only some Legos and a few books—no Ninja Turtles, no fun games, and only one old cuddly bear in Tini's room. The contrast with their bright yellow London bedroom, filled with bears, cars, dinosaurs, and other modern toys, was startling. Alexander seemed resigned, as if embarrassed by the destitution of their home. Tini, however, began to relax, as the two women had remained downstairs. For an instant he forgot himself and did a stand-up:

"Mummy, look at what I can do," Constantin called in German. His voice had livened up, and he laughed. But Alexander stood limp and silent, and I did not dare take him in my arms, instinctively aware that he had been ordered to reject me.

"Shall we play a game?" I asked instead.

"I'm not in the mood," Alexander answered. "We'd better go back downstairs," he added. He led the way, hesitating at each step. Constantin climbed on my back, then immediately jumped down, startled at the sight of the two women waiting for us at the bottom of the stairs. Alexander marched toward the sitting room and sat down. Constantin and I joined him at the table, followed by the women. The five of us started a card game. Alexander's expression had not changed. He remained impassive, as if he there were no child left in him. He lost first. In the old days he would have been upset. Today he sat quietly, watching over my game and helping me to collect my cards, as if he wanted to look after me and protect me. I was so impressed by his unnatural behavior that I became limp, unable to think. Constantin, however, was cheering up. He was making cute grimaces and laughing at what I said. If only I could be with them alone, away from this stifling environment. This was like a trip to hell—my flesh and blood, and I could not touch them, could not give them what they had been starved of for many months: their mother's love.

Suddenly, the room was lit up. I looked at my watch. Two hours exactly. Someone, probably Judge Monkmann, had switched on all the spotlights on the property to announce the end of the visit. Frau Kranitz turned to Alexander:

"This time your mother came to see you here. How would you like to meet her in Hamburg next time?"

Alexander looked panic-stricken, and before she had time to say another word, he shot out the door and into the hallway. A few seconds later Hans-Peter stormed in, Alexander shadowing him. Constantin, who had been sitting next to me, immediately ran to the other corner of the room and hid his head in the Lego box. Hans-Peter marched across the room and sat on the windowsill opposite, with Alexander on a chair beside him.

Alexander was looking at his feet, and Tini was motionless. The atmosphere was icy.

"Dr. Volkmann, this visit went very well," said Frau Kranitz. Hans-Peter's lip began to tremble. "And I suggested to Alexander that since his mother came all the way to Verden, maybe next time a visit in Hamburg could be arranged?"

Hans-Peter was raging with anger. He turned to his eldest son and said in a cutting tone: "Alexander, do you want to go to Hamburg?"

This sounded like an order, not a question. Without lifting his head, Alexander replied, "No."

I felt as frightened as my sons. Hans-Peter's voice had been so commanding, so filled with hate.

"But, Dr. Volkmann, you must understand . . . ," continued Frau Kranitz.

Hans-Peter exploded.

"She's accused me of being a kidnapper. She's talked to the press. Did you see what she said to them? She's a liar." Hans-Peter stood up, pointing his finger at me: "She must stop talking to the press. . . . " Constantin was inert, head deep in the Lego box, as if he wished it would swallow him up. Alexander looked down, head still lower, at his feet. I felt an overpowering desperation to halt Hans-Peter's delirious screaming in front of the boys. I rushed out to get the presents I had brought from London, to alleviate the tension.

I had been so shaken and distraught that I apparently tripped on the way to the car, Nicolette told me later. As I returned to the house, I saw Hans-Peter through the glass door leading to the drawing room, pleading with Frau Kranitz:

"*Bitte,* you must understand. . . . " I walked in, and Frau Kranitz stood up. She motioned to the children to move forward, and the three of us went into the kitchen at the side of the hall. I gave them their presents. They both stared at their parcels. I had never seen my children, any children, not unwrapping presents. I helped them and took out their favorite model, "Aliens." Both were quiet, as if they were frozen mummies. I turned my head toward the entrance hall to my left and saw Hans-Peter standing still, glaring intensely at Alexander, as if conveying an order to behave in a particular way. I was scared. I wondered if there were any relationship between his stare and the stare of the psychologist during the Celle hearing. I wondered how my boys had been trained to obey silent orders. I wonder how long these toys would remain in my boys' possession.

I was as subdued as my sons. I looked up and saw that Judge Monkmann was now standing beside Hans-Peter. Hans-Peter snapped his fingers. The children immediately stood up and walked over next to him. I did not know what to do. I tried to kiss them good-bye, but they stood frozen between the two men, too terrified even to say good-bye. I went back to the car and collapsed in Nicolette's arms.

Hans-Peter's house had large windows, and Nicolette, Alan, and Dr. Kram had watched all our movements from the car. They saw my boys and me go up the stairs, Constantin jump on my back, and Alexander's unnatural walk.

"Two hours alone with your sons, and they would be back to normal," concluded Dr. Kram. "I've dealt with cases like yours before, but I can tell you the bond between your sons and you is particularly strong. Constantin was nearly like a normal child at one stage. This is quite extraordinary, especially since his father remained in the house during your entire visit."

"What?"

"Well, as you walked into the sitting room right at the beginning, only Judge Monkmann left the house. Hans-Peter locked the front door from the inside and went into the cloakroom. He never left the house. Alexander knew he was there. We saw him run to the cloakroom to get his father." Nicolette went on: "We were sitting in the car looking at what was happening inside, when Alan heard a truck coming from Judge Monkmann's house. We saw it pass by and presumed it was a man working on the land. Dr. Kram thought it was rather odd and decided to go and see for himself. It wasn't a workman. It was Judge Monkmann. He had driven his truck across the driveway, blocking the property's exit."

"And this is illegal retention," Dr. Kram commented.

No one could have imagined such a remote, oppressive environment. There was something very sinister about it. The coldness of the house, the bareness of their rooms, and the sadness of their faces were haunting. I remembered the days when we used to snuggle together, how little Tini would tiptoe into my bed, Alexander behind him, and how I used to wake up in the mornings with them stretched across it. Today I saw how they had missed the warmth of our cuddles even more than I had.

All of this had only one apparent justification, one refrain rising from the past and echoing on the lips of those who defended this terrible injustice: German nationality. Two children and their mother had been torn asunder and stripped of all their legal and human rights on the sole strength of four words uttered by a tormented nine-year-old boy: *"Ich bin doch Deutscher."*

CHAPTER 14

Justice Denied

The report from Frau Kranitz was more or less as I had expected. I was still in a state of nervous indignation when I read it:

The visit of December 12 went well. Dr. Volkmann is prepared to have a discussion with his wife. Both children reacted positively toward their mother, and their initial angst was shed. At the end of the visit, Mrs. Volkmann suggested a meeting in Hamburg with the children. Dr. Volkmann adamantly refused, stating his wife would take the children back to England. Even with the effort of the youth welfare he would not change his position, although he finally agreed to a further visit of four hours in his house, in the presence of Frau Schwarz. The youth welfare would therefore suggest a next visit to be carried out according to Dr. Volkmann's wish.

"Brilliant! Another well-sealed report! Frau Kranitz is pretending to take a neutral stand and then blatantly sanctions Hans-Peter's demands!" I exclaimed furiously to Dr. Kram, who had sent a fax to Klaus reaffirming our request for a ten-day skiing holiday at Christmas. The offer I got back was to spend two hours with the children on the twenty-third, and four hours on the twenty-sixth and twenty-seventh, only in Hans-Peter's house and in the presence of Frau Schwarz.

"They must be joking! I am expected to travel to Verden twice—or do they expect me to spend Christmas alone in a hotel there?"

"Don't worry, I'll write to the court."

Dr. Kram sent an angry report stating that these conditions were entirely unacceptable, especially since last time Dr. Volkmann remained in the house and locked me in while Wilfred Monkmann blocked the exit from his property with a truck.

The Verden judge answered that since the parties could not agree he would hold a hearing on December 23 to resolve this matter and that I would be able to see my sons for two hours afterward.

This time my mother would accompany me. Dr. Kram intended to return to Munich after the hearing, and it was inconceivable to go to Verden without male protection. My mother is an elderly woman, and I was too terrified for words, so I asked Keith to accompany us. I had met Keith once, through a policeman I was in contact with. He had a friend he was visiting in Germany and did not mind chaperoning us.

Keith and I flew to Hamburg together, where we met my mother. Alan, who later became my friend, decided he would drive us to Verden. He had been shaken by the reception at our last visit and, as a father himself, felt deeply for me. Dear, kind Alan, who spoke fluent German, would protect me, then and later.

Verden had become a dreaded ordeal, and as soon as we drove into it I was filled with anguish. The memories were oppressive. Dr. Kram, my mother, and I walked into the red brick court building while Alan and Keith stayed in the car. We were ten minutes early. Again all was deserted, and I had a sense of foreboding. My mother, who was experiencing the strange atmosphere for the first time, was extremely nervous.

Suddenly, we heard men's voices coming up the stairs. Hans-Peter, Klaus, the blond lawyer, Frau Kranitz, Hans-Jorg, two unknown giants who looked like bodyguards, and a man in his fifties in a black leather jacket and a Russian fur hat surrounded my two children. My mother rushed toward the landing, looking for the grandsons she adored, who had stayed many times in Megève and Paris with my father and her.

"Alexander!" she called, bending down and trying to see his face, which was hidden behind the shield of tall men. Alexander did not answer but continued walking in the middle of the crowd.

"Constantin!" my mother murmured. Tini moved his head toward her but did not answer. The group of men, my little sons still in the middle, continued walking as a pack toward the larger waiting area. I stood behind my mother, unable to talk, unable to think. . . . I heard the judge calling us in. I looked back and saw my mother leaning against the wall, sobbing. I had never seen my mother cry before.

We sat in exactly the same place as on September 20, except this time I was alone with Dr. Kram. Opposite were Klaus, the little lawyer, and Hans-Peter. To our left sat Frau Kranitz and the man in the black leather jacket, his Russian fur hat still on. I understood he was the director of the local Youth Authority, the one who had insolently answered our consulate. His appearance frightened me; I shivered and looked toward Dr. Kram, the only ally I could expect to have in this antagonistic atmosphere.

The judge listened to the two sides and then asked the opinion of the social welfare workers. Herr Lecker spoke. The view of the Youth Authority was that the children should see their mother only in Dr. Volkmann's house. They felt they were German, etc., and they refused to go skiing with their mother, as they feared she would use this opportunity to take them back to England! Herr Lecker glanced at me as he was talking. He had never spoken to me, yet the contempt he seemed to feel for me as a foreigner was so violent that I felt overwhelmed by it.

The judge said he could not make up his mind as to whether I could have the children for Christmas and that he would announce his verdict on December 27.

"But that's after Christmas!" I whispered to Dr. Kram.

"Let's go out for a second. We must discuss a way you could see your children outside Hans-Peter's house this afternoon."

We asked for leave and went into the waiting area, where my mother was standing. A few seconds later Herr Lecker came out of the courtroom and walked toward us:

"Dr. Kram, if your client transfers custody to Dr. Volkmann now, I am sure we could come to some arrangements for Christmas."

"This is blackmail!" I exclaimed.

We went back into the courtroom to suggest my seeing the boys in a Verden public place of their choice.

"My client is prepared to surrender her passport to the court and for police protection to be brought if need be. My client has no intention of taking the children away."

Hans-Peter's face was red with anger. He started shouting, "I won't allow it!" The judge declared I should see the children in his house under the supervision of Herr Lecker!

As before, the Volkmann party rushed out of the courtroom with the social workers and disappeared downstairs. I groped my way out to find my mother. She was clearly very upset. While we were in the courtroom, she had tried to find the children. She had searched everywhere, until at last she found Alexander and Constantin in a bare room, guarded by Hans-Jorg and another man. She had tears in her eyes as she described the circumstances:

"Katia, they looked so frightened and tense, sitting still between the two men. They had no toys, no books—just a blank look on their faces. I have never seen children, let alone your children, capable of remaining motionless like this. ... Katia, I am frightened for them!"

We joined the others downstairs, and Alan drove us to a restaurant. Dr. Kram turned to my mother: "Oh, well, we'll just apply for another hearing," he said matter-of-factly and left for Munich.

.   .   .

The four of us met Herr Lecker as agreed. He sat in the passenger seat without saying a word, looking severe and hostile.

Alan stopped the car, and Lecker marched stiffly toward the house, my mother and I nervously scurrying behind. Herr Lecker opened the door, let me in, and turned to my mother:

"You wait outside. You are not allowed in."

"But I'm their grandmother, and I haven't seen the boys for over eight months!"

My mother returned to sit in the car, and Herr Lecker locked the door behind me. My children were standing in the drawing room as they had been last time, motionless and subdued. I kissed both of them and handed them their Christmas presents. They hesitated. I helped them with the wrapping paper. Tini sat down on the small sofa, and I followed him over. Alexander stood still with his new magnifying glass in his hand. Tini seemed pleased with his gift—a quiet pleasure I could detect only from the expression in his eyes—and we started assembling the pieces of the model car. Alexander walked slowly toward the window. Herr Lecker, still wearing his black leather jacket and fur hat, sat in an armchair opposite, his arms crossed, staring at me reprovingly. The atmosphere was tense and intimidating. Alexander was expressionless and lifeless.

An hour passed without the slightest movement from Herr Lecker; his eyes were tenaciously anchored on me. The doorbell rang, and Alexander walked over to unlock it. It was my mother, who was frozen to the bone and needed to use the bathroom. She then walked into the sitting room and told Herr

Lecker she wanted to take some pictures of her grandchildren. She first took one of Constantin and me sitting on the small sofa on her left, then one of Alexander in front of her.

"Alexander, smile. It's for your grandfather." Alexander smiled sadly.

My mother turned toward Herr Lecker and took his picture. I suppose she was so frustrated and incensed at the demeaning and vicious treatment we were receiving that she simply wanted to make a point. This was surely not very wise, but it was a minor demonstration of her outrage that she, as the children's grandmother, had not been allowed into the house and had had to sit in the car in below-freezing temperature.

Herr Lecker shot up:

"*Geben Sie mir die Kamera sofort!*" he ordered and blocked the door. My mother did not speak German but could not fail to understand his order.

"*Nein.* It's mine."

Herr Lecker stretched out his arm to grab the camera from my mother, who was holding it tightly to her breast. I panicked and ran to protect her:

"Don't you dare touch my mother. She is an elderly lady!"

"If you do not give me this camera immediately, I will write a negative report for the court!"

"This is blackmail!" I said in English, not knowing the German word for it.

My mother was terrified and managed to escape through the side door to the dining room, through the kitchen, and back to the entrance hall. Constantin was hiding under the table, and Alexander crouched in front of him as if to protect his little brother.

Herr Lecker continued to threaten me:

"I order you to give me your mother's camera. I do not want my photo in the press."

"Look, this is my mother's camera. These pictures are for her and my father. . . . " I was frightened, too, and tried to reason with him. He moved to the side, and Alexander, who had been observing each of his movements like a cat watching its prey, slipped through the door and ran into the entrance hall, through the cloakroom, and toward the Monkmanns' house. Constantin trailed behind him. I grabbed my bag and ran behind. As I reached the neighboring house, the children had already vanished. I walked in and stumbled on Ute, who was decorating a Christmas tree:

"Get out of my house!"

"But, Ute, I want to see my children. At least to say good-bye to them. . . . "

"Get out. This is private property, and I'm not allowing you in here."

My heart was thumping, my body trembling, and I walked into the adjoining room, where I found Hans-Peter sitting engaged in a conversation on his mobile phone. He stood up, his six-foot body blocking the way. I panicked and rushed out through the other door back into the entrance hall. My children were obviously upstairs, probably with the two bodyguards, Hans-Jorg, and tall Klaus. I did not dare go up, so I ran back toward Hans-Peter's house. Herr Lecker was standing in the hall. He let me in and locked the door behind me, taking me into the far corner of the sitting room, away from the peering eyes of my party outside.

"Herr Lecker, please. You must understand, I love my sons, this situation can't go on. . . . " In my desperation, I was trying to reason with a man who would rather die than move from his position. The doorbell rang. It was Klaus. I rushed to unlock the door and quickly slipped the keys into my pocket. There was no way I would be locked in, alone, with these two threatening men. In answer to Herr Lecker's explanation, Klaus put on a show of the conciliatory lawyer:

"Well, Mrs. Volkmann, I believe that you should surrender the camera to Herr Lecker."

"But it's my mother's property!"

"I'm sure you wouldn't want him to file a negative report in court."

"But you can't blackmail me like this. We are talking about my sons." I looked back and saw Keith and Alan standing beside the car, waving for me to come. I ran out toward them, and we drove off. I sat in the car, still shaking with fright and crying. Several miles down the road, I noticed I still had the bunch of keys in my pocket. We all laughed.

"Hans-Peter will have to change all the locks now!"

This moment of light relief was short-lived. I would be accused of having "threatened" two men (Herr Lecker and Klaus) and stolen the keys for the purpose of walking into the house and "stealing" my children away.

.   .   .

On December 24 I could not reach the boys to wish them a Merry Christmas. Although one concession had been made by the Youth Welfare—that I would be able to talk to my children once a week on Thursdays—the last time I was able to get through to them was on December 12, 1994.

On December 27 the Verden decision was delivered:

> The court rejects Mrs. Volkmann's demand for a Christmas holiday with her sons. . . . The children, especially Alexander, expressed a "wish" to remain in Verden, as he is afraid his mother would take the opportunity of such a holiday to take them back to London. . . . Herr Lecker stated that it would be against "the interests of the children to visit their mother in Megève. She [the mother] should, as an adult, listen to her children's 'wishes' and not the other way round."

I cried all through the night. Those two weeks in Megève were the bleakest days of my parents' and my life. Faced with bias and injustice, devastated by the absence of Alexander and Constantin, neither my parents nor I could weather our pain. My father was beyond outrage:

"'You should listen to your children and not the other way around'! Are they not even ashamed of what they write? When a nine-year-old wants to play truant, or take drugs, would Herr Lecker expect the parent to conform to his 'will'?"

I tried to contact newspapers, members of Parliament, human rights organizations—all were celebrating Christmas.

Dr. Kram had left for a holiday in the Far East. We decided I should look for a new lawyer. It was suggested to me that because Germany is a federation, it would be advisable for me to appoint a lawyer from Lower Saxony, where Verden was situated.

"You need to find someone who knows the local procedures and is known to the court. Not only will it be cheaper for you, as you do not need to pay their travel expenses, but a local lawyer will not be faced with the prejudice shown sometimes to lawyers from southern Germany."

Four lawyers (one from Bremen) refused to take on my case. They knew the Volkmanns or the Monkmanns and did not want to defend me against them. The stress, outrage, and panic I was under were barely describable. I was losing weight and could not sleep. I was surviving on nervous energy and strength of mind.

By early January I could not cope anymore. All my attempts to reach the boys on the telephone were blocked—even on the allocated Thursdays. More and more people, including politicians and authorities, knew about my case. But the situation remained unchanged. The Child Abduction Unit in London was not getting any results from Berlin. Dr. Kram was getting nowhere. Jane was unable to help me since matters were now in the hands of the German courts—and I could no longer live without knowing how my children were. I had written to the Youth Authority, the police, and the school they were supposed to attend, to obtain the boys' end-of-term reports. My letters were ignored.

On Thursday, January 5, I tried phoning yet again. Hans-Peter's answering machine was on, as usual. I asked the Lord

Chancellor's Office to telephone. They did and also failed to get through, confirming this in an official letter. On Thursday, January 12, I tried again with the same result. I was worried, frustrated, and beside myself. I just needed to know how my children were. I needed to see them, talk to them. . . . I was in a state of permanent panic. I decided to fly out and see for myself where my sons were. I asked Keith, who was in Germany, if he would accompany me. He came to pick me up at Hanover airport, and we drove to Verden in a rented car. I planned to wait outside the school and find a few minutes alone with my boys— talk to them away from the intimidating environment of Hans-Peter's house, away from Herr Lecker.

The school Alexander and Constantin were supposedly attending was in a tiny village, a mile down the country road from their house. The lane that led to it, up a hill, past five or six houses, continued into open fields beyond. From midmorning, Keith and I waited in the car park opposite. I had no idea what time it finished (in Germany school is a half-day affair), and I heard that some days schools closed as early as 11:30 A.M. It was freezing, and we had to start the car several times to warm up. At noon a school bus parked in front of us, and we saw children come out and climb into it. There was no sign of Alexander and Tini.

"Maybe they don't go to school here," I sighed, disappointed.

The bus left. It seemed there was no one else left in the school. We were about to drive off when we saw several cars drive into the small car park, and another school bus appeared. Maybe my sons were still inside! Soon more children started coming out, and there was a knot of people standing around and blocking our view. Keith switched on the engine and drove closer to the school gate. He spotted Constantin first:

"Catherine, look—there's your Tini, wearing the red hood!"

I jumped out of the car in excitement and called his name in front of all the other parents. He was surprised to see me, and to my incredible astonishment, after a few seconds' hesitation, he ran off in the opposite direction. I was shocked and continued to call, "Tini, Tini." A Volkswagen, which I recognized as Hans-Peter's and which I used to drive in Hamburg, pulled up near him. Ute Monkmann was at the wheel. She opened the passenger door, pulled Constantin in, slammed the door, and continued driving down the hill. I was shattered. I had come all this way to see my sons, and this ghastly woman was driving off with them. My immediate reaction was to run to her door and open it even though the car was still in motion. I wanted her to stop! She could not drive fast, as there were a lot of children, parents, and cars blocking the narrow country lane. I opened her door, but Ute continued to drive on, pushing me out of the car with her left arm and leg. Constantin started screaming hysterically. Ute is twice my size, and her determination gave her even more physical strength. I was sitting on the running board, hanging onto the door as she was hitting me—but I wouldn't let go.

Keith, still in our car, saw my struggle and rushed to help. Ute's car was close to the trees at the edge of the road. Keith made a run toward the other side and opened the passenger door. I looked at him in desperation. His reaction was to take Constantin, presumably thinking Ute would stop the car then. Tini continued his screaming, and Alexander, who was sitting in the back, started pulling Keith's hair. (I had not seen Alexander come out of the school and can only presume he attended another one or had been picked up earlier.) Finally, Ute switched the engine off. Keith let go of Constantin but stood by the open door to prevent her from driving off. Constantin continued to yell.

"What are you doing here?" Ute spat at me.

"Ute, they're my sons. I only want to speak to them."

"Leave your children alone!"

"Please . . . ," I begged.

She was yelling at me and interrupting every single word I was trying to say to my boys. Suddenly, a menacing woman marched toward the car. Ute immediately stopped screaming and smiled at her. This was the headmistress and, as I found later, an acquaintance of Ute's who had obviously been "warned."

"What are you doing here?" Her tone of voice was so dictatorial that I began to cry. "I'm their mother. I want to see my sons," I sobbed. There was instant peace. I turned to Tini, who had stopped his uninterrupted scream as abruptly as he had started it:

"Why were you screaming like that?"

Alexander answered for him in a cold, flat voice:

"Oma [grandmother] told us that if we ever see you outside school, we should run and scream. She repeated this to us this very morning."

"But I love you. I'm your mummy, and I want to see you— they just don't let me. . . . "

"You're lying. Daddy told us you could come whenever you wanted, but you never did."

"But that's wrong. Look, I'm here . . . and you're being taken away from me."

"That's not true. You're lying!"

"Alexander, I don't lie. I'm here to see you. I love you."

"We know, but you don't want to see us!"

In the presence of the headmistress, Ute had been forced to let Alexander speak. The words of a child, who had it endlessly drummed into him that his mother had abandoned him, had naively revealed all.

Three other women and a man marched toward us and surrounded the car. One of them told Ute to drive forward to the school gate. The headmistress opened the passenger door. Constantin and Alexander stepped out, and they all headed toward the school, encircling my little boys.

Keith and I followed them at a distance. The group quickly went into the school, and the headmistress blocked the door:

"You're not allowed in!"

"But . . . "

She slammed the door and gave instructions to the caretaker not to let me in. I stood leaning against the panel, trembling with cold and upset, tears rolling down my face. Finally, the doorman, feeling sorry for me, unlocked the door.

"It's much too cold outside. Why don't you stand here. At least it's warm."

"Thank you, thank you." It is extraordinary how grateful I felt for this simple civility. I could not stop my tears and went on, "I'm the mother. I need to know where my children are. I came all the way from London to see them. . . . "

"Come with me, they might be in the teachers' room."

Keith and I followed him through the empty corridors until he stopped in front of a door:

"This is the room."

Keith, who did not speak German, was worried. He went back outside to see whether his German friend (who was supposed to meet us to drive Keith back to Hanover) had found his way to the school. Alone, petrified by these people's hostility, my maternal instincts pushed me forward. I opened the door. Eight or nine teachers were sitting around a table, among them the four I had seen outside. No one acknowledged my presence. With tears in my eyes, my makeup running, my body shaking, I demanded, "Where are my children?"

Eight pairs of eyes looked up, stared at me silently, and returned to their conversation as if I did not exist. However, the man I had seen outside stood up, smiled, and led me back into the corridor. Naively, I thought he wanted to help.

"Now, tell me your story," he said.

I tried to explain who I was and why I was here.

Patiently he listened to my disjointed speech. He asked questions, appeared sympathetic, and I did not realize he was detaining me only to gain time.

Finally, a young policeman and a policewoman arrived. Keith's car had blocked the road, and the driver of the school bus had called them. I threw myself at them, glad to find some-one neutral who could enforce the law.

"I'm the mother. I live in London. I came to see my sons. I haven't seen them for months, and I desperately want to talk to them." I had barely started to explain when Gundel and Hans-Werner appeared in the corridor side by side. They were deter-mined, on home ground, and important people in Verden.

"Don't listen to her. She's lying. The children live with their father, on Judge Monkmann's property."

Keith had found his friend, and they were just walking in.

"Ah, look!" she pointed at them accusingly. "She has come to snatch the children. Here are her accomplices." Keith stood there numb; his friend wondered what on earth was happening.

"That's not true. I have custody. My children are wards of court in England. My husband has abducted them twice!"

Hans-Werner stepped between the policeman and me, look-ing important:

"I am Dr. Volkmann. Don't listen to this woman. She's lying. I want you to phone Herr Lecker, the director of the Youth Authority. He'll tell you the truth."

I was horror-struck:

"Keith, do you have a mobile phone? I must call my lawyer."

He looked at me regretfully. "No. I don't have a telephone," he said.

"Why don't you call the judge? Herr Lecker is completely on their side. The judge will tell you." I beckoned to the policeman.

The two young police officers were utterly bewildered. They had been called for a parking offense, as Keith's car was block-ing the country lane, but found themselves faced with screaming people and an unmanageable situation. Gundel was waving at me dismissively, blocking every word I tried to say to the police-man, Hans-Werner imposing his power as if he were an army commander. Suddenly, Hans-Jorg marched in, arrogantly point-ing at me:

"Ah. She's here to snatch the children. Look, two men are with her. . . . "

I was unable to talk, my eyes pleading for help from the policeman. He called the court: the judge had gone home for the day.

"Well, call Lecker!" Hans-Werner ordered. The policeman was unsure and decided to take a few notes instead:

"Tell me, please, your name and address," he gently asked me.

Gundel and Hans-Werner interrupted me, still pointing at my "accomplices" standing dumbfounded behind me. The policeman turned to me:

"Come with me." He led me into a quiet room to take down my details away from the commotion.

As soon as we returned, Hans-Jorg started attacking me. The policeman interrupted:

"This is a private matter. I can't intervene," and turning toward me he said, "You'll have to sort this matter out with the court on Monday. In the meantime, the children will have to return to their father." The Volkmanns were delighted. Having got their way, they could stop being aggressive.

"Yes, of course, officer," Hans-Werner quickly agreed with a smile.

"But can I see my sons? Please. At least to say good-bye to them?" I asked the policeman.

"Dr. Volkmann, you wouldn't object, would you?"

"Of course not."

"Will you come with me, please?" I asked the policeman, my fright probably written on my face.

"Of course."

He led me into the teachers' room and through to a room behind it. This was the headmistress's private office. She was sitting behind her desk telephoning, presumably talking to Hans-Peter in Bremen after she had alerted the rest of his family in Verden. Opposite, Ute was sitting poker-faced between my two boys. No one moved; only Tini looked up at me. The policeman stood at the door as I walked toward them. Ute sat implacably still. So did the boys. I went around behind her chair and kneeled on the floor, seeing my little boys in profile, their necks stiff.

"Alexander, I love you. Tini, I love you. Both so much . . . I brought your Game Boy, you know?"

Tini's eyes brightened, and he looked at me. I smiled, barely able to contain my grief:

"I suppose you don't have a Game Boy here."

"No."

Alexander was silent, but he, too, turned toward me. He looked sad and stiff at the same time, while Constantin looked straight into my eyes lovingly.

"*Wir gehen!*" Ute interjected.

Both boys immediately stood up, like two little soldiers under orders. I rushed toward the policeman beside the door. Ute, with Alexander and Tini trailing behind her, passed in front of me.

"Alexander? Good-bye. . . . "

"Bye!" and he marched forward behind his master.

"Tini? Bye-bye. . . . " I was bending down trying to steal a kiss from my baby. He leaned forward. "Bye-bye, Mummy"— he kissed me and he was gone.

"This is so sad. Poor kids," the policeman mumbled.

We walked out into the corridor in time to see Hans-Werner, Gundel, Hans-Jorg, and Ute triumphantly marching away. Only Tini dared to look back at me.

They were gone. The doors were closed. Silence. I was alone, lost in a pain that tore me apart, no shoulder to cry on. . . . I was forty-one years old, and yet I longed for my mother to be there and take me in her arms, like a child.

I returned to London, unable to face anything except the solitude of my sorrow. A week later I received a copy of Hans-Peter's court application for an "immediate transfer of custody, without a hearing," on the allegation that I had come to "abduct" the children on Friday, January 13, 1995. This was accompanied by a fourteen-page report stating that on my previous visit I had "stolen" the keys to his house and "threatened" two men, that I had come to the school with two "accomplices," one of whom had physically "attacked" Constantin, who had been bleeding and had to be taken to hospital. These claims were witnessed by Ute, who testified that I had "beaten" her. The bus conductor, the schoolmistress, and the four teachers supported these allegations.

The lies, the hate, the injustice were scandalous. How could they make such outrageous allegations? They weren't even credible! How could I physically be capable of beating Ute, threatening two men, one who was over six foot tall when I was not even five foot seven and weighed seven and a half stone! How could Constantin be bleeding when he was wearing an anorak and was seen by the policeman peacefully kissing me good-bye?

I was mad and panic-stricken. Dr. Kram had no time to help me prepare the answers to these accusations. Fourteen pages written in German had first to be translated into English before any lawyer could help me. Jane was busy with other clients, so another lawyer had to be found urgently, increasing my debilitating expenses. By January 23, I had found one. We spent the whole weekend working, but my answers still had to be translated into German, adding to the additional one thousand pounds I had already spent.

But on January 25—the day before my birthday—the Verden court transferred the residence of my children from London to Verden (the closest thing to custody, under German law), without even having given me the chance to present my evidence against the unproved allegations. The decision was based on Ute's testimony and a medical report, dated January 26 (the day *after* the decision and thirteen days after the alleged injuries).

Two months later we discovered that a police report dated the day of the decision stated that "as far as the police are concerned, Mrs. Volkmann had no intention of taking the children back to England ... no child was physically injured ... these claims were only put forward by the other party."

Haunted by the image of my children's faces, the hatred and barbarism of these people, the outrageous injustice, and the feelings of despair and helplessness that accompanied it, I saw no end to the dark tunnel my life had become. People speak of medieval tortures; I would have swapped anything for the mental torture that had been imposed on me.

I could no longer bear to stay in my flat, looking at the empty rooms filled with memories of happiness and laughter that would never be again. . . . Whatever happened, Alexander's mind was slowly being warped for life. I had to save my children, but I did not know how. I telephoned the United Nations in Geneva: they were not empowered to intervene in individual cases. The Luxembourg Court of Justice had no competence to deal with judicial matters other than those concerning disputes arising from Union laws. The Mediators to the European Parliament were under the same restrictions.

Europe was unable to protect its European children. I was alone.

CHAPTER 15

Things Turn Ugly

My two little boys had been barbarically kept away from me. There was nothing I could do to spare them the trauma. Hans-Peter and his clan had exploited a loophole within the Hague Convention. Irrespective of the English High Court orders, irrespective of Hans-Peter's abduction in Germany itself, the Celle higher court had sanctioned his illegalities. But the Celle court decision also meant that all further legal proceedings on custody and access took place on the abductor's home territory.

Suddenly, a new judge was appointed to the *Volkmann vs. Volkmann* case. This immediately resulted in Hans-Peter filing an application for sole custody. (I had been advised by my lawyer to withdraw my demand.) A hearing was set for February 23, 1995. In Germany, judges have full control of the proceedings. Again, no independent psychologist was appointed to examine the boys: the judge had deemed it unnecessary. Instead, another report from Frau Kranitz was requested. Apparently, English evidence was of no concern to the Verden court, as none of my witnesses who had flown in especially from London were called to testify.

Hans-Peter, who had brought witnesses for the custody hearing he had hoped to have on September 20, 1994, with Judge Moritz, brought none for this hearing with the new judge. This was suspicious.

Herr Lecker and Frau Kranitz testified with great determination. They alleged that I had threatened Herr Lecker, stolen the keys to the Volkmann house, and tried to abduct my children, who were living in terror at the thought that they might stumble on their mother in the streets of Verden. The references to "Nazis," to a "foreign environment," and to "life in England" were made again. I had the impression that I was part of a sacrificial ritual in a mock trial. Herr Lecker's blue eyes were staring at me malevolently as Frau Kranitz concluded that, in the "interest of the children," custody should be transferred to Hans-Peter. Any visit should be held in his house only and in the presence of a social worker.

I sat in the court, by turns despondent, resigned, incredulous, and outraged. I had no illusions. The verdict had been inevitable: this was truly Kafkaesque. But I still hoped that compassion would be shown to the children.

The *Volkmann vs. Volkmann* case had attracted the attention of the press, and the eyes of Europe were watching Verden. A crew from the German television station, Sat 1, had accompanied me to the hearing and were waiting outside the courtroom.

My new lawyer, Herr Struif, tried to present my defense as best he could. Children needed a mother; our bond was extremely close; I was a responsible mother who had promoted the boys' regular contact with their father; I came home from work every weekday at five-thirty, which meant that they would spend only two hours with a sitter. . . . On the other hand, Hans-Peter's actions had proven his irresponsibility and his determination to demolish the children's relationship with their mother; Hans-Peter worked in Bremen, and the boys were left all afternoon with a third party. . . . The children were happy in London, achieved excellent school results, and had many friends.

I stood up and presented to the judge a scrapbook Alexander's classmates had done for him: *Reviens vite* (Come back quickly), Sean had colored on its cover. There were photographs, drawings, words of friends. One wrote, "I am half-German like you, and I really miss you. Please come back soon."

The judge—a woman—did not look at it. Instead, she interrupted me, stating that all this belonged to the past and so did Hans-Peter's illegal behavior. The past was no longer relevant—we had to look ahead now. The fact was that the children were in Germany and that, when she had interviewed them a week before, they had expressed a wish to remain in Germany.

"But these children are totally manipulated and under pressure to express this 'wish'!" Herr Struif interjected. "Herr Lecker claimed that Ms. Laylle had 'threatened' him. You said that Alexander told you his mother had 'hit' Herr Lecker. This is clear evidence of how confused and pressured he is!"

The judge interrupted again. She did not want to spend the whole afternoon in court discussing this and would deliver her verdict on March 30, 1995. The Verden court—which last month had needed to make such an urgent decision (on the day of the police report) that it had not allowed me any time to present my defense—now required five weeks to make up its mind!

This was the justice of the fait accompli: possession had become the whole law. The children now lived in Germany; delaying the decision would strengthen the argument that they were settled there. I was in a no-win situation: little by little the system was validating Hans-Peter's abductions.

"My client has come all the way from London, and she would like to see her children today," my lawyer went on. "Since their abduction, she has only seen them twice and was not allowed to be alone with them. . . . "

"That will be difficult," the judge said.

"Why?"

"The children are not here," Klaus answered.

"Where are the children?"

"Somewhere."

Klaus refused to say where the children were. The judge did not intervene. In Verden a mother had no right even to know the whereabouts of her own children. I could no longer contain myself and ran out of the courtroom, in anguished tears.

As I rushed out, distraught, the cameraman filmed me. I had forgotten about them. My mother took me in her arms. She started crying as well. Nicolette, Leonard, Alan, and David (who had been Hans-Peter's boss in London) all stood in the waiting area filled with consternation. They had seen how Hans-Peter, his lawyers, and the two social workers had belligerently marched down the corridor, walking straight into the courtroom, as if none of us were there. I had tried to approach Hans-Peter: "Hello, Hans-Peter. . . . " But he didn't even look at me and walked away past me.

I finally composed myself and went back into the courtroom. Herr Struif was still trying to negotiate. But Klaus refused all his suggestions. Hans-Peter was silent, staring into emptiness. Finally, Herr Lecker made an offer:

"Next month, under my supervision."

"But that's impossible. He locked me in the house last time. I couldn't even speak to my sons. I am scared to go to Hans-Peter's secluded house. Do you know where they live?"

"Yes, I do," answered the judge.

I was dumbfounded.

She looked at her watch and declared the hearing over. Hans-Peter, his two lawyers, Herr Lecker, and Frau Kranitz stood up. The woman judge showed them through a back door, and the six of them disappeared together down the corridor. The cameraman immediately went after them and filmed Hans-Peter running off, the others speeding behind.

"How can you justify a mother not being able to see her own children?" shouted the journalist to Herr Lecker. He ignored him and rushed off with the others. In no time they had all vanished down the back stairs.

.   .   .

On March 30 the decision on temporary custody (that is, until the divorce proceedings) and on access rights was delivered to Herr Struif. Temporary custody was transferred to Hans-Peter "in the interest of the children." The arguments were similar to the one used by the Celle judges, with some additions—the "massive bodily harm" supposedly inflicted on Tini, my claimed "threats" to Herr Lecker, and my "disruptive press campaign." "The mother is not the most important person in the children's lives . . . especially since last summer. . . . Alexander used to love both his parents, now he loves his father more. . . . The mother works. . . . Since both parents work . . . the children feel German . . . they had no friends in London . . . the social environment is right in Germany. . . . " The Verden judge had granted Hans-Peter custody, although the children were wards of the High Court of Justice of England and Wales!

The decision on access rights was as follows:

The mother's right of access . . . is suspended until June 30, 1995. From July 1, 1995 the mother shall be entitled to spend three hours on one day each month with her children Alexander and Constantin either at the father's residence or at the District Youth Welfare Office in Verden. Commencing in October 1995 she shall be entitled to spend the period from 10:00 A.M. to 6:00 P.M. on the first Saturday of each month. . . . As a result of the incident on January 13 . . . the children feel insecure. . . . The court takes the view that the children's negative attitude to their mother is solely due to the fact that the children have no confidence in her and that their current experiences with her are entirely negative. In the view of the court a certain period of peace and stability is a matter of urgency, so that the children do not need to live in constant fear that their mother will appear unannounced and that they will be left to face her without protection. ... In order to enable the children to gradually reestablish trust in their mother, the Court deemed it necessary to ensure that the established periods for contact are not excessively prolonged. ... [Since visits can be held at the Youth Welfare Office] no particular day should be specified in order to ensure that they can be consulted as necessary.

I was up against a brick wall. English summons and wardship, European treaties, the UN Convention on the Rights of Children, evidence brought from England—none of these seemed to concern the Verden court. Verden belonged to another world—unconcerned with Europe, defiant of progress, and antagonistic toward "foreigners." Verden had its small, close-knit community, its hierarchic order and self-sufficiency. It even had its own court—and under German law, my case could not be transferred to another federal state. Decisions on custody and access rights could be made only in Verden, and appeals lodged only in Celle, the high court of Lower Saxony. Beyond that, there was no recourse, except to the constitutional court, which, as I had been advised, rejected most appeals.

Indeed, on March 9, 1995, the Karlsruhe constitutional court rejected my appeal against the Celle decision not to return the children. The verdict was summarized as follows: "The Celle court had formed their opinion following an interview with the children who express their strong wishes ... not in breach of constitutional law. ... This decision is unappealable." After yet more legal fees, there were no avenues left.

A few weeks later Herr Struif learned that Antje, Hans-Peter's sister (married to Klaus), had obtained a position in the Ministry of Justice of Lower Saxony. The fact that she had taken part in the abduction of the children after the first Verden judge had ordered their immediate return to England did not seem to have hindered her promotion.

I had come a long way from my former life. I had learned about family law, politics, the media, public relations, the human rights convention that stipulated that an individual has a right to be treated with respect, the right to freedom of expression, the right to a family life, the right to be heard equitably and without discrimination. But all of these rights had been denied me.

In December 1994, Lord Mackay, the Lord Chancellor, stated that he "regretted that he could not assist me. . . . It would be improper for him to raise questions about judicial decisions abroad." The ensuing correspondence with the Lord Chancellor's Office was contradictory and discouraging. The department had taken an initial position of not questioning Celle's dismissal of the Hague Convention. Although "no doubt" I was "disappointed" by the decision, I was, however, reminded that "an order refusing the return of the children under the Hague Convention was not an order granting custody." I had repeatedly expressed my concern regarding the possibility of a fair hearing in Verden but was still encouraged to make "an application for custody in the German courts" and to "continue to consult my legal advisers in Germany."

However, once my application was filed in the Verden court, I was informed that the Lord Chancellor's Office could not intervene while custody proceedings were pending in Germany. And when custody was transferred to Hans-Peter on March 30, 1995, I was told that the Lord Chancellor's Office could not intervene in court decisions abroad. What is the purpose of a wardship order made by the English courts if it can be ignored by foreign courts and the responsible department in England simply washes its hands of the whole affair?

Some members of Parliament showed concern, and many were outraged by the treatment my sons and I had been subjected to. Thanks in particular to Bill Cash's and Kate Hoey's kind support and energy, seven members of Parliament joined together on July 5, 1995, in a debate in the House of Commons. They questioned John Taylor, one of the Lord Chancellor's deputies, about European courts flouting the Hague Convention. John Taylor's answer mechanically repeated what his department had previously told me, ignoring the fact that Hans-Peter had abducted the children on two separate occasions. I was also astonished that the Parliamentary spokesman for the Lord Chancellor's Office was able to make the elementary mistake of characterizing the dispute as one of custody and not abduction:

It is not the unit's [Lord Chancellor's Office] role to intervene in private custody disputes that are being contested in foreign courts. . . . The [Verden] court ordered that the children be returned, but the father successfully appealed to the higher regional court. Ms. Laylle engaged lawyers in Germany. . . . While I sympathize with the difficulties in which Ms. Laylle finds herself, I do not consider that there is any more substantive assistance that the British Government can provide.

. . .

In essence, because I had acted legally—because I had abided by a legal agreement, trusted the law—I had lost. My husband—who had acted illegally and been in contempt of court—had won! My pain was at last turning into boiling anger. As if losing my sons were not traumatic enough, I was now faced with the realization that Britain, the country I so loved and respected, was failing me in my hour of need. A tenacious new will awoke in me and took over my entire existence. My life had only one aim. Nothing would or could stop me from attaining it. Justice became my obsession, and my sons were my raison d'être. I could talk of nothing other than my case, think of nothing other than my boys, and survive on nothing other than my new sense of consuming purpose.

There is a level beyond which one can no longer accept degrading treatment: one's esteem goes to pieces or rises like a phoenix with new resolve. There is no middle road. I had nothing left to lose. And this bolstered my determination to fight on until justice was brought to bear on my case, and others like it. In the name of my sons, in the name of all I had been raised to believe in, I would fight against this callous treatment. I wrote more letters, contacted more institutions, spending any free moments I had, all my evenings, trying to call attention to our predicament. My father became my link in Paris. Although no longer of an age to endure such stress, he galvanized himself into making appointments and writing letter after letter. He could not accept such flagrant injustice—but above all, he was a grandfather. He was depleting his finances, ruining his weak health, to help his daughter. But he would not surrender.

The Lord Chancellor's Office remained impassive and unhelpful, but the Foreign Office showed great sympathy. Our consul-general in Hamburg became involved in my story and gave his support. His kindness, humanity, and concern never wavered throughout my ordeal. He has done his utmost to assist me and gather support. Soon our ambassador in Bonn was informed, and he immediately reacted with compassion and deep concern. Both instigated interventions on my behalf.

Meanwhile, the French government, although not directly involved (since this case did not fall under its jurisdiction), treated my case with great concern and humanity. France is a country that cares for children. My father and I received extremely sympathetic letters from the Ministry of Justice and the Quai d'Orsay, from senators and deputies. They expressed their deepest sympathy for the "extremely distressing time we were enduring," and on February 16, 1995, the diplomatic adviser of Mr. Balladur (then prime minister) wrote to my father that France would intercede with the German authorities to try to find an equitable solution for the children.

The cooperation of member states in the European Union was being put to the test. The results were disillusioning.

First, the unofficial interventions made by our embassy in Bonn were rebuffed. The German authorities said that once a decision had been made by one of its courts, the government was unable to interfere.

Second, the German authorities took six months to reply to the French official intervention. It was received only on May 18, 1995, *after* temporary custody had been transferred to my husband. It was biting:

> Judicial decisions in custody matters are often perceived as an injustice by the defeated party, and attempts are often made to modify the decision through recourse to the media or political interventions. . . . Under German family law, it is not possible to go against the wish of the parent who has custody.

In the meantime, Jacques Chirac had been elected president in April 1995. Fresh interventions were made by the president himself, but Chancellor Kohl withdrew behind the argument that each *Land* was independent and he could not intervene. A few months later an acquaintance wrote a personal letter to the chancellor, whom he knew well: "Although I am aware of the independence of the judicial system in Germany . . . I am appealing to your commitment to Europe and your interest in family life, to find a human solution to this tragedy." Five days later he received an urgent fax:

> The chancellor has asked me to answer you. . . . The fact that Mrs. Laylle considers the decision as unfair cannot be used as a basis for polemics nor for media campaigns. . . . I believe that it would be in the interest of all—and the media should realize this—that a purely judicial "case" should not become an incident which spoils Franco-German relations.

I wrote to Chancellor Kohl himself, explaining my case in more detail and asking for help. My letter was never acknowledged. No articles were published in the German press, although two prominent weeklies had interviewed me and one had gone to Verden to investigate. At the last minute the editor suggested that, after all, this story was of no interest and things like this happened all the time.

"Well, then, even more reason to talk about it. Isn't it time someone protects children?"

.   .   .

The first access visit following the Verden court decision was supposed to take place in July 1995. But the Verden Youth Authority announced to Herr Struif that no access would be possible, as the children were on holiday with their father.

"Where?" asked my lawyer.

"I'm not telling you."

Then in August: "Dr. Volkmann says the children do not want to see their mother," stated Frau Kranitz.

In the first week of September, a television production company contacted me. They were working on a documentary for ITV about child abduction and the Hague Convention and had heard about my case.

"We would like to take you to Verden in two days' time," the journalist told me. I hesitated, aware that this could be used against me. It is always controversial to bring the media into a personal case. But since all else had failed, it was a risk I felt justified in taking. I was also within my rights: the Verden court had granted me a three-hour right of access, without stipulating day or time. I knew that if I did not try to see my children, this would be used against me; but I also knew that if I tried, I would be accused of trying to abduct them. Whatever I did or did not do was always turned against me. At least, if I were accompanied by the press, they could hardly accuse me of wanting to kidnap the children. I also held the faint hope that I might glimpse my boys and that a television program might provoke a reaction in England. I agreed to go.

On September 4, 1995, the producer, a researcher, and I flew to Hamburg. We drove to Verden and met two crews from Berlin. A photographer from *Paris Match,* which had already reported my case in an article in April, also joined us. We decided that I should ring Hans-Peter's house early the next morning and try to see the boys before they set off for school. This would be the first time I had seen them since January 13, 1995. I was apprehensive but determined.

It was 6:50 A.M. when the six of us reached the dividing line between the public path of the Monkmanns' property. Ulricke, the camerawoman, and Niko, the sound man, unpacked their equipment and started filming the sign declaring "Private Property," under which a handwritten board read, "No entry for the press." A microphone was attached to my anorak, and I walked on alone with my bag of toys and teddies on my back. All was quiet. The day had just dawned. I felt uneasy. I rang the doorbell. No answer. I rang again. And again. Odd. If the boys were still asleep, they would surely have woken up by now. I pressed my nose to the windowpane and suddenly saw Hans-Peter coming out of the shower-room opposite, a bath towel around him, sliding along the wall, into the drawing room. He had obviously seen me. His ridiculous behavior gave me courage. Hans-Peter could not even answer the door without the protection of his entourage.

I rang again, with more determination and whispered into the microphone:

"The children are not here. They would have heard the doorbell. Hans-Peter is hiding. I'm going around to the back of the house to see what he is up to."

I started off. My heart was thumping. I was very scared. I passed the kitchen window—no one there. I went on, past the sitting room—no one. It was silent: no birds were singing, even the leaves were still. I wished one of the journalists were there with me. But I went on. I reached the end of the sidewall of the house. Then I continued around to the back, where there were large bay windows into the drawing room. I looked in but could see no one. This was unreal! I had seen Hans-Peter walk into this room. I pressed my face against the glass. Yes. There he was—crouched behind the sofa, hoping I had not spotted him.

I knocked on the windowpane:

"Hans-Peter, will you open the door?" I shouted. He shot up, panic-stricken, grabbing his towel with his right hand and reaching for his cellular on the table in front of him. I knew he would be calling his friend, the judge who lived in the main house. I ran back toward the front of the house.

As I reached the front door, Hans-Peter was already there. He put down his cellular phone and opened the door: *"Was machst du hier?* (What are you doing here?)" he barked.

"I've come to see the boys. I haven't seen them for many months. I'm their mother." My voice was as calm as it could be in the circumstances.

"Well, they are not here!" Hans-Peter answered in German.

"What do you mean? Don't the boys live with you?"

"In any case, today is a holiday. They're going to Hanover with my parents," he said angrily and started to push the door shut. My right hand was on the frame. Hans-Peter pushed me out and slammed the door, nearly catching my fingers. I screamed as I tripped backward.

I started to walk back toward the journalists. They had obviously heard everything through the microphone. I was a little in shock, and I was shaking. One thought was uppermost in my mind: the boys don't even live with Hans-Peter. As I looked up, I saw Judge Monkmann. He had obviously come out of his house in response to Hans-Peter's telephone call. He was standing still. I ventured a few steps toward him. I was still trembling:

"Wilfred, I've come to see my children," I said in a half-begging voice, stupidly hoping that someone around here would have compassion.

"This is a matter for Hans-Peter and you," he answered coldly, without moving toward me.

"What do you mean?" I said. "He lives on your property, and you're the one dictating and protecting every single move he makes."

I looked back toward Hans-Peter's house. Feeling protected by Wilfred's presence, he had come out onto the porch and was standing, still holding his towel in one hand, talking on his mobile. I went up to him:

"I've got to go now, she's coming!" he said in a panicky voice. I presumed he had just telephoned his mother to warn her that I was in town and knew that the children were with her. I turned around and ran. I wanted to reach the grandparents' house before they had the chance to drive off with my sons.

"And I'll call the police now!" Hans-Peter screamed behind me.

Great, I thought. *The police are being called because a mother wants to see her children.* At least this time everything would be on film, for the world to see. Were even the Verden police controlled by the clan?

The media crew packed their equipment, and we retreated to our cars, which we had left parked on the roadside. Jacques from *Paris Match*, Jonathan, Debbie, and I got into one car, the crew in the other. A few seconds later we were on the road, heading back toward Verden. We had barely driven a few yards when we saw a police car driving in the opposite direction and turning into the track leading to the Monkmanns' property.

"Amazing!" exclaimed Jacques. "They took ten minutes to arrive, and it's not even seven-thirty in the morning!"

Jacques knew Verden. He had been here in March with a *Paris Match* journalist and had experienced the atmosphere of the place. It had taken them three hours to find the mud track, hidden in dense woodland. They had parked the car on the side road and had walked toward the Monkmanns' property. They noticed that someone was following them. Late that evening two policemen knocked on the door of their hotel room. They were startled and alarmed that the police could find out where they were staying. They had rented a car with German plates in Hanover and had talked to no one. Both had been shaken by this experience, astounded that the police should be checking people's papers in hotel rooms at ten-thirty at night.

We arrived in Rosenstrasse, where my in-laws live, and parked a few yards away from their house. The small residential street was quiet. No one had set off for work yet. We were tense. The Monkmann and Volkmann power in this town affected the whole group. None of us moved as we examined the house with its drawn curtains. It was still.

"They aren't there. This house looks as though it's been closed for the summer," Jonathan concluded.

"They *are* here," I said. Gundel never drew the curtains of the downstairs room, as she had nets at the windows. "They wouldn't have had the time to leave since Hans-Peter's call."

In a mad burst of courage, I stepped out of the car and walked alone toward the house. Both family cars were there. "They're here," I signaled to the others, ready to go to the front door.

Jonathan ran behind me:

"Wait. We need to unload the camera first."

My children were here, a few yards away from me, and still I had to wait! Ulricke and Niko took out their equipment, and I could now walk up the steps to find my sons. I rang the doorbell. No one answered. I rang again, then rang uninterruptedly. No one answered. My sons were behind this wall. What were they doing? I was at my wits' end.

I walked around the house calling, "Alexander, Tini, Mummy's here to see you."

The cloakroom window had no curtains. I pressed my nose against the windowpane. Among the coats hanging up were my boys' anoraks. Two pairs of children's shoes lay on the shelf beneath. I called again and turned to Jonathan:

"My sons are here!" But everyone was turned the other way. The camera was no longer filming me. It was directed toward the street. I looked up. A police car was speeding along it; it parked beside the group of journalists, and two policemen in uniform stepped out. I immediately ran toward them.

"My children, my children are in there. You must help me. I only want to see them, know they're still alive." This was surely not what the policeman had expected—a mother in distress surrounded by a camera crew. His expression softened. There was a genuine look of concern in his eyes.

Before we could say any more, a second police car and a police van blitzed in and encircled us. A few curious neighbors peered around their net curtains. They had never experienced such a commotion in Rosenstrasse. Ulricke was running her film camera trying to capture the action; Jacques was taking pictures. Niko was rushing behind me with his large micro-phone; Jonathan and Debbie were wide-eyed, trying to direct.

Two more policemen stepped out of the second car, one in uniform, the other wearing a black leather jacket and khaki trousers. Their expressions contrasted starkly with that of the policeman who had first approached me. They looked as if they meant business. The uniformed policeman walked determinedly toward me, gesticulating to the first lot to go—he was taking over. The first car drove off. The police van remained. I repeated what I had just said to his colleague. He remained impassive. I guessed that Judge Monkmann had called him to say that I had come to kidnap two children.

"But I am their mother, and I am within my rights. My husband is denying me all access."

The policeman wouldn't listen to my explanations. I was panicking:

"Debbie, get me the court order, please. It's in the car."

The court decision explicitly stated that "from July 1, 1995 the mother shall be entitled to spend three hours on one day each month with her children Alexander and Constantin." No days were specified. Poker-faced, the policeman started reading it, and his expression finally relaxed. Jacques came and stood behind me and whispered in my ear:

"This is the policeman who came to check our papers at the hotel room." *This cannot be a coincidence,* I thought. I began to feel seriously scared. I tried to reach Struif on Jonathan's mobile, but at 8:00 A.M. the office was not open. I redialed the number. Still no answer. Suddenly, there was a rattle behind me. A silver BMW whizzed past and parked recklessly: Hans-Jorg leaped out of the car and walked aggressively toward us, his right arm pointed at the camera:

"Stop filming at once," he ordered in an arrogant tone. Then, turning toward me: "What do you think you are doing here?" His lip curled in an expression of disgust. His voice was so commanding that I started to cry.

Ulricke continued filming as Hans-Jorg added, "If you resort to this kind of action, you'll never see your children again!"

"But, Hans-Jorg, I'm their mother. Can't you understand?" I sobbed.

He didn't even acknowledge what I'd said. Instead, he walked over to the policeman.

"I am Hans-Jorg Volkmann!" he said, expecting this declaration to cow the policeman into total obedience. "The children live with my brother. She has no right to be here and only wants to abduct them." I believe that even the policeman realized how ridiculous this statement was.

"She has a right to see her children," he replied in a slightly embarrassed tone.

"Well, the children don't want to see her!" He walked toward the house, unlocked the front door with his own key, and, before he opened the door, turned to the policemen: "And remove these people," he ordered with a dismissive wave toward us.

We were all speechless. Polite Jonathan had never experienced such a demonstration of aggression and arrogance. Even the stern policeman hesitated, his face registering doubt. Only Ulricke, a strong, resilient character, was bearing up. She was appalled by the behavior of these people and had been determined to capture every expression and demonstration of spite in Hans-Jorg.

"This place is incredible!" she exclaimed. "If I wasn't here, I would not believe it! In Germany!"

I walked over to the policeman in an attempt to gain his sympathy.

"The Volkmanns and the Monkmanns act as if they own Verden. I have no chance here. They have been blocking me from all contact with my boys." I was interrupted. Niko had turned around and taken the microphone behind me. There was some agitation. I turned around. Hans-Peter had appeared.

"Hello," I said.

He passed by me without looking and walked straight toward the policeman, putting himself between us to exclude me from the conversation.

"Hans-Peter, listen," I tried, standing behind him.

His lips were tense.

"She wants to abduct the children," he said to the policeman.

"Hans-Peter, they are *our* children," I mumbled.

He simply spoke over my head, and I couldn't attract the attention of the policeman. I turned to Ulricke and saw her camera directed toward a car stopped in the middle of the street. A man at the wheel. It was Judge Monkmann. Obviously here to check that everything was going according to plan. Hans-Peter started pleading with the policeman in his usual fashion. I was standing behind them but was ignored. They both walked away to speak in private. Monkmann was overseeing the situation. It was 8:15 A.M. Debbie had finally managed to reach Herr Struif. She passed the mobile over to me. I explained quickly and beckoned the policeman over to have a word with him. He walked toward me, passing Judge Monkmann's car. I saw them exchange a wink, and Monkmann drove off, satisfied.

Left alone, Hans-Peter immediately made a run for his mother's house. Debbie rushed forward, followed by Niko's microphone:

"Why won't you let the mother see her children?"

"The children are scared. Because she tried to abduct them."

"Why are the children scared?" Debbie insisted. Hans-Peter ignored her question and escaped in the direction of the house.

"Please, let me see them," I begged, running behind him. I did not dare walk into the small front garden that separated the house from the street. I was crying. The door was ajar:

"Alexander, Tini, Mummy loves you, Mummy hasn't abandoned you. . . . " Hans-Peter had already slammed the door behind him.

That was it. I turned to the policeman in a begging voice:

"Please. I only want to see my sons."

He seemed better disposed toward me now that he had spoken to Herr Struif, a member of the Verden community. I went on:

"We don't know what's happening inside the house. Maybe my children did hear me, maybe they're asking why they can't see me." He did not answer and walked toward his car instead. I was sobbing, my head against the front garden wall, the camera long forgotten. My boys were so close to me, only a few yards away, but separated by a wall.

The two policemen had gone back to their cars. Debbie approached them:

"How can you explain that a mother cannot see her children?"

"In Germany court orders regarding access rights can't be enforced. It's not like in England or France. I'm sorry, I can't help you."

"But how do you feel about this?" Debbie asked.

"I feel bad," one of them said.

They drove off.

I had no tears left. We all stood in silence, dumbfounded and shocked. Ulricke was angry. This was her country—things like this could not be allowed to happen:

"Who are these people? I have never seen anything like this. And Hans-Jorg's attitude. . . . "

They started packing up their equipment. Ulricke and Niko were still talking. I went to sit in the car, trembling all over. I looked at the white house imprisoning my sons. Where had they been taken—to the attic, or stashed away like hostages in the cellar? I wished we could just stay, sleep in the street, and wait until they finally walked out of the house. But filming was over. They had collected all they needed for the program, scenes that they had never expected. Now it was time to go back to London and edit the material.

It was my pain and mine alone. Except for Ulricke, who was still sharing it. She looked at Niko:

"But today's Tuesday, the fifth of September. There isn't any school holiday!"

We decided to have breakfast and then drive to the school in time for the break. We parked the two cars in the car park opposite. I was too scared to get out. This place carried so many horrific memories for me. Ulricke unpacked her camera and focused it on the school. She was right. A school bus appeared, and the conductor got down. He looked at the film crew and then walked back to his bus, reappearing with a pocket camera. It was the same bus conductor who had testified that I had come to abduct the boys on January 13. He proudly took a picture of Ulricke and the crew and walked into the school. As children began coming out, Ulricke filmed them. Hans-Peter had lied again.

Suddenly, the headmistress, followed by the four teachers I had encountered before, marched toward Ulricke:

"What do you think you are doing here? You have no right to film!"

They looked so menacing that everyone fell silent, except Ulricke, who was outraged:

"This is public property, and I can film whatever I want! In any case, with a scandal like this, you'd better get used to the press. This is only the beginning."

We turned and left—we hardly cared where we went, as long as it was out of this sinister, threatening environment. We were drained and shocked. We stopped in a small town nearby and found a coffee shop. Ulricke said:

"We're not in Iran! These people can't get away with such behavior. I really wonder what bonds them all together. Everything has such an eerie feel to it. This behavior must be exposed." She said she would contact the *Panorama* program on her return to Berlin. She warmly hugged me good-bye and set off with Niko. The rest of us left for the Hamburg airport.

.   .   .

Two days later, on September 7, 1995, the program went out on ITV's *The Big Story* at 7:00 P.M. I had gone to Nicolette's flat, around the corner from me, where a few friends had gathered to watch the documentary.

The presenter, Dermot Murnaghan, explained, "The Hague Convention, which is an international convention signed by forty-one countries, is designed to ensure the speedy return of abducted children to the country of habitual residence. . . . [It] does not seem to function as well as it should." He introduced four cases of British mothers who had married foreigners and had subsequently returned to England with their children. Their husbands had cited the Hague Convention, and the English courts had immediately ordered the children's return to their country of origin, irrespective of the conditions that awaited them and their mothers. Some were seen practically squatting while their husbands refused to give them financial support.

These cases illustrated that England abides by the letter of the law, systematically returning children. However, "foreign courts often won't play by the rules," he went on. Here was a clear-cut case of an abduction whereby the "father was completely in the wrong and should have been ordered by the German courts to send the children back to England. Instead, the father was awarded custody and Catherine given minimal access rights, amounting to three hours a month. But he refuses her even that. Catherine's children were not snatched away to some faraway land, but to Germany, a fellow member of the European community."

The film showed me walking along the path through the woods in a bid to see my sons. I looked small and vulnerable against the big trees, a large dog in the distance. A short clip of the conversation between Hans-Peter and me was heard, before I ran back toward the camera: "Let's go to the other house." Then the police scene, Hans-Jorg, Hans-Peter, and a shot of the pupils coming out of school. The program took a strong moral stand, conveying the mood of the Volkmanns' aggression toward me.

Then a switch to Dermot Murnaghan standing in front of the German embassy in London.

"The German embassy here in London refused to give an interview, although they said they were fully aware of Catherine Laylle's case. A spokesman for the embassy said that Germany always abided by the *International* Hague Convention. But when asked why they did not return Catherine's children to England, his answer was, and I quote, 'It had been settled correctly under *German* law,' and they had no comments to make when they were told Catherine was not even allowed to see her children."

Nicolette, her husband, and my friends sat in silence for several minutes, scandalized. The impact of the filmed scenes in Verden was certainly powerful. We mulled things over until midnight. I returned home exhausted. There was a message on my answering machine. It was my upstairs neighbor:

"Catherine, call me immediately. Your car has been set alight. The police and the fire brigade have been here to put the fire out."

A few minutes later two police constables came to take my details, which were later transmitted to the crime squad. Both had seen the program three hours earlier. The next day a small article appeared in the *Daily Express:* "TV Abduction Mother in Vendetta Claim."

I thought that this could not be Hans-Peter. He had been trying to serve me the German divorce papers to ensure that the proceedings would be held in Verden but did not know my new address. Serving me these papers would have been more important to him than setting my car on fire. But, then—who did it?

CHAPTER 16

The Trap

This latest incident worried my parents and friends. The police put on a special watch, and a detective came to see me the next day. A week after my car was set on fire, a note left by another neighbor informed me that someone had tried to break into my flat. It could have been a coincidence, but it seemed unlikely. There were too many odd circumstances. My friends advised me to be careful, and Nicolette asked me to give her copies of important documents and people to contact, just in case something happened to me.

But strangely enough, I was totally calm. Now I had lost absolutely everything. There was nothing else to go: my Renault 5 was a total write-off, I was overdrawn at the bank, and I had even been dismissed from my job. Despite my ordeal, I had remained the largest producer on the international desk, and the bank, or at least the director, had assured me of his support.

Then in June 1995 he was suddenly transferred back to Italy. Seven days later I was called upstairs and told that I had to leave immediately. On what grounds? No answer was given, but the bank was ready to make a settlement, which I was told I should not disclose.

Instead of feeling intimidated, I returned to my daily routine with more determination than ever: telephone calls, faxes, and letters to England, France, Luxembourg, Belgium ... the list went on. I now had seven files thick as phone directories on my case. If my friends could express their alarm, I could not. Any sign of weakness would be used against me: "She's hysterical, she has a persecution complex." Besides, if anyone thought I could be frightened away, I would show them how wrong they were!

These were my sons—my own flesh and blood—I was fighting for. Nothing would ever stop me. Furthermore, many people now knew about my case. It had been well publicized. Even in Germany leading papers had finally published full-page articles—they were the best and most powerful ones of all. If the government was not sympathetic, many Germans were. I received letters of support, and in Hamburg shop assistants who had recognized me came up and showed their concern. I felt that many were embarrassed that such events could take place in their country.

The French government had reacted warmly, and the public had read of my case or seen me on television. In Britain, where my story had been talked about most, people bid me courage and I received many letters of sympathy. If I was alone in my pain, I had discovered how many people cared. I would like to thank them all, in Britain, in France, in Germany, and in Holland, because they have given me the courage and the belief to go on.

If I was a political embarrassment to some, others showed their kindness and humanity many times over. Four very special people kept my faith alive: Michael Sullivan, our consul-general in Hamburg; Sir John Stanley and Kate Hoey, members of Parliament; Catherine Urban, representative of the French citizens living in Germany; and Philippe Perrier, the French consul in London.

.   .   .

On September 11, four days after the ITV program, Klaus submitted a fifteen-page application to the Celle court. Hans-Peter was seeking to cancel my visitation rights altogether (not that I had been able to exercise any!) on the grounds that I was a terrible mother. I had "threatened" Herr Lecker in December 1994, tried to "abduct" the children in January 1995, and appeared in Verden accompanied by the media. The allegations, which were also signed by Judge Monkmann, said that there had been ten journalists (in fact, there were five) and that they had trespassed on private property. (They had not, and there is film to prove it.)

I did not receive a copy of this application until September 17. Four days later Herr Struif received a notice from the Celle court asking us to present our defense. The allegations had to be answered point by point. I first had to have a translation made. Then I asked the *Paris Match* and ITV journalists to send me their statements. The British journalists had theirs officially sworn in. This took several weeks. But without informing either my lawyer or me, the Celle judges suddenly made a decision on October 4, 1995. They did not allow me to present my evidence against these false allegations. The decision was based entirely on Hans-Peter's unproven claims. That much for German justice!

The Celle court stated as fact that I had "threatened" Herr Lecker, attempted to snatch my sons (again ignoring the police report and the fact that at the time I had full legal custody), physically attacked Frau Monkmann, and injured Constantin. The media were given a lengthy mention, and the judges added a personal comment, namely, that I had referred to them as "provincials" in the press. They concluded that in the "interest of the children," who were now "scared" of their mother and needed "peace," visitation rights would be halved. Starting in October 1995, I would be able to see my sons four hours per month, instead of one day per month, as had been decided in March 1995! These visits would only be in Hans-Peter's house—but, as the court was "aware" that a mother should have contact with her children, I could see them without the presence of a third party.

The fact that I had not been allowed to present my evidence, let alone have my lawyer know that a decision was about to be made, no longer surprised me. Justice as I understood it simply did not exist in these courts. Judge Monkmann and Hans-Peter Volkmann had made their allegations, but my evidence was of little consequence, and so were my rights. The judges had even taken the opportunity to insert their own personal feelings against me (although it was a German journalist, not me, who had labeled them "provincial"). To add insult to injury, the visitation time was set for 9:00 A.M., in the knowledge that I had to travel from England and that this would add to my expenses (since it meant spending one more day in Germany). The only seemingly positive note in the decision was that I could be alone with my children. But these were only words: in Hans-Peter's house, how would I be able to be alone?

Not only had my constitutional and human rights been flouted, but the court had in effect asserted that I had injured my own child and beaten men and women!

I had not been with my sons since July 6, 1994, and I was beginning to doubt whether I would ever be able to exercise even these minimal access rights. But Herr Struif's persistence and the media's attention were such that Klaus finally conceded. But I sensed a trap. I was to walk alone to the desolate property, be locked in Hans-Peter's house, while next door Wilfred, Antje, Klaus, and Hans-Jorg's wife—all lawyers and a judge—would observe me and testify to whatever they saw fit. It would be my unwitnessed word against theirs, and I knew that this would be the end of the road for me. I sent faxes to embassies, consulates, ministries, politicians. . . . Mr. Sullivan immediately reacted and suggested that his chauffeur Alan accompany me, and the French authorities appointed Catherine Urban, an elected representative of French citizens living abroad.

The three of us left Hamburg at 7:15 A.M. to be in Verden by nine. I was apprehensive, convinced that something ominous was awaiting us. Yet how could I not go to see my children?

We arrived at the turning into the woods. A new wooden barrier blocked the public path. A red car was parked in front of it. We sighed and proceeded on foot up the icy half-mile-long muddy track. The three of us were silent and tense. Someone had put a barrier across a public road. Would no one dare complain in Verden? Soon we saw a man walking toward us in the misty distance. It was Hans-Peter's lawyer, Klaus. We crossed the abandoned railroad track and reached the "Private Property" notice just as Klaus approached us. Catherine Urban stopped in front of the sign "Do Not Trespass." Alan and I marched on, escorted by Klaus. All was quiet and still except for a German shepherd dog watching our advance. At the top of the drive we turned right toward Hans-Peter's house. A man stood there. He walked toward me and handed me some papers. It was a court bailiff.

This was the trap! They had allowed me to see the children— only to serve me with a divorce petition. Hans-Peter and I had married in London, and an English divorce petition had been served on him six months before. Under German law, this had established the competence of the English courts. But Hans-Peter had argued for a stay in the English divorce, saying that in our separation agreement (signed before I left Germany in 1992), we had agreed to divorce under German law, and he had claimed that divorce proceedings had already started in Germany. In my English court application, I had stated that no such proceedings had started in Germany. The court therefore required a confirmation from the Verden court to establish whether there were pending proceedings or not. Notwithstand-

ing Herr Struif's constant demands, the Verden judge never provided an answer. Now I knew she would—and that when she
did, my only chance to have the divorce hearing in the English
High Court would be destroyed.

I immediately telephoned Herr Struif on the cellular phone I
had brought as protection. There was nothing I could do but
accept the papers. The German divorce was officially served on
me. I felt physically sick. I had been allowed to see my sons only
to lose them forever. It was clear to me what a divorce in the
Verden court would mean for the three of us. I wondered how
much my little boys would despise those people once they realized how their own mother had been treated and betrayed and
how they themselves had been used for that end.

Paper in hand, Klaus led me into the sitting room. I could feel
how pleased he was with himself. To the left of the room, there
was a small sofa, a table, and an armchair. My two boys were
perched, stiff-necked, straight-backed, side by side, their backs
to the large window giving directly on to the Monkmanns'
house. Tall, skinny, her hair pulled back in a bun, Frau Schwarz,
the child-minder, sat rigidly in the armchair. No one glanced at
me as I walked in. Only Tini lifted his eyes as I came closer. The
atmosphere was tense and icy. The room had only the bare
essentials. There was no paper in the wastebasket, nor any
envelopes lying on the desk. It was as if this were a showroom,
uninhabited the rest of the time.

"Hello, Alexander. Hello, Tini."

Alexander answered curtly without lifting his head. Tini
looked up to me, quickly, and his head was back down. I put my
bag on the floor and sat down on the empty chair opposite Frau
Schwarz, to the left of Constantin, without another word, conscious of the strain my boys were under. They had not seen me
for a very long time, and they seemed to have been briefed
intensively on what they were allowed to do and not to do in my
presence. The three of them continued a game they had previously started, oblivious of my presence. Frau Schwarz then

invited me to participate. Between his dice throws, I noticed Tini looking at me attentively, as if he were trying to absorb every detail of my features. I wondered if he had forgotten what I looked like. Slowly I turned my head toward him and smiled, but he immediately turned his eyes the other way. Frau Schwarz was talking nonstop, with irritating enthusiasm. Alexander was silent, still looking down. His expression was somber and very tense. His face was pale, his features drawn, and his eyebrows knitted as they always were when he was stressed or angry. His movements were slow and deliberate. Sixteen months before I had taken a happy, boisterous child to the airport . . . today I was looking at a lost soul, neither boy nor man. I desperately wanted to take him into my arms and console him: "Your mummy is here. She will protect you . . . ," but I knew I wouldn't be allowed. Alexander might stand up and walk out. Frau Schwarz had probably received strict orders. It was agony.

We continued playing. As usual, Tini won first. He timidly passed the dice to me and advised me on which moves I should make. I knew he was happy to see me. He wanted his mummy to win, but there was nothing left in him of the energetic, jovial child he once was.

The game was over.

"Frau Schwarz, would you be kind enough to let me be alone with my children?"

"*Nein,*" she said. Then she addressed Alexander in an autocratic voice: "Do you want me to leave?"

"*Nein,*" Alexander answered without lifting his eyes, still frowning.

I did not insist. I was determined to see my boys whatever the conditions.

But Frau Schwarz agreed to go and sit on the sofa opposite us. She took up a newspaper, pretending to read it, but she never turned a page, monitoring every word my sons and I exchanged. Her back was to us, but I could nearly feel her antenna stretched out close to us.

I said something to Alexander in French, the language we had always talked in:

"*Du Muss Deutsch sprechen!*" he ordered me. I presumed this was another command he had received from his father to ensure that Frau Schwarz could interrupt when she felt necessary. Not wishing to add to the tension, I continued in my inadequate German. I started to remove from my bag the presents I had brought them from London, pretending to be cheerful. Both boys sat motionless beside each other, hands on their knees, their wrapped presents in front of them. I moved to sit on the sofa next to Tini and began to open them myself. What free, normal child would react like that?

I felt the nearness of Constantin's body next to mine. This was my son, whom I had carried in my womb, and today he was not free to touch his own mother. I gently stroked the back of his head and felt his body shiver with delight, but he did not dare to move. Alexander's face tightened. The torture was numbing me, but I continued in a jolly voice to unpack the boxes of Ninja Turtles. My sons still sat expressionless. I talked further. Finally, carried away by the sight of their new toys, Alexander quickly stretched his arm and literally grabbed his. Constantin followed suit. Suddenly, their voices lightened. Frau Schwarz turned toward Alexander. At once he put the toy back on the table:

"*Das ist doff* (That is stupid)."

"Will you show me your rooms?" I quickly asked, to distract their attention from this new difficulty. Tini did not answer. Alexander mumbled, staring straight ahead of him, "We can't. They are locked."

I was horrified. Hans-Peter obviously did not even want me to see their rooms. Why? What was he hiding? Last year I had been shocked by the bareness of their rooms. Had their few toys been confiscated? Was this part of a special training scheme to make them behave in a certain way, blindly obedient to their father? So many terrifying thoughts raced through my mind.

But Constantin was relaxing a little and ventured, "Are there any more things in the bag?"

I took out toys from their London bedroom. I had chosen to bring Alexander's Batman, Tini's Robin, their dinosaurs, and some Playmobil toys. They used to play with them often. I laid them on the table. Both looked down like two trained puppies who had to receive their master's order before being allowed to eat. What would happen to them if Frau Schwarz reported their disobedience?

It is difficult to express how I felt, faced with the horror of my children's existence, and with my inability to change it; I could not even take them into my arms. Finally, Alexander took a *Jurassic Park* dinosaur:

"This one's mine. Do you remember, Constantin? Mine had a mark on the back."

"*Ja*. And this one's mine. . . . " Their voices bubbled up again as happy memories flooded back. I felt encouraged. My boys were not lost. But Frau Schwarz turned once more. Alexander's excitement vanished in an instant, and Tini stood up. He picked up a ball I had brought him and decided to go outside to play with it. Frau Schwarz rushed after him, and I overheard her telling him to stay indoors. Alexander was still sitting on the sofa next to me.

"Alexander, tell me about school." He did not answer.

I picked up a toy and asked him which ones he wanted me to bring next time. He was motionless. He looked so sad. I patted him on the head:

"Alexander, I love you. I haven't abandoned you. I'm your mother and will always love you. . . . "

Tears welled in his eyes and his lips trembled; he stood up and ran out of the room into the entrance hall, past the cloakroom and out onto the lawn. I could see him through the window behind me, running as fast as he could, Constantin behind him. I saw them disappearing into Judge Monkmann's house. They were gone. We had spent one hour and twenty minutes together, watched over by this severe woman. The visit was over.

Frau Schwarz came back into the room.

"What happened?"

"I told my son I love him. When he heard these natural words from his mother, Alexander ran off in a panic."

I had said it automatically, more to myself than to this woman who had so interfered in our lives.

"Oh, but you know it is much better for your sons to live here in the country than in a big city. I love your sons as if they were my own," she went on.

It was difficult to control myself, but I had to. I had no choice. They had control of my sons.

"Frau Schwarz, wherever one lives, children need their mother. I would be very grateful if you could ask Alexander and Constantin if they want to come back to say good-bye to their mummy."

Reluctantly, she left the room. I telephoned Alan in his car to ask him to pick me up. Through the window, I saw Alexander and Constantin coming out of the Monkmanns' house. But Alexander hesitated and ran back. Constantin and Frau Schwarz walked back toward the house. Soon they were in the room. Tini stood leaning against the wall, looking at me fixedly as if he needed to absorb my features once more. I came up to him and asked him if he wanted to play with me. He did not answer. Instead, he looked at Frau Schwarz questioningly.

"Shall we clear up for your daddy?" I suggested, to distract him from Frau Schwarz's attention. Tini shot to the table and started packing the toys as quickly as he could. My heart sank at this demonstration of the authoritarian discipline they were subjected to. My sons never used to clear anything with such speed before! Klaus walked in with Alexander.

"Say good-bye," he ordered.

"Bye," Alexander obeyed, and he ran off. Tini hesitated. I managed to steal a kiss from him. Then, he, too, was gone.

Frau Schwarz and Klaus led me to the door as Alan arrived.

"This visit went very well. The boys need time to trust their mother again," Klaus explained to Alan. I signaled to Alan that we should go. I simply couldn't listen to their justification. Alan and I walked back toward the car where Catherine Urban had been waiting.

I was very upset as I described to them the conditions under which the boys and I were "allowed" to see each other and the depressed state I found Alexander in.

"But I thought the Celle decision stipulated you should see them alone."

"I know. But this is a no-win situation. They will claim that it was 'the children's wish' to see me in the presence of Frau Schwarz."

My situation was so hopeless, so depressing, that I could not get worked up about it. But the disturbing picture of my sons haunted me day and night. Would anyone be able to help them?

As I had expected, Klaus's answer to my lawyer's complaint about Frau Schwarz's presence was met with the claim that it was "the children's wish" since, and I quote, "Frau Schwarz was the most important person in their lives"—surprising, since one would expect it to be their father!

Struif's complaint about the road being blocked and our having to walk in freezing temperatures had little impact.

In the following months the roadblock was replaced by a permanent metal gate that was bolted. Catherine, Alan, and I proceeded on foot. Klaus stood in front of the entrance to Hans-Peter's house. He greeted Alan and led Catherine and me through to the sitting room. My children and Frau Schwarz sat in exactly the same position as the previous month. Klaus left the room, closed the door behind him, and returned to Judge Monkmann's house.

I kissed my sons and introduced them in French to Catherine. As there was only one spare chair, I went to the dining room to get another one for Catherine. But the door was locked. Obviously, Hans-Peter would allow me to see only one room in his house. I squeezed myself onto the small sofa beside Tini and could feel his body reacting warmly to the proximity of mine. Alexander, to his right, was tense.

Frau Schwarz and the boys continued their game of Mikado as if we didn't exist. Constantin was winning, and he brightened up, proud to show off his skills to his mummy. Alexander's face was somber, and his features were drawn. He spoke only to Frau Schwarz.

When the game was finished, I asked Frau Schwarz if she could kindly leave the room with Catherine, reminding her that the court decision said I could be alone with my children. She flatly refused, and asked Alexander.

"*Nein,*" he replied in the same monotonous voice as he had the month before. "The court decision says that Frau Schwarz should be here," he added without lifting his eyes from the table, his hands crossed between his legs.

I was stunned. Not only was my ten-year-old son being told about court decisions, but he had been lied to, obviously to make him believe that it was his mother who was defying the law.

Frau Schwarz suggested sitting on the other sofa and invited Catherine to join her. The two women moved over, and they started chatting together, in German, their back to us. Alexander relaxed. For a moment the three of us felt unobserved. I moved to sit between my sons, and I started to read a French book I had brought from London. The children relaxed, and both listened attentively. Suddenly, the door swung open and giant Klaus stormed in. Immediately, Alexander tensed up. His back straightened, and he was no longer listening to my words. All his attention was focused on his uncle, as if he were waiting for his orders. I continued reading as if nothing had happened. Klaus addressed the two women and walked out again. Alexander's back relaxed, and once again he became engrossed in the story. Ten minutes later the phone rang. Alexander answered and gave the receiver to Frau Schwarz.

"It's Klaus. He wants to speak to you."

I overheard Frau Schwarz:

"*Nein. Nein.* . . . Everything is going well. . . . I am talking to the lady. The mother and the boys are reading a book."

Again Alexander was on the defensive, but when he realized that Frau Schwarz had confirmed that all was well, his attention was back with me. Tini was happy, and as I stroked the back of his neck, his shoulders snuggled close to mine. I felt hopeful. Suddenly, the door flew open, and Klaus barged menacingly into the room, ordering Catherine to leave the house at once. Alexander froze up.

"It is unnecessary. Everything is peaceful," interjected Frau Schwarz.

Klaus ignored her, and pointing at Catherine, he repeated his order.

"Then Frau Schwarz should also leave," Catherine calmly answered. "The Celle decision stipulates—"

"In that case, I declare this visit over!" Klaus interrupted, looking straight at Alexander. Since Klaus had entered the room, Alexander had concentrated on his uncle's every word. Before I had time to notice, Alexander stood up and ran out at top speed. Tini hesitated for a second, then ran out behind him. Klaus followed them into Judge Monkmann's house.

The visit had lasted forty minutes. Frau Schwarz looked genuinely embarrassed.

"I don't understand him. Why did he have to interrupt the visit?" she complained to Catherine. I called Herr Struif on my cellular telephone. Klaus returned to the room. Frau Schwarz discreetly slipped out of the house with Catherine. I felt that she, too, was intimidated by Klaus. I was left alone with him. Before leaving, I asked him whether I could take the Lego bag I had brought into the boys' room. Without waiting for his answer, I walked up the stairs. There was a newly built door on the landing. I tried to open it.

"It's locked!" I exclaimed.

"Dr. Volkmann locks all the doors in the house because he doesn't want the press coming into the rooms."

Klaus's explanation was so ridiculous that I did not comment.

"I would like to say good-bye to my boys."

"They don't want to see you."

I left the toys on the landing and joined Catherine outside. The two of us walked toward Wilfred Monkmann's house. Klaus followed us. Tini and Alexander were standing at the entrance.

"Come here," Klaus ordered Alexander. Alexander came over immediately and let himself be kissed good-bye. He then looked at his uncle and ran back into the house. Tini seemed a little less scared, and he stayed beside me a few seconds longer, then ran to follow his brother into Monkmann's house.

In December the gates were wide open. The Monkmanns were selling Christmas trees, and customers had to be able to drive in. We parked our car in front of Hans-Peter's house. This time only Alan was with me. He waited in the car. As before, I found my boys sitting side by side on the sofa with Frau Schwarz next to them. The visit lasted one hour. Alan had seen Hans-Peter walk out of the Monkmanns' house, wave through the window—obviously to Frau Schwarz—and the boys ran out immediately afterward.

In January Alan was on holiday, and Catherine drove me to Verden. Herr Struif had written to Klaus to complain about Frau Schwarz's presence and to remind him of the court decision. He added that since Frau Schwarz refused to leave the room, Catherine Urban would be accompanying me. Otherwise, he stressed, the atmosphere would again be too tense for both the boys and me.

But when we arrived, Klaus wouldn't let Catherine into the house.

"But my lawyer informed you she would be coming!" I exclaimed.

"I sent him a fax yesterday afternoon to tell him this is not acceptable."

"But I was on the plane from London yesterday."

Klaus had sent his fax at 5:15 P.M., well aware that it would be too late for me to react to it or change my plans. I had spent another 470 pounds only to be subjected to the conditions they knew were intolerable for both my sons and me. Catherine had no choice but to sit in the car. Of course, no one asked her whether she would be all right waiting in the freezing cold. I walked in alone. My little boys were sitting at their usual place, their backs to the window from which their movements could clearly be observed from the Monkmanns' house. Frau Schwarz in the armchair was facing the boys and the Monkmanns' house behind them. Several cars were parked in the courtyard. Catherine told me later that she had seen several members of the clan walking around the house to double-check that she didn't step out of the car.

Frau Schwarz's attitude was entirely different this time. She refused to sit on the other sofa. She talked continuously to prevent me from having any conversation with my boys. But Alexander was not as tense as he had been during previous visits. Before, Alexander's body had been rigid, back straight, head down, eyebrows crossed, and he had not even looked at me. This time he was just resigned, his body lax, his eyes desperately sad. He stared at me, as if to say, "Mummy, save me. . . . But I know you can't." I knew my son was in danger. All the signs were there: in his eyes, in his movements, in his expressions. Alexander was weighed down with an intolerable burden. It was torturing him. I could feel his guilt, all the sharper for his not really understanding the emotions that were tearing him apart. His slow movements, his defeated, depressed expression were more eloquent than any words could describe.

Then this visit was once again interrupted in an ominous way. Suddenly, Antje's children were unleashed from Judge Monkmann's house into the yard separating the two houses.

And as if a school bell had rung, Alexander shot up and disappeared, Constantin on his tail. As soon as they reached the porch, Klaus came out, and all the children disappeared into Monkmann's house. Catherine and I left.

In February Frau Schwarz, the so-called most important person in the boys' lives, had been replaced by Hans-Jorg's wife, a lawyer who practiced in Bremen. The visit lasted one hour exactly. Alexander looked even sadder and more submissive. To cheer him up, I gave him his favorite London chocolate muffins. He opened the box and looked sadly at them.

"We've already had breakfast," he said before closing the lid.

Alexander had always had the greatest "sweet tooth" I knew. Now, even this had been squeezed out of him. Tini was also different. He was cold and indifferent to me. I could see all too clearly why. I had finally reappeared in his life. But I had been unable to change anything. He felt bitter and betrayed. His mother had failed to protect him. He snubbed me. This time it was he who ran out first when the visit was declared over.

The full horror of what was happening to my children dawned on me with a nightmarish clarity. They realized I could—or worse still, would—do nothing for them. They knew that they would be punished for the slightest deviation from their father's orders. They knew that the worst thing they could do in their father's eyes was to show me affection or to express the wish to be with me.

Their torment must have been beyond description, manifesting itself in bizarre, unnatural behavior. Constantin, with a keener, harder-headed instinct for survival, had put up a shield between him and me. That was his only defense against being terribly hurt. The dilemma for Alexander—more sensitive, more anxious by nature—was even more unbearable. He was old enough to perceive what was going on. He had been forced to do the most horrifying thing that could be asked of a child: to betray his own mother and to know he was lying as he did it. At the same time, fearful of alienating his father and losing his other parent, he was ready to believe I had abandoned him. In his rage and anguish, he had kicked me. But he had wept during his interview with the Celle judges. If there is a better definition of psychological child abuse, I cannot think of it.

.   .   .

A few weeks later the German current affairs program *Panorama* broadcast a documentary on child abduction. They were the first to succeed in interviewing Hans-Peter and Klaus. Hans-Peter admitted that the children were under stress:

"Constantin is very nervous, and Alexander has become very unsure of himself and is sometimes aggressive."

And Klaus commented:

"Of course, what Dr. Volkmann has done is at the borders of legality. But he felt he had no choice. . . . If the children had been returned to England, the proceedings [in Verden] could not have gone ahead, and the children would not have been heard by a German court."

A German lawyer who had been interviewed on another program a few months earlier had said that the Volkmann case implied that there was no legal sanction for kidnapping children and hiding them from the police. That was precisely what my children's case had demonstrated: Klaus proudly stood in front of the camera, leaning against the banister of Hans-Peter's staircase, boasting that by defying the law, Hans-Peter had managed to win his case. No small part of this victory was that all future legal proceedings would have to take place in Lower-Saxony.

CHAPTER 17

The End
of the Road

Klaus was entirely wrong when he assumed that an English court would protect me, a British citizen. Hans-Peter's application for the English divorce to be suspended was granted until the "final determination of the proceedings in Germany." In other words, the English judge gave priority to Verden in determining where the divorce would be heard.

These proceedings are a vivid illustration of the contrasting way in which members of the European Union view each other's legal systems. The German courts had overridden without compunction the English High Court. By contrast, the British Lord Chancellor's Office had been reluctant to intervene in proceedings abroad, and the English judge had given precedence to his German counterpart.

As early as September 1994 the Celle court had ordered the children to remain in Germany until the appeal hearing—it apparently feared that I would hide them in England. After that, all my demands for access were rejected on the grounds that I could "use this opportunity to take my children back to England."

Faced with the Lower Saxony courts' dogged protection of an abductor, their belief that they alone knew what was in the children's interest, and their dismissal of my and my sons' rights, I was horrified that an English judge could throw me back into the hands of the German legal system.

An old friend who had accompanied me to the London hearing was further outraged when she found out that Hans-Peter had received British "emergency" legal aid.

"British taxpayers' money is funding a German citizen who has abducted British children, defied English court orders, and denied a British mother access to them!" Incensed, she wrote to several newspapers, and the *Sunday Telegraph* published an article entitled, "UK Pays for German to Wrest Sons from Wife."

Germany's position on legal aid is in stark contrast to that of the United Kingdom. While Hans-Peter's legal expenses had been minimal (with his brother-in-law, his sister, and Judge Monkmann as his advisers), I had been ruined financially by mine. Most of our case had been fought in Germany, and on top of the exorbitant lawyers' fees, I had incurred heavy travel, phone, and fax bills. (To date I have spent over $200,000.) For almost a year I had been unemployed and unable to survive on welfare benefits—yet I had still not been granted German legal aid. Since the decision rested with the Verden court, the German judge had it in her power to help or hinder my plea before her court.

· · ·

My financial situation had become alarming. I was dreading the day when it would prevent me from pursuing my case. I was mortified by the idea that I would be paralyzed, while my children's basic human rights were at stake, just because I had no more money. For Verden, needless to say, such an outcome would mean victory, a dream come true: the mother would have laid down her weapons, abandoning her children ... there would be silence at last, and in time Verden's behavior would be forgotten. But for the generosity of my German lawyer, Herr Struif, the pursuit of my case would have been almost impossible.

Now that the divorce papers had been served on me, the Verden judge declared her jurisdiction over all matters: divorce and final custody would be decided in Germany. Herr Struif immediately requested that the children and both parents be examined by an independent expert from a neutral country. He suggested a world-famous child psychologist from Switzerland who spoke German, French, and English. Herr Struif insisted that unless the boys were interviewed in French and/or English, a proper assessment could not be made. These were the languages with which they associated their mother and their lives in London. My German was also not fluent enough to do myself justice in an interview conducted in German.

Our requests were rejected. The Verden judge ruled that "since the court's language was German," any alternative arrangement was uncalled for. Furthermore, the children spoke German fluently, and the mother's knowledge was deemed sufficient. So the judge duly appointed a German from Bremen! Bremen, where Hans-Peter had his practice, and where he was presumably also a member of the Chamber of Doctors. Bremen, the very place where much of Hans-Peter's family had influential positions and where several lawyers had refused to take my case.

Adding insult to injustice, I discovered that the appointed person was not a child expert but simply a court-registered general psychologist. There was no way a professional, impartial report could be written like this. After almost two years of isolation and indoctrination, only an independent specialist in children's behavior, examining my sons away from their new environment, would be able to determine their true mental state.

But Verden had its own way of defining children's interests and human rights. If I was not German-bred, and German was not my mother tongue, this was my problem. If my sons only knew how to relate to their mother in a language other than German, that, too, was my problem, even if it meant undermining my children's birthright and leaving them motherless.

An appointment for me to meet the psychologist was made. She at least agreed to interview me in Hamburg, where I felt more comfortable, but refused to come to London and see at firsthand how the boys had lived.

Again I had no choice, and in May 1996 I flew once more to Germany. In my rudimentary German, I tried to explain how we had lived in London. I talked about our daily lives, our weekend outings, their school, their friends, our holidays in France. I had brought some photographs with me, in an attempt to illustrate our life together, show how happy my boys had been and how many friends they had in England, and prove that they had not been clothed from "cheap shops," as the Celle judgment had claimed (not that cheap shopping would be evidence of a deficient mother in most people's opinion). She quickly looked at what I showed her, but I could sense I was wasting my time.

She was a woman in her sixties, of average height with long hair tied back in a bun. She informed me that she had interviewed Hans-Peter and his parents and that she had seen the Monkmanns and the boys' school.

"Would you like to talk to my parents?"

"No, that will not be necessary."

"But what about their London teachers?"

"No. You've shown me their school reports. That's sufficient. Next week I'll pick the children up from their father's property, and we'll drive to the Verden Youth Authority, where I will interview them for a couple of hours."

"Is this how you'll base your report? Just talking to them at the Verden Youth Authority? Taking them out for a couple of hours and bringing them back to their father?"

"Yes."

I did not make the obvious comments that were racing through my mind, too aware that anything I said could be detrimental to my sons and me. I had serious doubts about the neutrality of this woman. She had been appointed by the Verden judge. I was living far away and was of no importance in her life, whereas the Volkmanns and the Monkmanns were prominent members of the Bremen community where she herself lived. Once again I could do little more than endure in silence what lay ahead. Tomorrow we would meet my boys to see how they reacted to their mother—but, of course, this meeting would be held at the Youth Authority and considered my visit with them for the month of May.

The next morning Alan and I set off for the thirteenth time. We sat in silence when we reached Verden. Neither of us found it necessary to comment. We both knew what was in store for me. We parked the car in front of the red brick building, and Alan helped me up the stairs with the suitcases full of the boys' remaining London toys. As we reached the first floor, Frau Kranitz walked toward us and muttered, *"Guten Morgen."* Her expression was hostile. Alan gave my arm a squeeze and returned to the car. Frau Kranitz remained standing in front of me, without saying a word. A few minutes later the psychologist appeared. She gave us a courteous smile. Alexander and Constantin, upright and stern-looking, marched in behind her. They looked stiffer than I had ever seen them. My sons barely greeted me:

"Hello," they said, without raising their eyes. We went into a tiny room. Both boys were tense, and neither of them looked at me as we sat down around a Formica table. Only Alexander ventured a few quick answers to my questions as to how they were. Constantin sat motionless, and I could see how rigid his body was. The psychologist tried to look cheerful. Following the usual ritual, she suggested playing a game. I could sense how bored my sons were. I wondered how Hans-Peter had trained them to sit still and act in this way when their mummy was present. There was practically no conversation. My questions were answered by "yes" and "no." I quickly realized that the boys' reaction would be cited by the psychologist as evidence that they did not want to see me.

Precisely an hour later Alexander stood up, fidgeting and impatient:

"We must go back. I have to do my homework, and Constantin wants to play in the woods."

And they both rushed out toward Frau Kranitz's office. I tried to explain to the psychologist that these were not the reactions of "normal" children. She simply smiled. We left the building.

I returned to the car, distraught and filled with fear.

"Hans-Peter was here. I saw him walking in the car park," Alan announced.

It explained everything. Hans-Peter had remained outside, manipulating his puppets with an invisible thread. My poor, poor boys. They were probably terrified of him. Children do not behave the way mine did unless they are scared. Hans-Peter had also repeatedly told them that I was a threat to their safety: they were scared of seeing me, and they were scared of being rebuked by their father if they did not do as they were told. I had to do something. I knew that this was not the way: coming here, straight into the lion's den. Hans-Peter had probably been panic-stricken before my visits to Verden. He must have ordered the boys to behave in a certain way—or else . . . Alexander and Constantin knew they had no choice but to obey. What hell it must have been for them. No wonder my children were angry with me. My coming to Verden only served to increase the distance between my sons and me: precisely Hans-Peter's intention.

As if he had read my thoughts, Alan broke the heavy silence:

"Catherine, you can't go on like this. These visits are destroying you, and it is exactly what Hans-Peter wants. Unless you can see your sons in normal circumstances. . . . "

Alan was right, and I knew it. But would I ever get normal, decent access? I doubted that Hans-Peter would ever allow this. He had too much at stake.

Under article 21 of the Hague Convention, the German Central Authority had a responsibility to secure me a "peaceful enjoyment of access rights." But the German Central Authority informed its British counterpart that since the Verden court had granted me *some* access, its obligation to me under the convention had ceased. There was nothing further they could do to help. The police could do nothing either: in Germany, access rights are not enforceable. It was up to my lawyer to see that my access rights were respected. Our only solution was to file yet another court application. Yet again the Verden judge cast it aside and yet again requested another report from Frau Kranitz.

By now I knew the lines by heart, and predicting Verden's moves was not difficult. Court applications were rejected on the grounds that there was no urgency. The judge would then delay the proceedings still further by requesting a report from the Jugendamt. These reports would say that "the children's wish" was not to see me. Accordingly, in the "interest of the children," no normal visitation rights should be granted for the moment. The last step in this performance would be a court decision based on the Jugendamt recommendations.

Frau Kranitz faithfully played the role allotted to her and confirmed that the limits on my access should stand. She was not always careful with the truth in setting out the arguments behind her conclusion. For instance, she asserted that Dr. Volkmann had allowed a third party to be present during the access visits because Frau Laylle had also brought in a friend on *"many occasions."* Catherine Urban had been permitted to enter Hans-Peter's house only once, and her presence was then used as an excuse for ending the visit prematurely!

We now had clear evidence of the local authorities' sympathy— to put it mildly—for the Volkmanns. But I knew this would end up as whitewash just as before. Time and again, things so brazen in their injustice had happened that I had felt that surely *this time* they had gone too far, that surely this time their basic unfairness would be unmasked and stopped . . . but it never had been.

The harsh reality was that decisions emerging from Verden had one after the other added to the distance—both spiritual and physical—between my sons and me. No system of justice that deserves the name can allow a situation in which for almost half a decade a mother is never allowed to be alone with her children. But that, as I write—six German lawyers and more than half a dozen German court hearings later—is the situation in which I still find myself. Its particular cruelty is that my sons were given a choice when they had none. All this has been accomplished in the name of the "children's will," a will that has been systematically pressured and indoctrinated over the years. What do you say to your child when, after years of agonizing and fruitless effort to see him, he turns on you—as Alexander did on me again in February 1998—and calls you a liar for abandoning him?

I had trained myself not to think about my sons, and recently my nights had been free of the recurrent nightmares that had haunted them for so long. But no sooner had I found some calm than I would suddenly feel their little bodies wrapped around mine, feel what it had been like to hold them in my arms. It was a physical sensation, and at times I had no control over it.

I tried to settle down, cast out the memories, and turn my attention to what most needed to be done: telephone and fax everyone who needed to be informed. Catherine Urban, who is also the president of French Women Abroad, intensified her campaign to raise the French government's awareness of my plight. Her brief encounter with my boys had deeply distressed her. No normal child behaves as my children did then. She was certain that they were terrified, manipulated, and in psychological danger.

In London Sir John Stanley, cochairman of the All Party Group on Child Abduction, mobilized the other members of Parliament who had been involved in my case, and together they secured at last the support of the Lord Chancellor's Office, in particular of the new minister responsible for these matters,

Gary Streeter. An investigation of the workings of the Hague Convention was under way.

Sir John instigated another debate in the House of Commons. Further approaches to Germany were made by both France and Britain. The German authorities remained unmoved, even though the German media had begun to ask questions. We got the usual boilerplate answer, resting on the independence of the courts and the children's wishes.

.   .   .

A school report reached Herr Struif—the first in twenty months. It was a scrap of paper that had a short listing of subjects with marks beside some of them. There were no teachers' comments, and the name of the school had been whited out.

Several weeks later, in June 1996, the first written information on the children reached Herr Struif. There were no words from the boys themselves. Hans-Peter had typed a "report" summarizing his views on how the children were. It was a matter-of-fact account of the boys' activities to illustrate how happy they were in Verden, how they had become friends with the Monkmanns' and Uncle Klaus's children. But, Hans-Peter went on to say, both had been "traumatized" (to such a degree that Constantin had been frightened to walk up the stairs of the house alone!) by the uninvited appearance of their mother in January 1995 and by the media campaign she had instigated.

This report was accompanied by a recent photograph of the boys, dressed in Bavarian gray flannel suits. I showed this photograph to Erica, a new friend, whom I had recently met through mutual friends. She was appalled:

"This is sheer provocation."

Erica came from Bremen, where she had spent most of her life before moving to France, and then to England. She had two teenage daughters, and six years ago had adopted a Brazilian orphan who "fell into her arms" and whom she couldn't bear to leave behind in the shocking conditions in which she had found him. Erica was an amazing woman, and her love and compassion for children were boundless. When she heard about my case, she phoned me, and from then on committed herself to doing what she could to help.

By an extraordinary coincidence, Erica had once had dealings with Ute Monkmann's pastor and his wife. Though she had not been in touch for a long time, Erica decided to write to Frau Neumann and appeal to her as an advocate of children's rights. Frau Neumann campaigned publicly against abortion and for children to remain with their mothers, even in difficult circumstances.

Erica received an answer: Frau Neumann agreed that although children should normally stay with their mothers, my sons were much better off living with their father. They had been very unhappy in London and had a bad relationship with their mother. Furthermore, since their mother had "hired private detectives" and had alerted the press, they now lived in constant fear of her.

"This is astonishing," said Erica. "She is just repeating Hans-Peter's words. How on earth can a woman in her position make statements about someone she does not know and about conditions she has not seen? She herself campaigns on television—yet you shouldn't for your own children! What do they expect? For you to just lose your children in silence? Will they then say you are a good mother?"

"Oh, no. If I didn't fight for them, they would also say I was a bad mother. This has been going on for nearly two years: I'm damned if I do and damned if I don't!"

Erica had not lived through my story since the beginning, and she found it impossible to imagine.

"Catherine, I am going to Bremen to speak to her. See if I can make any sense out of these people and try to come up with a solution. I just cannot accept that this is happening. Bremen is my hometown."

Kind, generous, and compassionate, Erica set off for Bremen a few weeks later for a roundtable meeting with the pastor, his wife, and Hans-Peter. The children, of course, were not there. She returned to London thoroughly depressed but even more determined. The Neumanns and Hans-Peter had reduced her to utter frustration.

"They wouldn't listen. They closed ranks against you. How can a priest, a representative of God, take sides? And the side of an abductor! Punish children! The fact that Hans-Peter had abducted the children was past and irrelevant. The fact that you had come to Verden uninvited on January 13 last year was given as the absolute reason why your sons should never see you."

Erica began to alert everyone she knew in Germany. Such a travesty of justice had to be exposed. Fate had brought her into my life. Erica was a godsend. Her determination and faith revived mine, and for the first time I had the feeling that the wind might be turning: a miracle might yet happen.

Although I found solace in the fact that Germans like Erica were supporting me, I was no longer able to endure the monthly trips to Verden. A week before the next visit was due, I would start panicking, overwhelmed with anguish. I would develop stomach cramps that prevented me from eating and would spend my nights tossing and turning. The thought of Verden, the two lone houses, the eerie room, Frau Schwarz's insidious presence, the treachery, were heart-rending. The tension inside me would become unbearable as I found myself walking up the lengthy, muddy track with Alan in silence, my heart pounding. What would await me this time? What device would they use to ensure the visit broke up after exactly one hour?

And then, with a knot in my heart, I would enter the cold, soulless drawing room, find my little, sad, and frightened angels, and share the agony of their existence. I was forced to speak in broken German, confined to a locked space, barred from any intimacy, observed, and unable to hold my own sons in my arms. Did Hans-Peter punish them when Frau Schwarz reported any wrongdoing? I was there for only an hour, but they were the ones who were left behind to face the consequences of any forbidden word or gesture. How can I ever describe the turmoil or find the words to capture my agony? How can a mother be expected to witness the suffering of her own children, to watch them craving love and freedom, while she is utterly powerless to protect them? I felt myself crushed by the weight of this cruelty. My whole being cried out in pain.

My father took a firm view.

"Catherine, you shouldn't go anymore. You can't continue to spend over one thousand dollars a month to give Hans-Peter the satisfaction of ruining you. By accepting his terms, you are securing exactly what Hans-Peter wants: to demoralize you and destroy Alexander and Constantin's image of their mother. It would be better for them to remember you as you were, a cuddling and free mummy, than see you like this. These conditions are utterly humiliating and abusive. It's not a question of abandoning your children—quite the opposite."

I knew that my father was right. I had seen Tini's recent reactions to me. He had become cold and dismissive, angry with his mummy for complicating his existence and, as he saw it, making things worse, not better.

My friends voiced a similar opinion. They, too, had observed how my trips to Verden profoundly affected me. Two years had gone by. Dedicating my whole existence to my fight, I had forgotten to live and was incapable of allowing myself any form of distraction. They could see how it was eating away at me. They were concerned:

"Catherine, you've done more than anyone could expect. When they are free to think for themselves, your children will realize that you did not abandon them. But now you need your strength—for them—and if you continue at this pace, you'll burn out."

The thought of what lay ahead of me loomed like an ominous dream. The unimaginable was becoming reality. Hans-Peter was succeeding in excluding me from my sons' lives. He had written in his letter after abducting the boys that he had no intention of "sabotaging" my relationship with the boys, no intention of "not letting me see them"! There had been so many lies.

I often wondered how Hans-Peter was able to reconcile his behavior with his conscience. After all, he had to be aware that one day Alexander and Constantin would be adults and feel the need to find out the truth. They would be able to read their father's letters, the court depositions, the press articles. . . . Didn't he realize how betrayed they would feel then? Didn't he realize that what he had done would hurt his own children most of all? But then, this is what obsessions do—kill judgment, conscience, and common sense.

I decided that I had to do something. I could not go on seeing my sons under these conditions. I had to secure access to my sons on neutral ground. I had to be able to speak to my sons alone and let them know that I loved them. I sat at my desk and wrote to my children. Each word had to be carefully chosen to try to convey my message, while not giving Hans-Peter any pretext to attack me. "Mummy loves you. Mummy has not and will never abandon you. . . . These visits are too degrading for the three of us. . . . Every child has a mother. Every child is allowed to see her. . . . I will go on fighting until we are able to be together again normally."

I informed both the French and British embassies, and Catherine Urban offered to drive up to Verden to deliver my letter personally on June 15, 1996, the day of my entitled visit. We were all nervous, I most of all.

As has been customary throughout this case, nothing happened the way any of us had predicted. Catherine arrived at exactly 9:00 A.M. She saw Frau Schwarz's car parked by the house, but Klaus was not there to greet her. The door of the house was locked, so she rang the bell. A young girl, sixteen, perhaps seventeen years of age, opened the door. Catherine had never seen her before. She introduced herself and asked whether she could see Klaus.

"Dr. Volkmann is not here," the young girl answered, unsure.

"Ah. I wanted to see Klaus, if it's possible."

"Who is Klaus?"

Catherine was taken aback by these odd and seemingly staged answers. The conclusion she drew was that Hans-Peter had thought that this time I would appear with a court bailiff to attest to his and Frau Schwarz's presence.

For once we had wrong-footed them, and Catherine was able to ask whether she could see the boys and give them a letter from their mother. The girl called out, and Alexander slowly walked out of the drawing room and toward Catherine. First she spoke to him in German, and as she recounted to me, Alexander's eyes were glued to the floor. Then she proceeded in French:

"*Ta maman vous aime. . . .* " At this point Alexander looked up into her eyes.

As she later recounted: "I wanted to take him in my arms. . . . He looked so sad. It was as if once I had spoken French to him, he could hear your voice instead of mine. His eyes were begging for love, your love."

Catherine explained to Alexander that I was not abandoning them, quite the opposite, and that I had written them a letter. He took it in his hands and slowly went back to the drawing room. "I then talked to this girl, as I wanted Alexander to be alone with your words. I think he read your letter, but, of course, we will never know for sure—not until you can see him alone."

But would I ever see my children alone again? We filed a new application for "better conditions." Hans-Peter replied by filing a counterapplication requesting that all my access rights be revoked. This was boosted by a claim for child maintenance (through the Youth Authority) backdated to March 1995! At this stage, everyone supporting me was speechless.

The judge rejected both applications. No changes in the access provisions would be made until the judge received the psychological report. Until then, there was nothing else I could do or hope for. My sons' and my future together was now entirely at the mercy of a woman who had met me for a couple of hours and who had deliberately decided to interview only Hans-Peter's side of the family. Final custody and access rights would be determined on the basis of a Bremen psychologist's report.

My parents had obtained from the High Court of Justice in Paris the right to two weeks' access to their grandsons each year. (In French family law, grandparents are entitled to visitation rights.) They clung to the remote hope that they would see Alexander and Constantin on July 15, 1996. Predictably, Klaus faxed their lawyer at the last minute to say that the children would not be coming "since this was their wish." Not only did my sons supposedly not wish to see their mother, but they were not interested in seeing their grandparents either! Klaus went on to add that "the Verden Jugendamt supports the children's opinion, and their [Verden Youth Authority's] view should take priority over any decisions made by the French High Court of Justice."

I may still, one day, see my sons. But my parents probably never will. They will die without seeing them again. Alexander and Constantin were the only grandchildren my father ever had. This is why I become so angry when the media describe my case as a "tug of love." It is about basic human rights and their abuse by a system that appears to have forgotten nothing and learned nothing.

At the end of August the psychologist's report was finally submitted. There was an introductory résumé of the situation. As usual, the fact that Hans-Peter had abducted the children twice, been in contempt of court, and denied me any form of access or telephone contact with the children was omitted. As usual, my relations with the media were used as a stick with which to beat me.

My "fight" for my sons was interpreted as a negative aspect of my personality. The psychologist considered me "a woman who was accustomed to succeed in all things" and that when I lost the battle for my children, I had formed an idée fixe: the need to fight on instead of adopting a reasonable attitude and letting my children be. She quoted passages from the letter Catherine Urban delivered to my sons to reinforce her point. Apparently, as their "biological" mother, I had no particular claim to my children.

Without knowing anything about my life in London, without talking to anyone in London, the psychologist decided that I was a "bad" mother who had never had any time for her sons. By working (and earning the money to support the boys), I had shown my complete lack of interest in the children. The fact that Hans-Peter left the boys in the hands of others while he worked in another town was not relevant.

She described Hans-Peter as oversensitive and highly concerned about his children. But the report acknowledged that he was unable to keep his feelings under control and that this was affecting the children, deeply impairing the restoration of normal relations with their mother. The psychologist described Gundel, Hans-Peter's mother, as a very "dominating woman who prevented the children from articulating, or even being allowed to articulate, their own feelings when they did not agree with the grandmother's ideas." Furthermore, she constantly said bad things about me to the boys and openly made derogatory comments about foreigners. Her narrow-mindedness was such that she had in the past warned Hans-Peter "that under no circumstances should he find himself a foreign wife."

We learned from the report that Hans-Peter had a girlfriend whom he had known for several years. She was the one who opened the door to Catherine Urban. They worked and lived together. Although some twenty years his junior, she was described, unsurprisingly, as the dominant partner in the relationship. She often had to remind Hans-Peter to get on with his work. But the psychologist viewed her as exerting a "very positive influence" on Hans-Peter, whereas I had been overdemanding in my expectations. The report, almost as a casual aside, revealed that she had spent several months in a hospital because of a severe but unexplained psychological problem. This was the woman into whose care my children had been placed. But the Bremen psychologist, while quick to condemn me for wishing to be with my children, never thought to ask whether this woman was fit to look after them.

The psychologist described one of her tests on the children. The children had to draw a castle. Alexander at first refused. He wanted to know what the purpose was. According to the psychologist, Alexander was expressing an inner resistance and "was attempting to convey a specific picture of his feelings." He was afraid that the psychologist would interpret his drawing in a way different from the one that he wanted (or was told) to convey.

Constantin made the point even more clearly. He drew the castle, and when the psychologist asked him if his mother should have a room, he immediately said yes. But when she asked which was her room, Constantin suddenly realized what he had spontaneously said. He frantically corrected himself, insisting that his mother was not "allowed," and he asked the psychologist if she could delete his yes answer. He then repeated several times that he had made a mistake. When she brought him home later on, the first thing he told his father was that there had been a misunderstanding. In her conclusions, however, the psychologist insisted that the boys had not been "manipulated" and—at least with Alexander—it had been his "will" to remain with his father.

Surprisingly enough, the psychologist confirmed that Constantin still had a strong bond with his mother and that Alexander had positive feelings at his "subconscious level" and that he had loved his mother in "earlier times." But, again, this did not seem to represent a major dilemma for the psychologist when she drew her conclusions. The boys' relationship with their mother "had been seriously disturbed." These were the "current conditions." And if they had a "disturbed relationship with their mother," this was "the result of her own behavior." The fact that I had seen my sons for only a few hours, and never alone, since they had left London in 1994 was ignored. The report was full of contradictions, and I found it extraordinarily biased. Quotes from what I had said were twisted to work against me, and I did not recognize some of my supposed statements. Everything about me was unremittingly negative. Having a babysitter looking after my sons each working day for one and a half hours until 5:30 P.M. confirmed that I had neglected them. But she made no comment on Hans-Peter's returning home at 6:30 P.M., nor on the children's spending all afternoons (school finishes at lunchtime in Germany) in the care of their paternal grandmother—even though the psychologist herself considered Gundel's "authoritarian character" and prejudices a very harmful influence on the boys.

The report also confirmed the very significant fact that Frau Kranitz had offered Hans-Peter her support as early as the summer 1994 holidays, when he was laying his plans to keep the children.

The Bremen psychologist's report was essentially as I had expected. The children's whole environment was favorable in Verden with their father and unfavorable in London with their mother. Final custody should be transferred to Hans-Peter. This was bad enough. But there was worse to come. She would examine access rights only *after* the decision on custody had been made. This meant further delays. Until her report was submitted, there would be no review of my access rights.

All was set for the final act. The Verden court would soon be at peace. Backed by a psychological report, final custody could be transferred to Hans-Peter "in the interest of the children." And since, as a letter from Chancellor Kohl's office had explained, under German law "it is impossible to go against the wish of the parent who has custody," I appeared blocked at every turn.

But had anyone proved that I was an unfit mother? No. I was nonetheless denied the basic human rights that even women in prison are allowed. My parents had been denied their human rights as well. Before Hans-Peter kept our children, they were allowed to see and to love both their parents and grandparents. Now they were not. This in itself would be a determining factor in countries where the courts genuinely had the interests of children at heart—but not in Verden. There, the mentality was different. Apparently, children did not need both their parents, and a foreign mother had no intrinsic right to her children. No wonder some people make a connection between this mentality and Germany's past.

I had fought for my sons as best I knew how. But had I run my course? Should I turn the page and forget that I had two children? Forget I was a mother and find a way to cut the cord to my boys? I could see no way out.

I had kept going for over two years, sustained by a mother's love for her children and the belief that one day I would get justice. I had thought, naively, that it was only a matter of time, only a matter of endurance. Now I no longer knew what life was about and how I could go on living it. There was so little left to believe in, to live for. My friends tried to comfort me. "The boys will be back," they would say. I did not doubt this. One day, in years to come, they will want to know who their mother is. But I had moved beyond the shock of separation. My agony was to be helpless before the destruction of their happiness, useless to stop what was being done to them. I wanted to sleep forever, and forget.

I was sinking. I sat at my desk and started to write my will. I was talking to my children, telling them our story, how I had fought to see them—and how the law had failed us. I talked about life, about death, and about how much I craved seeing them. The next day I left my flat and started to walk aimlessly in the streets of London. I went wherever my legs happened to take me. I wandered along the quiet tree-lined streets, through the garden squares, across the busy roads. The simple act of putting one foot in front of the other brought me a kind of peace. I felt separate from the world around me. Street noises lulled my mind. I was able to escape the obligation to think and to feel. It was late when I returned home. I stripped my clothes off and fell asleep.

There was nothing left for me here. A part of me had already died when my children left; now that my trust in life had vanished, I felt free to go. I no longer wished to linger over my shattered hopes. I no longer wished to remember how it had been to hold my boys in my arms, suddenly waking up from one of those dreams, so real that I felt the imprint of my children on my body.

CHAPTER 18

The Hand of Fate

On September 16, 1996, I was woken up by a telephone call from BBC Television: the Lord Chancellor's Office had released its report on the workings of the Hague Convention. They wanted to interview me on *Breakfast TV.* So did another news channel. I was carted from one TV station to the next. The next day several articles appeared in the British press. The *Times* had a big headline: "Government Accuses Germany of Failing to Observe International Accord." In a highly unusual step, the Lord Chancellor's Office accused the German courts of hiding behind legal technicalities to block the repatriation of abducted children. My case was cited as being central to the government's strong response. I was ecstatic. The British government had at last taken a position, showing that it cared for children and that it was determined to ensure their protection. Gary Streeter, Parliamentary undersecretary at the Lord Chancellor's Office, pledged that Britain would take the lead at a Hague Convention meeting in March 1997 (the first in years) to review how its procedures were working on the return of abducted children.

Overnight I had regained my faith in Britain. In France the then Minister of Justice, Jacques Toubon, who had taken a personal interest in my case, also ordered an inquiry into Germany's adherence to the Hague Convention. After these years of fighting I was still unable to see my sons, but at least the issue of international child abduction was becoming a matter of concern to both the French and British governments.

The following day I set off for Paris. At President Chirac's request, I was invited to the Élysée to meet his European adviser. This was a major breakthrough.

My parents picked me up at the Eurostar train station. My father looked tired and aged. The strain of the last two years had left its mark on all of us. But today we were inspired by the realization that these months of relentless work had not been in vain. The president himself had taken a personal interest in my case, and we allowed ourselves to be excited at the prospect that there might yet be some hope.

It was a hot September day. Paris looked beautiful. I felt alive. A certain feeling of pride took me over. After all, I had managed to attract the attention of the most important person in France. I had done it practically alone, supported by my family and friends. I felt confident and cheerful as I walked toward the Élysée.

The European adviser was very sympathetic to my story. But after I had spent an hour explaining my case, he sighed. There was little he could do. My case was in the hands of the German courts. But he would see that it was mentioned again to Chancellor Kohl, who was due to be in Paris on an official visit the following week. As I stood up to leave, he added, "The president has asked me to give you his sympathy. He feels for you and will continue to give you his support."

That evening my parents and I went out to dinner. We discussed the situation: if the president of France could not help—

if, as his European adviser feared, the chancellor would fall back on the independence of the German justice system—what next? My parents were worried. They felt that I should stop giving my whole life to my case.

"Katia, you should get a job. You can't go on like this. If even the president can't help you, what else can you do? You are ruining your health. Isn't it about time you started looking for a job and doing something else with your life?"

My father continued:

"Alexander and Constantin will know that you haven't abandoned them. But what good will you be for them if you continue like this? You are too thin, too tired, and I am worried for you."

"Yes, yes. . . . " I understood my parents' concern, but I couldn't accept it. It wasn't that simple. I couldn't simply bow to the pressure. The civil rights movement in the United States had taken years of determination and perseverance to achieve results. I certainly wasn't a martyr, but I had not run my course either. This issue was too important for me. It was my life. I had not chosen this destiny, but it had chosen me. I could not turn my back. How could I return to the mundane preoccupations of my earlier existence when my sons were asking themselves why their mother wouldn't even visit them? If I did not fight for their rights, who would? Children are resilient. They have no choice but to adapt. But it is precisely at the point when they are being forced to adapt that they are vulnerable to deep, and possibly irreversible, psychological damage. I had talked to several child psychologists and had been horror-stricken at their description of the psychological consequences of childhood trauma. My only consolation was that children's very early years are formative in the emotional makeup of their adult selves—and at least for Alexander and Constantin those years had been trauma-free. But the belief that their mother had deliberately abandoned them could create feelings of betrayal, anger, and deep, deep hurt. They would feel discarded and rejected. These feelings of alienation would pursue them throughout their lives. It was impossible to predict how, or even whether, they would be able to come to terms with those feelings as adults.

As soon as I returned to London, I was back to work. Working on my case allowed me to exist. It had become my solace. Through it I could justify my existence. It was the only way I felt I could narrow the distance separating me from my sons. If I did not spend my day telephoning, faxing, and writing, they would be forgotten. Wherever I happened to be, whatever else I happened to be doing, my mind would always drift back to my sons. There were always avenues that had not been explored, and I would often discuss them with my friends in the evenings. Had I written to all the right people? Had I thought of contacting this or that member of Parliament? Had I talked to that other organization? The list was endless. No one could be overlooked because maybe it was precisely that person who could make a difference to the outcome of my story. What I dreaded most of all was the idea of not having done enough. I was always in search of a new idea.

The first edition of my book was about to be published in France. It was entitled *Two Children Behind a Wall*. The wall referred to the wall of silence that was surrounding my boys. But I had also made the connection with the Berlin Wall. As implausible as it had once seemed, the wall had finally fallen. Maybe this wall would fall one day, too.

Writing my book had been a kind of exorcism. But it had all happened by chance. I had spent many evenings writing résumés of my case. Some in English, others in French, some briefly describing the events, others outlining in detail its legal evolution. I would also spend hours writing to my children, letters that I could not send but that allowed me to feel a part of them. It was the only way I had left to communicate with them. As I wrote, I felt their presence. Their spirits were close, and I hoped they would feel my thoughts around them, although they were physically hundreds of miles away. It was a friend of mine who finally suggested I write a book. It was a good idea, but I would not be capable of writing it on my own. After all, I had never written a book before. My command of English would not lend itself to an accurate account of my feelings. I approached someone I knew whose writing I admired. Unfortunately, he was busy with another project.

"Catherine, you should write it. Of course, you are capable of doing it. Just try it. You'll see, it won't be difficult, and it will be your book. If someone else writes it for you, it will be their reconstruction of the events you have lived and felt."

I began to write. The first pages were difficult. I kept stumbling on every word, weighing them, changing them, never feeling satisfied. I wanted to retrace events exactly the way they had been, and I pondered the meaning of each sentence. I wanted to be fair, but I had much more anger to deal with than I had ever realized. Soon, though, words started filling my blank pages. It was as if I had unlocked a door. I kept on writing, propelled by the flow of what I had been wanting to let out for so long. And before I knew it, I had written a whole chapter.

I felt exhausted, yet liberated. I sat down on the sofa and read through what I had just written. It was terrible. The anger revealed itself in every word. I threw away the twelve pages, and I started again on the book. It took me seven weeks to write. My French publisher had set me a strict time limit. It was exhausting, but writing our story became a compelling force. I would wake up early in the morning, sit at my desk with a mug of coffee, and until dark, I would bury myself in the task of bringing our experience into words. The nature of the book made it easier—the outline of the story was set. But I felt inhibited, knowing that every word I wrote could be used against me in the German courts.

For seven weeks I almost never went out and saw practically no one. I confined myself to my apartment in Egerton Gardens. I thought of nothing else, did nothing else. Even when, late at night, I drifted to sleep, I would be tracing the skeleton of my next chapter. Writing this book was a combination of deliverance and hell. I had to retrace the horrors of the past two years, walk through the labyrinth of endless legal steps that had led me nowhere, and relive emotions that I did not want to reawaken. But at the same time it allowed me to talk to my sons and record the events as I had experienced them.

People could now read the book. From that moment on I freed myself from the endless explanations about my case. Most people had been unable to believe that a story like mine could be true. I had found myself endlessly answering their questions. But as the months went by, I had found it more and more difficult to satisfy their interest. Each explanation meant describing details I did not want to relive. Through my book, I had liberated myself from the sensation that I could not move on.

The other major change in September 1996 was my awareness that I no longer had to defend or justify myself. My case was so extraordinary that some people thought either that I had been a complete fool—or at least that my lawyers had been—or worse still, that there was a serious flaw in my character that made it possible for the courts to take the children away from me. "Oh, well, there are always two sides to a story. You don't know what she did. Maybe she deserved it," a few people had said earlier on. This reaction was extremely difficult for me to cope with. It was traumatic enough to deal with the loss of my sons; being confronted with criticism and having to justify myself to others was unbearable. I had had to do it in Verden. I simply could not endure the prospect of having to do it in London. Thanks to my dear friends, who would loyally defend me, I was spared some of this humiliation.

But now, even the more skeptical observers were beginning to accept that something must be wrong. The real breakthrough came when the British and French governments spoke in my defense. I was publicly acknowledged as a victim and a spokesperson, as it were, on the issue of child abduction. The entire perception of me changed—and I with it.

Over the months I had come across scores of parents in Britain and France whose children had been abducted to Germany and who, like me, had been blocked at every turn by the German legal system. Some had not seen their children for years. I now felt myself part of a wider cause. This gave me strength and a certain feeling of recognition for what I was trying to achieve.

I had been unemployed for two years, barely able to survive on welfare checks, and my debts were mounting. Herr Struif's complaints to the courts about the conditions for access visits had had little effect. The judge would not review the provisions until the psychologist had filed her report. For the time being, I decided to abandon the visits to my children under the oppressive conditions imposed by the Verden court. It was quite clear that visits on these terms were so difficult for both the boys and me that, far from building normality between us, they were feeding Alexander's and Constantin's sense of alienation from me. I assumed, as I still do, that this was the deliberate intent of the Volkmann family and their supporters in the German system. I was not going to fall further into their trap.

But I had to have an alternative strategy. I could not just sit at home waiting for the psychologist to present her report. The wheels of the German legal system seemed to turn extremely slowly when it was a question of considering my wishes and rights. In turn, I had no expectation that when it finally came to a decision the court would do anything to help me see my children alone and in normal surroundings.

If I could not get justice for my children, the least I could do was to raise awareness of this appalling international scandal. Of course, I would not rest until I saw my little angels again. But I was also determined to wage war on international child abduction and to lobby for the implementation of the Hague Convention as it had originally been intended. I decided, though it was full of risks for my case, to intensify my public campaign and my lobbying of the British, French, and German authorities. I knew that this would infuriate Verden and that going to the media would be used against me in court hearings. But the alternative was to submit passively to injustice—to play the Volk-manns' game as they wanted it played—and that I could not agree to do.

I started to give regular press interviews in England and in France. One French father who had been separated from his daughter since 1994 decided to set up an organization called "SOS Abduction to Germany." The membership grew rapidly. We became a voice that could no longer be ignored. In December 1996 we decided to gather in front of the German embassy in Paris. Since none of us had any contact with our children, we wanted to ask the embassy to deliver Christmas presents to our children in Germany. Catherine Urban informed the German embassy and asked to be received to present a petition.

On December 18 approximately sixty people, including several politicians wearing their French tricolored bands across their chests, stood in silence in front of the German embassy. The gates were closed, and several policemen were stationed in front of the courtyard. Catherine Urban was not allowed in. A few journalists and photographers were present. Each parent held at least one Christmas present in his or her arms. A few more had brought placards; one read, "Kohl, give us back our children." Catherine switched on a tape recorder. It played Christmas carols. Inside the embassy several people discreetly peeped out of the windows to see what was happening, but no one came out. After an hour we asked the guard if we could at least bring our presents inside the embassy. He refused. He had strict orders. We pleaded. Someone came out of the building. The best he could do was to allow us to deposit our presents in the courtyard. The gates opened, and we walked onto German territory to leave the gifts for our children.

A few days later Catherine Urban received a letter from the German embassy's legal adviser: the presents should be picked up within the next ten days or they would be given to charity. French congressmen and senators were informed. Most were outraged at the way we had been rebuffed. The French government reacted immediately, and a few days later Catherine Urban obtained an audience at the German embassy. The chair of the parents' organization accompanied her. The embassy grudgingly agreed to forward the presents through the regular postal service. On the issue itself, the embassy could do nothing: the justice system was independent, and it was not in the embassy's power to intervene. But we still hoped that with the latest events and the publicity attached to it, the German government would react. It did not.

.   .   .

In March 1997 my book was launched in England. (I wrote the original version in English, but a French publisher approached me first.) Thanks to my supporters among members of Parliament, I held my book launch on March 6, 1997 in the House of Commons. This got me good publicity in the British media. It also boosted my self-confidence and determination to press ahead with my war against child abduction. For the first time in my life, I was forced to overcome my shyness and to speak in public. In a modest way, I was becoming a public figure and an acknowledged expert on child abduction.

More important, I was gaining a new lease on life, a new purpose for my existence. I realize now that to achieve this, I had had to survive an emotional crisis that had almost destroyed me. Without children, without hope, without career, without money, surviving on welfare, I had begun to wonder whether I had the strength to go on. Life had lost its meaning, and I was tempted by the peace that only death can bring. But I suppose that it was at just the moment when suicide seemed attractive that the instinct kicked in to live, to struggle, not to desert my children when they most needed me. These feelings are not easy to describe. But once you find consolation in the thought of death, then nothing else can touch you or frighten you anymore. You gain an inner peace that becomes an inner strength. You become tougher. You prepare yourself, like the great Russian generals of history, for the long, arduous campaign. You become determined never to give up. You feel pity and contempt, not hatred, for those who have taken and manipulated your children. You realize how twisted and impoverished their inner lives must be. In a sense, you know that you have already won, because you will never descend to their level.

It was in this resolute frame of my mind that I set out for Germany on April 14, 1997, for yet another dramatic and totally unexpected turn in my life.

.　　.　　.

A few weeks after my book launch a German television station called me. They were producing a program on child abduction. They had several parents on the panel and had heard about my case. Would I come to Cologne and participate in a live interview? I panicked. Going to Germany had become a grueling nightmare for me. It's harsh to say, but at that time Germany was equivalent to enemy territory for me. It was the place where my children were kept prisoners. It was the place where the system of justice had made it possible for us to be forcibly separated. I was scared to go there. I called Mr. Perrier at the French consulate. Three years on, he had become a friend, and I knew I could seek his advice. He immediately understood my concern and phoned Paris to let them know that I intended to fly to Cologne. An appointment was set up for me to see the French ambassador in Bonn. I had met him several times in the past, and he had been following my story with compassion, intervening whenever he could.

I then called Michael Sullivan, the British consul-general in Hamburg:

"And, Catherine, will you take this opportunity to meet our new ambassador? I've recently seen him, and he has assured me that he would continue the support Sir Nigel Broomfield used to give you. I think it would be a good idea for you to make an appointment. I'm sure you'll like him. He's young and dynamic."

In fact, I had already written to Christopher Meyer, who had arrived in Germany as our new ambassador in March 1997. I

knew he was aware of my case. My file had been at the embassy
long enough, and a member of Parliament had approached him
about me before his departure to Bonn. But I thought it would do
no harm to introduce myself and send him a copy of my book. I
decided to take Michael Sullivan's advice, and I placed a call to
the embassy. His private secretary informed me that the ambassador was in a meeting but that he would pass on the message.

Less than an hour later, the embassy was on the phone:

"I am putting you through to the ambassador."

"Hello. Miss Laylle? This is Christopher Meyer." His voice
sounded extremely friendly, and I was somewhat taken aback,
expecting a more reserved tone.

"Ambassador, yes, hello. I am sorry to trouble you. . . . But I
am coming to Germany for a television interview next week. . . . I
was wondering whether I could possibly come and see you."

"Yes, of course. When will you be here?"

"The interview is on Tuesday."

"Tuesday I am in Hanover. But I could see you on Wednesday."

"Yes, Wednesday. That's perfect for me."

I had not intended to stay overnight, but I decided that I
could not pass up this opportunity. He had sounded unexpectedly accessible for an ambassador.

On April 16, Catherine Urban was waiting at the Cologne
airport. A friend of mine who knew how scared I was to go to
Germany had kindly offered to chaperone me. The three of us
drove to the television station. Herr Bloch, a lawyer from Berlin,
and two German victim parents joined our party. We were all
nervous and apprehensive. This was a live show. The two other
parents and I sat on the stage; Herr Bloch and Catherine Urban
sat in the first row of the auditorium. The interview was conducted in German. But the show went well. The presenter was
excellent, and although I had made the mistake of speaking
German rather than have a translator speak over my voice, the
message was strong.

The next day Catherine, Herr Bloch, and my friend set off
early in the morning, still exhausted from our previous day, to

meet a Bundestag member in Bonn. He was sympathetic to my story and promised to ask about it at the Ministry of Justice. The meeting took much longer than we had expected, and we were running late for our lunch appointment with a French newspaper correspondent. I phoned the British embassy to ask whether it would be possible to postpone my meeting with the ambassador. A new time was scheduled for 4:30 P.M. After lunch we headed for the French embassy. As always, M. Scheer, the French ambassador, was attentive. But on that day he was more talkative than usual. I was becoming anxious and discreetly looked at my watch. I was running late again. As soon as possible, I said good-bye to the ambassador and joined the others, who had been waiting outside. Catherine had to leave for Frankfurt, and I asked the receptionist to call a taxi for us. When the cab finally appeared, it was already well past four o'clock. Herr Bloch was in a state. During lunch he had set up an appointment with another Bundestag member for 3:45 P.M. He wanted me to come with him. The taxi driver did not know his way around. He was not from Bonn. Maps were unfolded. Bloch was agitated, the driver grumbling. I was becoming frantic. It was nearly four-thirty, and the driver suddenly stopped the car to look at a plan of the city.

"Don't you know where the German Bundestag is?" Bloch shouted at the driver. "Catherine, phone the embassy and tell them you'll be late. You must come to the meeting with Frau von Renesse. She's important for your case."

"It's impossible. I cannot cancel my meeting with the British ambassador. The plane is at 6:30. There wouldn't be enough time to see him later."

The cab drove on. The driver kept on making wrong turns. Herr Bloch was more and more agitated. Suddenly, I recognized the embassy building.

"Stop here," I shouted to the driver, and before Herr Bloch had time to argue, I stepped out of the car. Something told me that I had to go to this meeting. Herr Bloch sighed and went off with my friend to the Bundestag.

My heart was pounding. I could feel on my forehead the cold perspiration that too much stress brings. I took a deep breath and walked up to the guard at the gate.

"I have an appointment with the ambassador."

The gate opened, and I entered the building. Suddenly, I felt calm. The private secretary soon came to pick me up, and he led me upstairs. He knocked on the ambassador's door, and we stepped in. I was immediately taken aback. A tall, attractive man walked swiftly toward me. He enthusiastically put out his right hand. I immediately noticed his fair hair and blue eyes. A youthful smile lit up his face. We shook hands:

"I'm so pleased to meet you, Mrs. Laylle."

His forthright and unaffected way made me like him instantly. Mr. Sullivan had been right. But I had never imagined that our ambassador to Germany would be so young and easygoing. I suddenly became aware of my disheveled hair and the signs of fatigue that I knew marked my face.

Without any protocol, the ambassador asked me to sit down. His secretary left the room. Christopher Meyer sat in an armchair to my right. He leaned forward, smiled warmly, and we began to discuss my case. I felt myself blushing. I became confused. I tried to compensate for a sudden feeling of shyness by being more businesslike than usual. He listened attentively, his blue eyes fixed on me. He asked questions. I detected a genuine concern and compassion, tinged with an attraction to me personally. I felt myself warming to him.

There was little time. I had to catch a plane back to London. But we talked about all sorts of things. Before he had taken up his post, the Foreign Office had sent him to Hamburg to brush up on his German. He had stayed with Michael Sullivan for several weeks. What a coincidence! Michael had often talked about me. We returned to the subject of my sons.

"There is something I ought to tell you," the ambassador interjected. "I am separated from my wife." There was a sudden pause. My mind was racing. An hour earlier the French ambassador had mentioned that his wife was French, so this came as a surprise to me.

Christopher Meyer went on: "We have three sons, and this is why I have some insight into what you are going through." From then on, our conversation took on a slightly different tone. A common bond had been established between us, but at the same time both of us became more conscious of each other. We talked about my children, his children, life in Germany. One minute we were serious, the next lighthearted. This gave me a strange feeling that I couldn't analyze.

"Your mother is Russian? I was posted twice to Russia." And away we went into a discussion about life in Moscow. I felt comfortable in this man's company, but I did not know what to think. I was confused. His unexpected interjection about his personal life was echoing in the back of my mind. My cellular phone, which was buried in my purse, started ringing. I knew that it must be Herr Bloch or my London friend wondering where I was. I discreetly looked at my watch and ignored the call. We went on talking. The phone rang again. I answered it. It was Herr Bloch. We were running terribly late. They would pick me up in a taxi. As we stood up, the ambassador gave me his business card. His manner was slightly awkward, and I felt more self-assured.

"And please call me anytime," he added as he gave me his card.

He led me out of his office and followed me down the stairs. I was conscious of his presence behind me. Instead of taking his leave, he waited with me for the taxi. It was a warm and sunny day. We stood side by side, talking to each other, but not looking at one another. I wondered what the girl at the reception desk behind must have thought. The ambassador did most of the talking, and I cannot remember what the conversation was about. We simply enjoyed standing next to each other. The taxi finally pulled up, and I left. A strange feeling of calm and well-being had taken me over. As the plane took off, my London friend started chatting away, but my mind was miles away. There was a moment of tranquillity up there in the air, and in it, I was thinking of Christopher Meyer.

.   .   .

From then on, things moved very fast. And no one was more surprised than I.

On my return to London, I wrote to the ambassador, thanking him for seeing me and giving him some additional information on my case. But I also decided to attach a separate card to my official letter. It took me several days to write these few lines. I wanted to convey a slightly more personal message yet at the same time be discreet. The message was ambiguous. It said nothing if you wished to read nothing into it. But if you were looking for more. . .

The following week I took the Eurostar to Paris. I had an appointment at the Ministry of Justice and a second one with President Chirac's European adviser. On my return journey to London, my cellular phone rang, and a voice I didn't recognize at first was at the other end.

"Hello. This is Christopher Meyer." I was flabbergasted. "I got your letter. Thank you so much. I only read it yesterday. I was in Berlin for a few days. . . . I was very touched by what you wrote. . . . "

"Hmm . . . yes, hello. I'm sitting in a train. . . . "

"Ah, would it be better if I call you at home?"

"Yes, I'll be there at 7:00 P.M." Apparently, my voice was very businesslike. So much so that he wondered whether he had made a mistake and had misinterpreted what he felt was a message in my note. But I had been taken by surprise. Calling me on my cellular phone . . . when he could have left a message at home . . . I was over the moon. As soon as the train arrived at Waterloo Station, I jumped out and ran to the taxi stand. I had miscalculated my arrival time. I still had to get home. The phone rang as I opened my front door.

"It's Christopher Meyer. I'm sorry, I can't talk to you now. I have Lord Menuhin for dinner. May I call you at 9:30 P.M.?"

"Yes, yes of course. . . . I'm first going out to dinner myself, but I'm sure I'll be back on time. . . . "

When I returned home, there was a message on my answering machine. It was an hour later in Germany. He was sorry that he had missed me. He'd call tomorrow at six. I listened to the message twice over. He had such a nice, cheerful voice! I fell asleep looking forward to the next day. I had almost forgotten how it felt to look forward to anything. At six o'clock sharp, the phone rang. We started talking. We were both slightly shy, but the conversation was easy. We talked again the next day, and the day after, and by the third day we were talking to each other twice a day. By the seventh day we had spent hours on the telephone. We were never short of things to say to each other. It felt so easy and natural. There was never a misunderstanding. It was as if we had found a soulmate in each other.

The May bank holiday weekend was approaching.

"So, when are we going to see each other again?" Christopher asked me.

"Why, are you coming to London for the bank holiday?"

"No, I have to stay in Bonn during the British general elections this weekend. There will probably be a change of government, and I need to be here to receive the incoming ministers. You'll just have to come to Germany."

"But I have no excuse to come to Germany," I said, just a little flirtatiously.

"Oh, yes, you do. The British ambassador is inviting you for a private meeting."

We decided on the second weekend in May. On May 1, 1997, Tony Blair and New Labour were elected with an overwhelming majority of 179 seats in the House of Commons. Two days later I was on the phone in a state of panic:

"I can't come to Germany. It would be mad. I have a problem with the German authorities. You are the ambassador to Germany. . . . Of all the women in the world. . . . It's too dangerous for your career. . . . " My mind had been made up. I was not going to Germany. It wouldn't be right for his career, and I was scared of going to Germany myself. But his mind was made up as well. He wasn't afraid, and whether it was risky or not, he wanted to see me again. On May 5, 1997, I was on the plane to Bonn, apprehensive, weary, and excited at the same time. We had gotten along so well on the telephone, but why had fate sent me back to Germany? Wasn't life just too bizarre?

We immediately hit it off as if we had known each other for years. It was terrific. We talked and talked incessantly. We forgot about the outside world. On the second night we went out to a well-known Bad Godesberg restaurant. The owner, an elderly lady, who had known many German politicians since the end of the war, came up to us with great excitement.

"Ambassador, welcome to Bonn. . . . Oh, and it's so wonderful to see two people so in love. . . . " We looked at each other. She had noticed something we had not been aware of. I returned to London two days later. I was a new person. Besides a few old and trusted friends, no one knew about Christopher Meyer. I was too terrified, and I felt too much was at stake for both of us. Two weekends later we met in Berlin. There, we had the most magical and romantic days together. We drove into the countryside. We played tennis. We had long, lingering dinners. We talked and laughed, oblivious to the outside world. We were in love. The summer was approaching, the days lengthening and getting light. Irony of ironies, it was in Germany that our love blossomed. But by falling in love in Germany, I found myself able to make peace at last with part of it.

CHAPTER 19

A Change
of Course

Meeting a man, let alone starting a serious long-term relationship, was possibly the very last thing on my mind. Since the
abduction of my children, my attention had been devoted quite
exclusively to Alexander and Constantin. I had no other
thoughts or feelings. My days and most of my evenings were
spent working at home on my case. The only people I saw
socially were a few very close friends. Nicolette, who also lived
in Egerton Gardens, often dropped in on her way back from
work, and we would spend hours discussing my case or writing
letters together. She was extremely bright and efficient. She was
able to guide me through the maze of legalities and, with her
sensitivity, helped me hold my emotions together. During the
first two years, Nicolette was the bulwark behind my survival. I
came to rely on her, and she wound up becoming as emotionally
involved in the recovery of my sons as I was.

My other friends would regularly check in with me. But over the months it had become more and more difficult to talk to those who were not directly involved in my plight. My case was so complicated and so absurd that, unless you followed it step by step, it was incomprehensible and unbelievable. I would find myself drawn into providing long explanations that drained me emotionally. By the end of 1995, I had cut myself off from the outside world. I felt comfortable with no one except five friends and my parents. If I met anyone else, it was only to advance my case and the struggle against international child abduction.

But by June 1996, my parents and my close friends had become extremely worried. They feared the worst as they saw me fall to my lowest ebb. So they masterminded a scheme to get me out of my misery. My cousin, who was involved in the Sochi International Film Festival, needed a Russian interpreter for the French actors and journalists who were attending. It was, of course, an amazing opportunity. But I felt I could not be absent for ten days. I was almost forced by my parents onto a flight to Russia. The first days were agony. I was in a state of near panic without a fax machine, proper telephone lines, or a laptop. I felt extremely guilty that I was doing something other than fighting for my sons. But there was nothing I could do. I soon found myself engrossed in the festival and in my work. The drastic change of scenery, the activity around me, and the feeling that I was needed created space for a different kind of life. I had fun and I laughed. For the first time in years, I was able to put my case to one side. By the time I got home, I was no longer thinking about ending it all.

By September 1996, I began to take a new lease on life. Though battered and bruised, I began to compartmentalize my life. I worked on my case all day, but I went out in the evenings. I had been a hermit for over two years; now I was ready to socialize, albeit very tentatively. I was simply starved for laughter, and I knew that I had to give myself time off, away from my papers. But I was not looking for relationships of any kind. Going out and meeting people was more a retreat from my reality.

In any case, as soon as men heard about my predicament, they would shy away. It did not upset me. I felt I could never trust a man again. I preferred the intimacy of my friends. I was certainly not ready to risk more disappointment or hurt. But when I met Christopher, everything was different. It was as if the question of trust, or of whether to get involved with him, never arose. We met, we liked each other immediately, and we became partners. He was my best friend, and I his. We shared our thoughts and our fears, and we never hid anything from each other. The more we knew each other, the more indispensable we became to one another.

The British ambassador's residence in Bonn became our refuge. I would turn up most Fridays, and we would spend the weekends together walking on the bank of the Rhine, eating in local pubs, talking endlessly. We had so much to say to each other, so many experiences to share. I was very interested in his work. We discussed political issues, had lively debates about Europe and Germany. We both had strong personalities and determined views, and neither of us liked to lose an argument. These studentlike debates could have been the end of us— instead, they bonded us together. Even arguing was fun. We felt young, alive, and happy together.

But I had a lot of heavy psychological baggage. The past three years had made me anxious, mistrustful, and weary. I found it very hard to expose my deep emotions. I do not know if anyone other than Christopher could have managed to break through the thick protective layers I had built around me. But he was patient and understanding. He made me trust him. It took much courage and determination on his part, and I realized how much he loved me. Few men would have wanted to take on a hurt and blistered soul like mine.

Still, I needed the approval of my friends. I felt I could not trust my own judgment. On his first visit to London, I introduced Christopher to my old and trusted friend Claudine. We had lunch with her and her husband, Dennis. The next visit, he had to meet

Nicolette; then Leonard, then Lila. . . . They all approved and felt terribly excited for me. I began to dare to hope. . . . Our relationship flourished. Soon, there was talk of marriage.

Christopher and I talked a lot about my case. It was a part of me, and had he not been receptive, or had he grown weary of my talking about it, I would not have been able to trust and love him. Christopher would listen and sympathize. He was concerned and kind, but I still felt that he thought, like many others, that I exaggerated the negative attitude of the forces ranged against me in Verden. But he would soon change his mind.

It took the court-appointed psychologist nine months to file the report on my access rights. Any fair-minded observer would ask how it could take so long to draft a report that simply rehashed an earlier report and did not involve further interviews with the parties. The arguments were the usual ones: of course, a mother should see her children. But since they and their father were so "terrified" that I would re-abduct them, a third party had to be present during access visits, and these should be restricted to four hours per month so as not to "overwhelm" the children.

The report had its own logic. But behind the logic was a set of twisted and perverse assumptions: that a child does not need two parents; that it is better for a child's development to live in Germany and be exposed to German culture; that German blood is superior to others; and that nationalities are transmitted by blood, not by birthplace or residence. Alongside these assumptions was the belief that a biological parent has no entitlement to her children. All this is the legacy of the German legal system of the late 1930s. Much of the family law of that period has still not been revised and remains to this day a part of the German legal system.

This explains the psychologist's apparent astonishment that I should claim a right to be with my children, as she put it, "simply because she is their biological mother." She was either unable or unwilling to acknowledge what most normal people would consider a basic law of nature: the close, instinctive bond between a mother and her children. Nor would she accept that the presence of a mother was essential to the healthy, well-balanced development of her offspring. But when the psychologist interviewed me, I had no idea that fundamental common sense and humanity would be brushed aside. I was dumbfounded when she took a position that ran counter to human experience from the beginning of time. One has to ask where this dangerous and perverse nonsense comes from.

As in her August report, the Bremen psychologist built her thesis on what the children had said about me. Since I had been absent from Alexander's and Constantin's lives for three years, it would have been logical to dig more deeply into why they had a negative view of me: could the boys' apparent hostility toward me be the direct consequence of our enforced separation? Might there be some connection to Hans-Peter's and his mother's openly negative attitude toward me, which the psychologist had noted in her first report? But her professional curiosity stopped short of asking these obvious questions. Instead, she simply concluded that since the boys viewed me negatively, it would be wrong for them to see me. Her recommendation was that Hans-Peter have custody and that my access rights be limited to a few hours each month, under supervision by a third party.

I showed the reports to Christopher. For him, this was the final realization that I had not exaggerated my plight.

Christopher was not the sort of man who would shy away from difficult problems. It was no accident that he had climbed through the echelons of the Foreign Office to become a top ambassador at a relatively young age. He had been posted to several countries, including Soviet Russia, and had long experience of the most intractable problems and how to solve them. My case was becoming a challenge to him. But it was more than that. Christopher was becoming emotionally involved, and he could not bear the unfairness of it all. He often reflected on how he would have felt if his own children had been wrenched away from him.

While we sat in the sunshine at Claudine and Dennis's house in the South of France in the summer of 1997, Christopher applied himself to reading the two reports. He had spent an entire career identifying the strong and weak points in an argument and had an amazing ability to strip a report down to its essentials. Much of our first holiday together was spent working on my case.

I was no longer alone. The closer we became, the deeper his commitment to my struggle for my sons became. Alexander and Constantin were a part of the woman he loved. Now they were becoming a part of him as well.

Meanwhile, the fates conspired to accelerate our lives together in a completely unexpected way. A few weeks before our summer holidays, Christopher received a phone call from London. It was another strange twist of fate. The head of the Foreign Office was retiring. Sir John Kerr, then British ambassador to the United States, was called back to take over his post. Our new prime minister and foreign secretary decided that they wanted Christopher as their ambassador to Washington, even though he had spent only a few months in Germany.

"Catherine, what would you say about a move to Washington?" Christopher asked over the phone one morning. "Would you come with me?"

I was thrilled for Christopher. As always in my life, destiny was taking over. Move to Washington? I thought about it all night. The idea appealed to me more and more. This would be the beginning of a new chapter in my life, and with Christopher at my side, there was so much to look forward to. I would be further away from the children. But staying on in Germany would have created its own stresses and complications. Christopher, for example, would have had to recuse himself from my case to avoid a conflict of interest. But behind all these calculations lay one decisive, paramount idea. Christopher and I wanted to share our lives, and it would not have mattered to me if he were sent to the moon.

For the moment, the notion that I would have to take on the role of ambassador's wife hardly entered my mind. There were too many other hurdles to overcome. I had stopped believing in my good fortune long ago. In fact, deep down I wondered whether Christopher's new assignment would actually come to pass. My deeply ingrained Russian superstitiousness stopped me from thinking too much about the future.

Christopher was to leave Bonn on October 14 and take up his post in Washington on October 30. He was adamant: "We must arrive together. I do not want to turn up alone and settle in without you. We've done enough commuting, and Washington is just too far away from London."

"I agree, but I don't think we'll ever make it." The prospect was daunting. The divorce hearing in Verden was scheduled for September 30.

On September 28, I flew to Bonn to meet Christopher. We were both very apprehensive. Would the Verden court grant me the divorce in time? Would I finally obtain decent access rights? Would there be more surprises in store for me? I could not imagine that things would run smoothly in Verden. Thank goodness, Christopher was by my side.

The next day we flew to Hamburg and went on to Verden. We had booked ourselves into a little inn a few miles away. Herr Struif met us for dinner. He was delighted at the new turn in my life.

"I advise you not to fight for custody. It would be futile and would delay the divorce. You would not stand a chance. The judge will say that the children have adapted to their new lives in Verden, and she will rely on the psychologist's recommendation that final custody should be given to the father. Tactically, it will put you in a better position to secure regular access to the children if we give Volkmann his divorce and custody."

"But even then I doubt the court will grant me proper access," I interjected.

"Well, there is one piece of good news," Struif went on. "Yesterday I received a fax from the IAF [an independent organization that mediates between German and foreign spouses]. They have offered their help to set up an access meeting."

"In Hamburg?" I asked.

"Yes, and the International Social Services have sent a fax to the Verden judge to inform her of the IAF offer."

This was not much to go on, but it was an opening. The letters that both my mother and I had recently written to the secretary general of the ISS in Geneva had borne some fruit. I could only hope that the Verden judge would agree.

On September 30, we woke up at dawn and drove along the misty country lanes to Verden. My stomach was in a knot. I could not speak. Christopher and I were silent. The landscape was gray and ominous. I hated being there. The potato farms, the woodlands, and the small villages were associated with too many frightful memories. I could not remember a time when I had not been apprehensive on approaching Verden or outraged and in tears when leaving it. Each visit had put more distance between my children and me. I felt limp. My hands were cold and sweating.

We arrived at Struif's office at 7:30 A.M. Michael Sullivan, our consul general, Dr. Meincke, the consulate's legal adviser, and Monsieur Perdu, the French consul, arrived a few minutes later with Alan, Michael Sullivan's driver. He had just recovered from a bad illness but had been determined to be there. He greeted me with a warm hug. He had heard about Christopher and me and was delighted. His expression of warmth gave me courage.

Christopher stayed in Struif's office while the rest of us walked to the courthouse.

As always, the other side arrived at the last minute. As always, Hans-Peter walked straight past us without turning his head. On the grounds that this was not a public hearing, the judge refused to admit Mr. Sullivan and Monsieur Perdu to the courtroom. But to our surprise, Dr. Meincke was allowed in. I felt this was a positive sign.

Hans-Peter did not look at me once during the hearing. It was strange to sit opposite him and observe the effort he made to look disdainful and above it all. Suddenly, I felt calm. The knot in my stomach was gone. The thought of Christopher nearby gave me strength. Herr Struif presented our case. Klaus, Hans-Peter's brother-in-law, argued his. The first part dealt with the divorce. Both sides agreed. The judge declared us divorced. I sighed in relief.

The two lawyers went on to discuss custody and access rights. The Volkmann side probably sighed with relief when Herr Struif did not contest their bid for custody. The judge seemed friendlier than usual. Maybe she also was relieved about this. Herr Struif then presented our case for an access arrangement outside Verden. The other side immediately argued furiously against it. Frau Kranitz, who was sitting in her habitual place opposite the judge, presented her familiar arguments. The children were scared that I would abduct them, they were scared of me, they did not want to see me, I had gone to the press and had written a book full of lies. If these allegations had not concerned my sons, I would have laughed. It was like a black comedy in which the humor lay in the endless repetition of the same words and actions. The whole performance was maddening and depressing. Struif went on:

"I have an offer from the IAF. It is a professional body that employs trained psychologists. It is recognized by the ISS and the Jugendamt. There could be no question of my client abducting the children under their auspices, and this would be an excellent way to facilitate a first meeting."

The judge hesitated, then agreed that it would be a good idea. I could sense panic in the opposite camp. Hans-Peter started whispering in Klaus's ear.

"My client would like a few minutes to discuss this matter."

The judge agreed, and the two of them hurriedly left the courtroom. Several minutes later, they were back. Hans-Peter looked tense.

"Okay, okay," said Klaus, "but not before January 1998."

"Yes, it wouldn't work before January 1998," continued Frau Kranitz. "I talked to the IAF yesterday, and they cannot do it before then." I later found out that this was untrue.

The judge appeared, for the first time, to take a more reasonable attitude:

"Well, that is settled. The first visit between the mother and her children will take place at the premises of the IAF in Hamburg, as soon as possible. It will be up to the IAF to specify a time. And Dr. Volkmann, this amounts to a court order. You will have to take the children to Hamburg when a date is established, probably in January. I do not want to see you back in my court in a few months claiming that it is the will of the children not to go to this meeting."

The hearing was over. Hans-Peter and his party left quickly, and we walked back to Struif's office. Everyone seemed extremely pleased with the outcome. It was a cause for celebration. The divorce had been granted, and for the first time in three years I would be allowed to see my sons outside Verden. I rejoiced with them, but deep down I wasn't sure. Klaus had agreed too quickly. I felt he had something up his sleeve. But I did not want to sound too pessimistic in front of the others, who had genuinely hoped and prayed that this time there would be a breakthrough.

.   .   .

A week before Christopher was due to leave Bonn, I received the written judgment from the Verden court.

I immediately realized that something was terribly wrong. There were two different decisions. One dealt with the divorce and the custody, and for some reason a separate one dealt with access rights. I talked to Herr Struif, but he did not seem bothered about it. Even Christopher, who was much preoccupied with the move to Washington and his own divorce, was not too worried.

I decided that I was probably being oversuspicious. After all, the Verden judge had accepted the offer of the IAF. Then, against all odds, I had received the final divorce papers in time: I was free. This was a day to celebrate, not to be pessimistic. Christopher and I had overcome a huge hurdle, and we could look forward to our lives together. That evening we went out to dinner, and I soon forgot about my worries.

The next day I returned to London, where the movers were packing my belongings. I was busy separating the items that needed to be stored from the ones being shipped to Washington. Christopher called:

"So, do you believe it now?"

"I suppose so. The reality is that the flat is nearly empty—but I still can't imagine everything will happen as we hope."

"Well, every day you'll believe it more. The movers have started to pack my things as well. We are going to Washington together, you'll see."

On October 14, Christopher officially left Germany. I felt relieved. As much as Bonn represented a happy time, I never felt that I could fully make peace with Germany—not until Germany gave me back what it had stolen from me: Alexander and Constantin.

.   .   .

Christopher had only two weeks in London before taking up his post in Washington. This was madness. There were so many things he had to do: have an audience with the queen, see a whole range of people at the Foreign Office, talk to the prime minister, the foreign secretary, see his parents and his children, organize his personal papers, and settle his own divorce.

We were supposed to arrive in Washington on Friday, October 31. We booked our wedding at the Kensington and Chelsea Registry Office for the previous day, in the hope that Christopher would be free by then. He was—just! His divorce came through on Monday. I called Claudine. She was nearly crying for joy. Christopher and I phoned all our friends to tell them the happy news and to invite them for a celebration party on Thursday evening. My friends were delirious. Finally, a happy event in my life! If I had not been aware before, nothing could have shown me more clearly how wonderful my friends were. Whatever their previous engagements, none of them would miss this celebration!

On Thursday, October 30, Claudine and Dennis, who had become Christopher's friends as well, came to pick us up, and we drove to the Registry Office in King's Road. Our close friends were already there, impatiently waiting for us. Everyone was excited. It sounded like a school reunion. There were hugs, kisses, laughter. An official came down to tell us we were making too much noise in the corridor.

Finally, we were led into an official room. There were more giggles and commotion as we took our seats. Christopher and I sat in the front facing the desk, his friends and mine mingled together in the rows behind us. The registrar read out the marriage vows. Lila, Nicolette, Claudine, and I were nearly crying when we heard the words:

"Christopher Meyer, will you take Catherine Laylle as your lawful wedded wife?"

It was a fabulous, sunny day, and we were all delirious, Christopher and I most of all.

That evening sixty of our friends crammed into my flat in Egerton Gardens. Everyone I had managed to reach turned up. It was magic. Our friends mingled, laughed, and rejoiced. It was the loudest party I had ever been to. At midnight Christopher and I collapsed into bed, exhausted but ecstatic. We had made it!

.   .   .

The next morning, an official car took us to Heathrow Airport. We sat in the backseat, sleepy-eyed, holding hands and feeling warm. We were on our way to a new life. Not that new for Christopher, but a complete turnaround for me. It was not until we were in the plane that Christopher and I first talked about what Washington would be like.

"Our life will be incredibly busy. We will have to make a huge effort to find time for ourselves. I have already told the embassy to ensure we always have each week one evening and one lunch alone together. If you don't set rules immediately, we will end up having no time to ourselves."

Overnight I had become the wife of the British ambassador to the United States. I had not really thought about it. Somehow it had hardly even entered our conversations. We had too much else on our minds. I was not scared or apprehensive. I had Christopher at my side, and after my experiences, I felt I could cope with anything. Once you lose your children, nothing seems daunting in comparison.

.   .   .

Landing in Washington was the first taste of my new life. We were led off the plane before anyone else, and an official from the White House escorted us into a private room at the airport. A small welcoming party from the embassy greeted us. We were immediately separated. Christopher was placed in one car, I in another. I was a little overwhelmed. But this would be the last time. Christopher gave firm instructions that his wife was not to be on a separate schedule from his. We arrived at the splendid Lutyens Residence on Massachusetts Avenue. We were met by the staff and led to our room. As soon as we were alone, Christopher took me in his arms:

"Now do you believe it?"

"I do."

On that very evening, we went to our first reception, hosted by Christopher's deputy and his wife. It was a strange feeling, but I was so exhausted and jet-lagged that I remember little of it. Then, after a weekend break to settle in, we began our busy lives. Christopher was terrific. On his first day, he took me to his weekly staff meeting, attended by representatives of all the embassy's departments. It was probably the first time an ambassador had brought his wife to the Monday morning meeting. But if anyone was surprised, no one showed it. Through this action, Christopher made a statement—for his colleagues and for me. We were a partnership, professionally and personally.

But I still had one worry: that I would no longer be allowed to express my own views. Christopher calmed my fears: "Just be yourself. And if your views are different from mine, so much the better."

His wonderful support, his confidence in my abilities, and his respect for my opinions allowed me gradually to assert myself and feel part of it all. There was an unusual quality about our relationship. The more we grew to know each other, the more we respected and relied on one another. Of course, we had to make a few adjustments at first. After all, we had not known each other for that long, and as in any relationship, we needed to define our own space while adapting to each other. But in hindsight, it was amazing how quickly we melded into each other, especially given the many outside pressures and commitments crowding in on us.

CHAPTER 20

The Double Cross

In November, Frau Barrera from the IAF contacted me. She felt that, as a professional mediator, she should make her own assessment of the children and their parents. She wanted first to interview Hans-Peter and the children, then Christopher and me. I felt uneasy about this. I was convinced that it would delay matters even more.

Sure enough, Hans-Peter began to stall, saying that he was too busy to come to Hamburg. Frau Barrera was doing her best, but she could not move without Hans-Peter's cooperation. This was the basis of her mediation, and Hans-Peter knew it. The months passed, and I got more and more depressed about my situation.

Christmas came. Frau Barrera had still not managed to see Hans-Peter. On Christmas Eve, I tried to reach my children. I telephoned their grandparents' house. This was the only number I had since Hans-Peter had refused to give me his. But I knew that each year the Volkmann family gathered at the grandparents'. Gundel answered:

"No, the children are not here."

"When will they be back?"

"At six o'clock."

At six o'clock, I called. My heart was pounding as I dialed the long-distance number. I hadn't talked to my children for so long. The line was busy. I tried again, and again, and again. The line was permanently busy. I must have tried twenty times. They had obviously taken the phone off the hook. Two hours later I phoned again. No answer. I was in a desperate state.

The next morning, I called once more. Gundel answered:

"The children are gone." She was about to hang up.

"Where have they gone to?"

"They went skiing with their father."

"I would like to wish Alexander and Constantin a Merry Christmas. Can I please have their telephone number?"

"I don't have it."

"Come on, Gundel, of course you have the number. You just don't want to give it to me."

She hung up.

Christopher heard the conversation. He was stunned at the length to which Hans-Peter's clan would go to block my having contact with the children. His sense of outrage mounted. Having gone to great lengths to shield his own children from the worst consequences of his divorce, he was all too aware of the damage being done to mine.

The months were passing. Then, Frau Barrera informed me that she had finally managed to see Hans-Peter and the children. A date for my first visit was set for February 22. A few days later, I received a letter from Hans-Peter. It had been redirected from my London address. Obviously, Hans-Peter had no idea that I was living in Washington and that I was married to the British ambassador.

This was his first letter in years. Hans-Peter declared that for the "sake of the children," he wanted us to have a more normal relationship. But first of all, could I please send the children the rest of their toys.

This was odd. I had brought all the toys to Verden long ago. I had always wondered whether my sons had ever got them. Was this unexpected communication some ploy to show Frau Barrera that I was a vindictive mother who had refused to give my children their toys?

Christopher and I composed a brief but courteous letter saying that there was nothing I wished more than to reach an agreement over the circumstances in which the boys and I could see each other. Our past difficulties should be put behind us so that the children could enjoy a normal relationship with both parents. I invited him to discuss this with me over the telephone.

Instead, Hans-Peter faxed me. He wrote that he agreed a meeting should take place on neutral ground: a priest's house in Bremen! And while the priest would be present during the visit, I should come alone. He then went on to say that the IAF was unprofessional and insensitive. "After a talk with the IAF, which essentially took place without me, the children said they did not want any further visits. They are fed up. They feel very insecure and under pressure and their reaction to this pressure is total refusal." Hans-Peter's letter was full of underlinings and repetitions, and it stressed that it was Alexander and Constantin's "will"—not his own—to refuse to come to the IAF in Hamburg.

I could only conclude that Hans-Peter was trying to wriggle out of the agreement and that "the will of the children" was once again his pretext.

I wrote back insisting that we stick to the terms of the agreement we had reached in the Verden court and faxed this correspondence to Frau Barrera. She advised me to come to Hamburg nonetheless. Herr Struif suggested we should immediately apply for a writ to enforce the access agreement.

Christopher and I flew to Europe. The next day, we learned that the Verden judge had refused to issue the writ. She claimed that she needed the originals of the divorce papers (which she had herself issued). My copies were in Washington. Struif made an application for duplicates. The judge rejected it. Herr Struif immediately filed a second court application to force Hans-Peter to bring the children to Hamburg. There was no reaction from the court. For the next twenty-four hours, things got complicated as they begun to unravel. There were constant phone calls, exchanges of faxes, last minute changes of plan, offers and counter offers. At one point, it seemed that Hans-Peter might bring the children after all. This set off a new flurry of confusing phone calls between the two sets of lawyers, the British consulate, and us. It was a false alarm. Hans-Peter would not bring the children to Hamburg.

On February 20, Christopher and I went to see Frau Barrera for our scheduled interview. She suggested that my lawyer send a final fax to Klaus, Hans-Peter's lawyer. We asked for a reply by 6:00 P.M. We waited in her office, and we started talking about the children. Frau Barrera could not tell us much because Hans-Peter had refused to sign a form allowing her to disclose the content of their meeting. Still we learned that Klaus, contrary to usual IAF practice, had been present at the meeting. We also learned that her separate meeting with the children had gone well. She felt that they wanted to see me, but that they were under enormous stress. They were extremely worried about saying or doing something that their father would disapprove of.

By six o'clock, no fax had arrived. We left. Christopher had to go back to Washington. Very reluctantly, he took the last plane to London, and I went to stay with my friend Brigitte Pahl.

The next morning, I was awakened by a phone call. It was Michael Sullivan. He had just found a fax from Hans-Peter with a covering letter from Struif's colleague. The time registered was 11:08 P.M. To show his "goodwill," Hans-Peter would bring the children, accompanied by his sister-in-law, Dr. Volkmann (a lawyer practicing in Bremen), to Struif's office at 10:00 A.M.

By this time, it was not physically possible for me to be in Verden by 10:00 A.M. since the drive there would take an hour and a half. I was in a state of panic and I called Herr Struif. He tried to reach Hans-Peter. He could not find him anywhere, but would wait for him in his office. At 10:00, Herr Struif called me back. Hans-Peter had not showed up, nor had the children. He suggested that I go back to Washington. There was nothing more he could do.

"On Monday I will make a court application for new access arrangements."

I had flown in from the United States to see my sons. I was not about to give up. Michael Sullivan, Brigitte, and I decided that I should try to call the grandparents' house. No one was home. I kept dialing the number. Finally, Hans-Peter's sister, now employed at the Ministry of Justice in Hanover, answered.

"Hans-Peter is out shopping. The boys are out as well."

"Well, could you please ask him to call me at this number."

"Yes, of course," she said in a surprisingly courteous tone.

Equally surprisingly, Hans-Peter rang me back. It was now well after 1:00 P.M. His tone was aggressive.

"I told you that you could come to see the children at ten o'clock."

"But how could I be there? The fax only reached us in the middle of the night."

"It's your problem if you weren't there."

"But I've come from the United States in order . . . "

"Well, the children did not want to go to the IAF. They were unprofessional, and I simply won't force the children to do something they do not want."

"Why don't you bring the children to Hamburg? If you are scared, you could stay . . . "

He interrupted me all the time. I could not finish a sentence. It was maddening. Brigitte stood beside me, listening to the conversation and trying to encourage me to go on. Finally, he ended the conversation by saying that if I wanted to see the boys, then I should come to his house at 3:30.

"But even you agreed in your letter to me that I should see the boys on neutral ground."

"Take it or leave it. You can phone me back."

"Can I have your telephone number?"

"No. Call this number. Antje will pass on the message." He hung up.

If I wanted to see my boys, I had no choice, but I knew that I could not go on my own. Michael Sullivan and Brigitte kindly agreed to accompany me to Verden. Alan would drive the three of us.

We set off as soon as we could for Verden. We reached the private property just after four.

Hans-Peter, his twenty-five-year-old girlfriend, and the two boys stood in the hallway of the house as we arrived. The boys looked stiff, controlled, and despondent.

Brigitte went out and sat in the car. Hans-Peter and Mr. Sullivan left the house as well. For the first time, Hans-Peter did not seek refuge in the judge's house next door. Mr. Sullivan felt that Hans-Peter wanted to talk to him. The two of them went off for a walk.

I followed my two boys into the sitting room. Hans-Peter's girlfriend did not leave the house. She simply walked into the kitchen to be in earshot. The boys stood inert, leaning against the wall. I tried to talk to them in English, but Constantin told me I must speak German. At my suggestion, Alexander agreed to sit on the sofa. Constantin remained standing. Alexander stared straight in front of him. I tried to explain to my sons that I loved them and wanted to see them, but that I had not been allowed to do so. Constantin remained impassive, an ironic expression on his face.

"You lie. Papa told us that you could come to see us whenever you wanted, but you never did," said Alexander.

"But I wanted to. I wasn't allowed."

"You wrote a book full of lies."

"Have you read my book?"

"No. But Papa told me it was full of lies."

Constantin was still standing, leaning against the wall.

"*Ja, ja.* And you came with two paid bodyguards and tried to abduct me."

"Of course I didn't want to abduct you. I wanted to see you. Would I stand in front of the school, in front of other parents, calling your name, if I had planned to abduct you? You must have seen movies. There are helicopters, getaway cars, hooded men. . . . " I was trying to make a joke out of it and show them how ludicrous it all was. But Constantin did not smile. The ironical expression on his face remained. Alexander went on:

"You've made the press write lies." Alexander's tone was aggressive. He repeated these sentences as if he were a robot. There was no expression on his face, and he kept looking at the wall straight opposite him. I could feel the anger in him. I ignored his words and repeated in a gentle voice that I loved him and Constantin. Alexander blushed. I stroked the back of his head. I felt that he found this comforting, but he still did not turn toward me.

I wanted to change the subject and try to create a more relaxed atmosphere. I stood up to get the presents I had brought for them. Immediately, both boys left the room like two little robots and went to the kitchen. I had spent thirteen minutes with my sons. I asked Brigitte to come into the house. We joined the boys in the kitchen. They stood motionless next to Hans-Peter's girlfriend, who had her back turned to us, pretending to be cooking. Brigitte started talking about her children, whom Alexander and Constantin had known well in the past. My sons said they didn't remember them. Brigitte's children remember mine.

In fact, Constantin said he didn't remember anything of his past life:

"Don't you remember Karim? You used to be inseparable."

"No." Constantin kept on glancing at the girlfriend before answering any question. She seemed to give him orders by eye contact. Brigitte went on:

"And Alexander, you must remember that day when you came to our house and the four of you took a bath together. You laughed so much. . . ." Alexander seemed to remember. His body language changed, and a semblance of a smile appeared on his face. At that point, the woman stared at Constantin, as if to indicate an order, and before Brigitte or I could react, she walked out of the room. Constantin marched behind her, and Alexander followed. The three of them disappeared outside, walking off toward the woods. I looked at them in the distance. My sons walking on each side of the girlfriend, as she was talking. They looked stiff, controlled—no normal children would walk like that. Maybe she was already "programming" them to forget all that I had said to them.

Hans-Peter and Mr. Sullivan were walking toward us. I tried to say something, but Hans-Peter's tone became immediately aggressive. It was not possible to have a sensible conversation. He would not discuss anything. I should write to his lawyer. But at least in front of Michael Sullivan, he was finally forced to give me his phone number.

. . .

This was the last time I saw my children.

I flew back to Washington more depressed than I had been in months. I could not watch the movies on the plane, I could not talk, I could not sleep, I only thought of my boys. Christopher came home immediately, and I cried and cried while he held me tightly in his arms. He felt so frustrated. Somehow we had hoped that now that I was married, Hans-Peter would become more reasonable. After all, now that I had a husband who had brought up three children, including a stepson, Hans-Peter would be reassured to know that our sons would always be in sensitive and caring hands when they visited me. I could offer a comfortable, stable, and loving family environment in one of the great capital cities of the world. But all this probably had the reverse effect on him, as many of my more perceptive friends pointed out. Indeed, soon after returning to Washington, I received a letter from Hans-Peter's brother, Hans-Jorg, full of threats and bile.

Then I received a letter from Struif's office. With it was the court's decision on our second application to enforce my access rights. The judge rejected the application on the grounds that the access rights she had granted me were not enforceable. The letter confirmed that the September 30 judgment as it related to access was different in kind from the divorce and custody provisions: the latter were enforceable, but the access arrangements were not.

.   .   .

It is extraordinary, at least by British, French, and U.S. standards, that a court can rule on divorce and custody while neglecting to protect a mother's rights of access to her children. And given the contradiction between what the judge had said in September and what actually happened, it is hard to avoid the conclusion that there was more to this than incompetence.

CHAPTER 21

A Broader Canvas

I was now in a worse situation than ever. I had—reluctantly—not challenged Hans-Peter's custody application, and I had accepted that the children's main home would be in Germany. All I had asked was, first, to see them alone in Hamburg, and then to have them spend part of their school holidays with me in America. But Hans-Peter got what he wanted, and in return, I had nothing.

The Verden judge then administered the final blow, ruling that all legal proceedings were now at an end. If I wanted access, this could be established only by starting all over again with a new court application. You did not need to be a conspiracy theorist to wonder whether the judgment had been framed precisely to ensure that the planned access visit in Hamburg could not be enforced.

So yet again, I was back to square one. Hans-Peter's strategy of endless delay had won him another victory.

Michael Sullivan advised me to find a new lawyer. That made me angry. After five German lawyers, two British lawyers, and the expenditure of every penny I had, I could not bear the thought of starting all over again. After the repeated setbacks of the last four years, I was convinced that I could not win justice. Meanwhile, the recent sight of my children, so traumatized and robotic, had revived my deepest fears. The memory haunted me. A flood of suppressed fears and anxieties swept through me. At night I could not fall asleep. When I finally did, I had horrific dreams. Some of them were so realistic that I could not shake them off on waking. It took me weeks to bring under some control the shock of that terrible February encounter with the children. Christopher tried to comfort me, but he too felt disappointed and angry. The hopes that we all had invested in the decision of the Verden court on September 30, 1997, had once more proved illusory.

My new Washington friends tried to support me as much as they could. Among them, Sheelagh Taylor became my biggest advocate and my most active helper. She could not accept that a situation like this could remain unchallenged. She spent hours on the World Wide Web and unearthed numerous psychological studies on "parental alienation syndrome." The syndrome was already widely recognized in U.S. courts, but as in so many things, Europe was only just beginning to catch up with the United States.

Sheelagh and I plowed through the research, and we came to realize that Alexander and Constantin's reaction and behavior fit exactly the description of what the experts labeled "severe alienation syndrome." What was particularly surprising was that the Bremen psychologist had unwittingly confirmed the strong presence of parental alienation syndrome in my children in her two reports. For example, she recorded that Alexander had painted an exclusively positive picture of his present situation and an entirely negative one of his previous life in London, that he had an idealized picture of his father, that he needed his father's constant attention and felt that he solely related to his father. She explained that Alexander felt betrayed by his mother, that he found it difficult to express positive feelings for her, and that his relationship with his mother was characterized by insecurity and a defensive attitude.

As time went by, it had become ever easier for Hans-Peter and his family to coach the children into believing that I had abandoned them. And having asserted that Alexander now had a bad relationship with me, the psychologist concluded that it would be harmful for him to see me under normal circumstances. No child expert worthy of the name would prescribe continuing separation from a parent as the remedy for PAS. But that was precisely the conclusion that the Verden court–appointed psychologist drew.

I was trapped in an impossible situation. The German legal system required that children—even at a very young age—be heard by the courts, but on the other hand, the courts did not recognize that there was such a thing as PAS.

Additionally, if I gave up my increasingly costly and debilitating fight for access, I would be accused of abandoning my children. If I continued the fight, I would again be accused of being a bad mother for not accepting that my children did not want to see me. I was in a terrible Catch-22 situation, and I did not know how I could ever get out of it.

.   .   .

It was also becoming more and more difficult to avoid other people's questions. Christopher and I met thousands of people in Washington and on our travels. Quite naturally, they would regularly ask me whether I had children and whether they were with us in Washington. These were extremely taxing moments for me. A voice inside me would almost cry out, "stop, please don't ask me more," but I had to remain calm and find a way to discreetly change the subject. Normally this worked well enough, but I soon realized that it was only a matter of time before journalists put two and two together and worked out that Catherine Meyer used to be Catherine Laylle. When this finally happened, the requests for interviews came pouring in. Since meeting Christopher in April 1997, I had avoided the media. At first this was not too difficult. But now I was in a different position. After marrying Christopher and coming to Washington as the wife of the British ambassador, I had obviously become a more public figure. Events involving the ambassador and his wife routinely attract publicity in the United States.

My first instinct was to publicize the continuing injustice. But it was not that simple. In the past, I had always been seen by the press as a victim. Occasionally, an attempt was made to portray me and Hans-Peter as partners of equal moral culpability in a classic "tug-of-love" case. But I had always found that the simple facts of my case were sufficient to demolish this unfair portrayal. Now it was not so easy to depict me as a victim. By marrying Christopher and becoming wife to Britain's senior ambassador, I was catapulted into the public gaze through what was seen as a highly privileged lifestyle. I was still the same person who had lost the most precious thing in her life. But I worried that people would view me differently. I also knew that Verden would use further media attention against me.

Yet I was so incensed by the injustice toward my sons, and other children in the same situation, that I wanted this scandal exposed. And if God had given me the extraordinary privilege of being an ambassador's wife, I owed it to victim parents and to myself to do something useful with it. I felt very strongly about this. I decided that whatever criticism I attracted, it would be a small price to pay if I could expose the abuse of human rights that is child abduction.

In the end, the decision was made for us when it became clear that articles would be written about us, with or without our cooperation. So we cooperated, in the hope of getting accurate stories. By and large, we succeeded.

More important, I was able to use my case as a window on the growing international problem of child abduction, an arena in which, regrettably, Germany loomed large. A new chapter in my life was beginning.

As a result of one of my interviews, I was contacted by the National Center for Missing and Exploited Children, the biggest nonprofit organization of its kind. They had read about my predicament in the *Washington Post*. Ernie Allen, the center's chairman and CEO, came to see me. We talked at length about the problem of cross-border child abduction. We decided that we should tackle it together.

"Why don't we try to organize a small meeting of experts and discuss ways in which we could improve the workings of the Hague Convention?" I suggested.

"That would be an excellent idea. We know most of the experts in the United States, some in Europe, and I am sure you have been in contact with others. We could invite them over and have a two-day workshop at the NCMEC center in Arlington."

"Yes, and maybe we could publish a white paper on our findings afterward. . . . " I was getting very excited about the idea and began to dream ahead. Ernie and I discussed the shape of our meeting and what we wanted to achieve. Needless to say, it took months to organize. Sheelagh and two new friends from the embassy became involved as well. The four of us began making lists, drafting letters, phoning, faxing, and searching the World Wide Web for more information. The NCMEC was delighted with its enthusiastic new helpers.

Most people are still unaware that there is a serious child abduction problem in Western democratic societies. Despite the existence of the Hague Convention, most cases remain unresolved, and every year more and more children are separated from one of their parents. But there had been no international action to tackle the problem and remedy defects in the Hague Convention. Our meeting would be a first.

·   ·   ·

In Washington the situation of my children was becoming common knowledge. One day I had lunch with some new

American friends. One of the women's husbands was the distinguished attorney and former White House counsel, Lloyd Cutler. She went home and immediately told him my story. The next morning he was on the telephone to me: "Polly told me about your case. This is quite appalling. We must do something to help you. Send me all your papers, and I'll look over them."

A few days later Lloyd came to see Christopher and me with a plan of action. He had talked to a distinguished German lawyer with whom he had had many dealings. We would immediately start new legal proceedings for enforceable access rights. Lloyd realized how difficult the case was, but he saw it as a challenge. "We need to have a solid strategy, and maybe we'll achieve a breakthrough."

Christopher was hopeful; I was despondent. It seemed to me that even the best lawyers in the world would not be able to advance my case. But I had to give my new legal team a chance. I also wanted to show to my sons, one day, that I had tried absolutely everything.

My new German lawyer immediately filed two court applications—one for an emergency access visit at the end of May and one for long-term enforceable access rights, beginning in Germany and then for half the school holidays in Washington. Now we had to wait—as ever—for the court to answer.

.   .   .

On Sunday, March 29, the phone woke us up. Catherine Urban was on the line:

"There's been another abduction. But this time on French territory."

"What do you mean?"

"Remember Cosette Lancellin? I've told you about her. Well, yesterday evening, she was returning home from her brother's house. She was driving on a country lane. It was dark. Her two children were sitting in the back of the car. Suddenly, three cars appeared and blocked the road. She had to stop. Five men jumped out and opened the front doors of her car. It all happened very quickly. The children started screaming hysterically. One of the men started pulling Cosette out of the driving seat and a second man who had got into the passenger seat started pushing her from the other side. She fell in the ditch, and the men drove off with the children."

"What?" I could hardly believe what I was hearing. Catherine went on.

"Her husband had told her that he would be calling the children at her brother's house. So he knew exactly how long she'd be staying there and when she would be leaving. He then called the hired guys to tell them to be ready for the ambush."

"You mean, he wasn't even there?"

"No, he stayed in Germany. He gave instructions and waited for the children to be delivered back to him."

"What about the police?"

"The French police were alerted. But Cosette had to walk a few miles to get to a telephone. The police reacted quickly, but it was too late. They found the getaway cars abandoned at the Franco-German border. The men must have had another car waiting for them there. But can you believe it? They actually went into French territory to abduct the children and drove straight home."

Christopher and I were dumbfounded. During the next few days Cosette's case was everywhere in France: newspapers, magazines, television. . . . It even hit the front pages and was reported on the evening news. France was shocked. I saw Cosette being interviewed on television. She looked lost. She was clutching a picture of her children. Her big brown eyes were staring at the camera. She was unable to comprehend what was happening to her. She could hardly talk. The reporters took over. I felt terrible. I knew she would have a titanic struggle to see her children again.

Child abduction to Germany was becoming a huge topic in France. It had gone too far now, and politicians, journalists, and the organization called SOS Abductions to Germany rallied together. There were more news reports, more talk shows interviewing other parents whose children were held in Germany. The minister of justice, Elisabeth Guigou, and the secretary of state, Monsieur Vedrine, promised that the issue would be at the top of their agenda. Hired men could not simply walk into French territory and snatch children away.

But nothing happened. As I write today, Cosette has still not seen her two children—Mathias, age seven, and Caroline, age three and a half. The father's actions have not been condemned by the German courts, the hired men have not been prosecuted, and the French police can do nothing. Cosette's children, like mine, remain motherless, and as the months pass, her chances of getting them back are becoming more and more remote. The courts will say that the children have adapted to their new environment and that it would be against "the interests of the children" to make them go back to France. You do not have to be a psychologist to be aware of the devastating trauma for a child of three and a half to be violently snatched from her mother by total strangers. But so far the German courts have been oblivious to this issue, and to the long-term damage that separation from a mother causes.

What was even more extraordinary was that Cosette's husband lived in a small town just a few miles from Hans-Peter Volkmann. He too was involved in local politics. He was the director of his town's administration. His lawyer was Dr. Kram, the very same lawyer from Munich who had at one time handled my case. Cosette's lawyer was Herr Struif's colleague and the responsible youth authority was the Verden Jugendamt. There was something deeply disturbing about these connections.

Anyone besides me would have thought that this time the German authorities would react. But I knew that their answer would be that the courts are independent and that they could not intervene in judicial matters. I had heard this argument over and over again. Several weeks later, I learned about another case in Lower Saxony. This one concerned an American woman. Her German husband lived in the next town, even closer to Volkmann. She too had been separated from her children in a similar way.

.   .   .

Depressing news kept on pouring in. On May 15, the Verden court rejected our application for an access visit in May on the grounds that there was "no urgency in the matter" and that since the children had not seen their mother in four years, immediate access would be too overwhelming for them.

Interestingly enough, back in December 1994, my application for access was rejected on the same grounds of "lack of urgency." Obviously, whatever the time or the circumstances, it was never urgent for children to see their non-German parent. For the second application, the judge ruled that she would not decide on future access without first holding a hearing. And before then, she needed to see the children and get another report from the Jugendamt. I was back to square one, and I could expect long delays.

.   .   .

My expectations were correct. Frau Kranitz took two months to file her report. Her position was predictably unhelpful. Her report recommended that I should see my children once every *two* months for five hours at a priest's house in Bremen. This proposal was as inhumane as it was impractical. But to top it all off, it was almost identical to the proposal Hans-Peter had made earlier that year.

Now that the Jugendamt report was in, the Verden judge informed us that there would be an oral hearing. But with the court's lack of any sense of urgency, it took us almost five months to agree on a date.

First, the Verden judge said that she would be on holiday and would not be able to hold the hearing before early September. We subsequently offered the first two weeks in September, when we would ourselves be on holiday in Europe. The judge rejected this. She was too busy. The earliest date she could give us was September 17, knowing full well that we would just have returned to the United States. Frau Stadler-Euler tried to persuade the court that, living four thousand miles away and with inescapable obligations in Washington, Christopher and I could not leave at the drop of a hat.

Finally, after much to-ing and fro-ing, we agreed on November 25, when Washington would be shut down for the Thanksgiving holiday. We booked our flights to London and from London to Hamburg. Then, out of the blue, on October 6, Hans-Peter's lawyer announced that he would be on holiday at that time. Despite our protests, the judge agreed to the postponement, saying that we had ourselves not accepted the previous date she had offered us.

Needless to say, living four thousand miles from Verden, our position was not comparable to Klaus's, a local lawyer. The fact that we could not meet the judge's previous date had nothing to do with our personal wishes. It was the result of our official commitments as representatives of the British government. My ex-husband and his lawyer had no such obligations. Furthermore, we were perfectly willing to sacrifice our summer vacation to come to Verden, and now the Thanksgiving holiday. We ourselves would not have dared to use a holiday as an excuse for postponing a hearing. As it was, the judge used our scheduling difficulties to suggest that I was not serious about wanting to see my children!

·   ·   ·

A new date has now been set for December 10, 1998—fourteen months after the divorce hearing. In the meantime, all our out-of-court attempts to reach an amicable solution have been rejected by Hans-Peter and Klaus.

In February 1998, Michael Sullivan tried his hand at mediating a solution. He even managed to meet Hans-Peter, offering him all sorts of guarantees and his house for me to meet the children. Hans-Peter said he would think about it and write back. He never did. Christopher decided to help out as well:

"He cannot talk to you. There is too much anger and resentment there. Maybe if I write to him, on a man-to-man basis, he'll find it easier to communicate."

"I doubt it. But we certainly must try."

Christopher wrote to Hans-Peter. His letter was low-key and very conciliatory. It provoked a ten-page torrent of abuse against me. Christopher wrote a second letter. It remained unanswered. He wrote a third letter, this time inviting the children and Hans-Peter to come to Washington at his expense in an explicit gesture of reconciliation. Several weeks later, Hans-Peter answered. He declined the invitation, on the grounds that it would all be too much for the children. Instead, he proposed yet another visit in Verden.

.   .   .

My only consolation was that the NCMEC workshop, which started as a modest affair, had ballooned spontaneously into a large forum. My three embassy friends and I became increasingly busy, helping the NCMEC organize the event. Larger premises needed to be found, venues changed, programs printed. . . . The last three weeks required a rush of activity, and I was about to go off on holiday. Luckily, Sheelagh was there. She took over my responsibilities. She was terrific.

We were all exhausted, but the forum was a great success. Congressman Benjamin A. Gilman (R-NY) opened the event and brought with him a concurrent resolution of the House urging increased international cooperation in this area. We ended up having over sixty participants from eight different countries. The fact that so many people attended was in itself an indication that international child abduction was becoming a worldwide concern. The participants included the permanent secretary to the Hague Convention on Private International Law, professors of law from different countries, representatives of nonprofit organizations and the Justice and State Departments, a Belgium senator, members of the European Parliament, the French parliament, and the French Ministry of Justice. Many issues were discussed, and we all agreed that the Hague Convention was not working as it was originally intended. Germany was singled out as one of the worst offenders. Professor Nigel Lowe of Cardiff University will write a white paper with our recommendations. Our hope is to announce them at a second event in Washington in April 1999.

This first initiative led to my invitation, together with three U.S. parents, to testify before the Senate Foreign Relations Committee on October 1. Attorney General Janet Reno was invited to give her evidence first, then the parents spoke about their experiences.

If I could not advance my own case, I could at least pride myself on helping to raise the profile of the general issue. This gave me an enormous boost of self-confidence and a feeling of purpose. But the situation of my boys was an ever-present worry.

Luckily, our lives were extremely busy. This was a blessing in disguise. I became so involved in the demands of our job that I had little time left to concentrate on my problem. We had cabinet ministers staying at the residence, parliamentary committees, fund-raising evenings for charities, think tanks, delegations. . . . We also did a great deal of traveling across the United States. It was a stressful life, but the more I got used to it, the more I enjoyed it. Every day was different. There were interesting debates on different subjects, ranging from politics to trade development to medical research. I sat next to interesting people—and there was so much to learn and to discover. My days were interesting and fun. It was the nights I dreaded. The reality was that as much as I tried to compartmentalize my life, I could not switch off what was happening in my subconscious. I could not stop worrying about my children and felt extremely frustrated at my inability to do something to help them. I could not stop the nightmares.

Now I dream for the most part of Alexander. It is he who needs me most. I know it. I hear him so often at night, in my dreams. The bond between mother and child is so deep that I believe I can sense what is happening to him.

Constantin had blocked me out—for the moment. But Alexander, who had turned thirteen in May 1998, was beginning to question what had happened to him.

When I had finally seen him in February 1998, two years had gone by since our last meeting. He had grown so much that I had hardly recognized him. He was nearly my height. His voice was breaking. He was coming out of childhood and into puberty.

.   .   .

Lloyd Cutler put me in touch with a psychologist, Betty Anne Ottinger. She had read my book and had felt very concerned for my boys and me. She was kind and understanding. We discussed my children and their development.

"You must talk frankly to Alexander. He is old enough. He should know that you want to see him and that you cannot. Let him make his own judgment. If you don't tell him, no one else will. His father certainly won't." I listened to her advice.

Since Michael Sullivan had succeeded in obtaining Hans-Peter's phone number in February 1998, I had regularly called my children. Of course, I could reach them only once in a while. They were either out or asleep or having a bath. But I persevered. At first, when I did manage to talk to the boys, our conversations were extremely short. Alexander would listen a little, and then he would suddenly cut me off and say that he had to go. Constantin would not even listen. He'd get on the phone and tell me he was off to play or to sleep—literally "hello, got to go," and he would hang up on me. Gradually, though, they started to talk a little. But our conversations were stilted. On some occasions, I heard their father in the background whispering to them; then they would tell me they had to go. It was a chilling experience.

Constantin seemed genuinely uninterested in me. I could sense that he wanted to get off the phone. He did not want to deal with the hurt again. His mother had abandoned him, and he did not want to be faced with the emotions my voice would revive. For the moment, he had blocked me out. Alexander, though, was different. As the months went by, I could sense a change in his reaction. He did not want to get off the phone. He usually said little, but he listened carefully to what I would say. I could sense that he was absorbing everything, that he wanted to talk to me but could not.

Until one day:

"Hello, can I speak to Alexander, please?"

"He's sleeping."

"But it's only seven o'clock." There was a pause. I felt Hans-Peter had been interrupted. Maybe Alexander had just walked into the room.

"Well, there he is, he'll tell you himself."

"Hello."

"Alexander, it's Mummy. How are you?"

"I'm fine." His tone was stern, detached, and very sad, but he didn't repeat in a robot fashion what his father had wanted him to say to me. I went on:

"I just wanted to see how you are and tell you that I love you. . . . And what did you do today? I went to . . . "

"I think it's better if you call me back tomorrow." Alexander interrupted.

This conversation haunted me for days. Was Alexander starting to rebel? It was the first time he did not repeat to me what his father had ordered him to say. I was excited, but it also worried me greatly. Alexander was suffering.

The next day, of course, I could not reach him. And Alexander probably believed that I had not called back. It was awful. I finally reached him several days later. He was cold again and ended our conversation abruptly. But several weeks later, I had another "good" conversation with Alexander. I told him that I would be coming to Germany in December, that I wanted to see him, and that I had been trying for months on end but it was never allowed. He no longer called me a liar. Instead, he listened carefully, absorbing each of my words. I could sense that he wanted me to talk on and that he needed to hear the sound of my voice, his mother's voice. I felt that he had started questioning what had been said around him. I felt that he realized it did not make sense. Why would his mother be calling him and saying she loved him if indeed she had abandoned him? My poor, poor Alexander. How he must suffer today. He has come out of childhood. Soon he will raise questions and Hans-Peter's answers will not be enough.

I often wonder how my children will ever be able to come to terms with what has been done to them. Maybe they never will. And one thing is certain: they, and all the other children in similar circumstances, do not deserve such inhuman treatment.

.   .   .

Today Cosette Lancellin's children are among the latest victims of this treatment. On November 25, 1998, the Constitutional Court of Germany decided that her two children, Mathias and Caroline, would not be returned to France. The judges ruled that, since the children had been living in Germany for nine months (since their kidnapping), it would be against "their interest" to change their environment once again. The Constitutional Court, in taking six months to make a decision, had created a self-fulfilling prophecy.

President Jacques Chirac of France expressed his outrage at the press conference following the Franco-German summit in Potsdam on December 1, 1998: "I was shocked by the method used by one of the perpetrators, who, under totally unacceptable conditions, organized a real hold-up on French national territory to kidnap two children. We cannot accept such behavior because this would mean that the law of the jungle prevails over the rule of law."

Cherie Booth, wife of British Prime Minister Tony Blair, has also made a strong public statement expressing her commitment to the struggle against international child abduction. Her words were those of a renowned lawyer, but also of a loving mother. "Child abduction is a subject in which I have always been interested as a lawyer. To lose one's children must be torture for any parent. Even worse, imagine it from the child's point of view:

snatched from the security of a family environment, often at an age when the breakdown of family relationships is hard to understand."

After sixteen years, a new government has come to power in Germany. It has promised greater social justice and a righting of the wrongs of the past.

A new government, a new beginning, a new millennium—maybe a new hope yet for our children?

APPENDIX

This paper was the basis of my statement before the Senate Committee on Foreign Relations on October 1, 1998.

Introduction: The Problem

Most people associate child abduction with countries where laws and customs are very different from ours. But child abduction within Western societies is much more common than supposed, and there has been an explosion in the number of incidents since the mid-1970s.

There is an obvious link between this phenomenon and the decline in marriage as a stabilizing factor in our societies. The sharp rise in divorce rates and children born outside marriage provide fertile ground for disputes about custody and access.

At the same time the problem of child abduction has over the last two decades acquired a new and sometimes insoluble dimension. Statistics point to an increase in marriages between people of different nationalities. This is hardly surprising. With the explosion of international travel and tourism, the social consequences of a global economy, and the increasing irrelevance of national frontiers, especially in Europe, traditional impediments to transnational marriages have fallen away. But those unions are no less prone to divorce and to quarrels about children.

Whenever marriages break down, a decision has to be taken on where and with whom the children will live. This can be a bitter and contentious business. But when parents of different nationalities are involved, disputes over custody and access can be further exacerbated by differences in culture and in the legal systems of the two countries involved. Some of these situations result in cross-frontier abductions by one of the parents. When this happens—in contrast to abduction within a single national jurisdiction—experience shows how difficult it is to secure the safe return of children and to protect them from the psychological damage inflicted by abduction. If anything should transcend frontiers, it is the interests of children. Sadly, children's issues remain an area where national interest is often allowed to assert itself.

Judicial cooperation between states can be a highly contentious area, as the recent negotiations on an international criminal court have shown. One of the reasons is that judicial systems lie at the heart of national sovereignty. This often inhibits cross-border cooperation, which requires the competence of national courts to be limited by international obligations. The issue of child abduction is a prime example of the limitations of international cooperation in the judicial area.

There are no international conventions regulating custody matters. Every country has its own judicial system. Custody orders made in one country are not necessarily recognized in another. When noncustodial parents abduct their children from the country in which custody has been given (usually heading to their home country), the chances of recovering them through judicial process can be slim. Every year more and more children find themselves separated in the most harrowing circumstances from one of their parents.

The effect on children can be devastating. But the victim parents themselves are also plunged into a bewildering world where helplessness, despair, and disorientation compete. The emotional trauma is compounded by the daunting practical obstacles to retrieving the children, or even to gaining access to them. Simply finding out where to get help can be very difficult. Parents often face unfamiliar legal, cultural, and linguistic barriers.

Their emotional and financial resources can be stretched to the limit. In the meantime, the abducted child is often led to believe that the victim parent has abandoned him, so leading the child, in his anger and hurt, to assert that he does not want contact with the victim parent. This vicious circle complicates still further a resolution, and will continue to do so until courts recognize that there is such a thing as parental alienation syndrome (PAS). As the years pass, the chances of recovering children before their adulthood become progressively more remote. Many victim parents feel that it would be easier to come to terms with the shock of bereavement than with a situation marked by prolonged uncertainty and anxiety.

Some abducting parents may believe that their actions have an objective justification (for example, to rescue their children from domestic violence). But a common thread in all too many cases is the sustained, vengeful effort of the abductor to deprive the other parent of contact with the child to the maximum degree possible. The aim is to flee one judicial system and to destroy the other parent's relationship with the child.

The International Hague Convention on the Civil Aspects of International Child Abduction of 1980 was designed to ensure "the protection of children from the harmful effects of their wrongful removal or retention." Should one parent break a custody agreement, either by illegally retaining (on an access visit) or abducting a child, the Hague Convention requires the child's immediate return to the country where the original custody agreement was made.

The purpose of the Hague Convention was to provide a simple and straightforward procedure. In this, it has largely failed. Different national approaches to implementing the Hague Convention, the slowness of procedures, the lack of legal aid in some countries, and the excessive recourse to the loophole clause, has meant that most cases of international child abduction remain unresolved. Some children are never located. Others are not returned to their country of origin.

The exact figures for transnational child abduction are not known. Many parents are reluctant to go to the central authorities. Others are not even aware of the existence of the Hague Convention. The official figures could well understate the problem. Even so, they are alarmingly high. In the United States alone, the National Center for Missing and Exploited Children reports that 165,000 children are abducted by a parent every year. More than 10 percent of them are taken abroad. In recent years the number of abductions has grown sharply. In England, Reunite, the National Council for Abducted Children, has recorded a 50 percent increase since 1995 in the number of children abducted abroad by an estranged parent. In France a similar upsurge has been recorded.

Despite the rapid increase in abduction cases, there is little awareness of the phenomenon in the governments and legislatures of convention signatories. Nor is there much awareness among the populations at large. As a result, very little is being done to tackle the issue and to make the Hague Convention work as originally intended.

The Hague Convention: What It Does and What It Does Not Do

The Hague Convention on the Civil Aspects of International Child Abduction is an international treaty currently in force between fifty-two countries.

The objectives of the convention are "to secure the prompt return of the children wrongfully removed to, or retained in, any Contracting State; and to ensure that rights of custody and access under the law of the Contracting State are effectively respected in the other Contracting States" (article 1). The convention is not concerned with the "best interests of the child," that is to say, with the merits of a custody case. Criticisms or complaints about the custodial parent or the terms of a custody award are matters to be dealt with by the jurisdiction of the child's habitual residence. The paramount objective of the Hague Convention is to return the child to the country of habitual residence and to confirm that country's jurisdiction.

The Hague Convention provides for a civil proceeding to be brought by the country from which the child was removed or retained. If proceedings are filed within one year, the judge of the country of retention is mandated to order the return of the child to the country of habitual residence. (Return is discretionary if more than one year has elapsed and the child is settled in the new environment.) The abducting parent can raise objections to the return. But the intent of the convention is not to allow these objections except in the most narrowly defined circumstances.

The exception to the requirement for the immediate return of the child to the country of habitual residence is to be found in article 13 of the convention.

The judicial or administrative authority of the requested State is not bound to order the return of the child if . . . [article 13b] there is a grave risk that the child's return would expose him/her to physical or psychological harm or otherwise place the child in an intolerable situation. The judicial or administrative authority may also refuse to order the return of the child if it finds that the child objects to being returned and has obtained an age and degree of maturity at which it is appropriate to take account of its views.

A main intention of this article was to draw a clear distinction between a child's objections, as defined in the article, and a child's wishes, as commonly expressed in a custody case. This is logical, given that the convention is not intended as an instrument to resolve custody disputes per se. It follows, therefore, that the notion of "objections" under article 13b is far stronger and more restrictive than that of "wishes" in a custody case. A failure by courts to grasp this distinction, and to see it as a key defense against the manipulation of a child by the abductor parent, is a root cause of the difficulties described below in the implementation of the convention.

To sum up:

1. By allowing an exception, the Hague Convention does not set an absolute rule. Children are not automatically returned.
2. Article 13, in constituting this exception, can offer abductors a way of legitimizing their actions.
3. Whether or not article 13 serves this purpose depends on how the judge interprets its meaning.

The Hague Convention: What Has Gone Wrong

The discretion given to judges has in practice resulted in a wide variation between signatory states in the outcome of proceedings. The American Bar Association reports that judicial returns vary between 5 percent and 95 percent from country to country. Article 13b, originally intended as an exception, has in some countries become virtually the rule. This is jeopardizing the convention's effectiveness and perverting its original intent.

THE EXCEPTION IS MADE THE RULE

Evidence is accumulating that a major cause for the discrepancy in rates of return orders is the level of court allowed to hear convention cases. When cases are heard centrally by High Court judges, return orders are usually made. But the system tends to fail when the courts hearing convention cases are local family courts without convention experience. This is particularly significant when article 13b is raised as an objection.

In England and Wales, convention cases are exclusively heard *centrally* by a small number (seventeen at present) of specialist High Court judges. The High Courts of England and Wales usually hear cases expeditiously, based on paper evidence and without the child's view being heard. Judges usually make a decision quickly to return the children, relying on the foreign court to make a fair decision at any subsequent custody hearing.

The consultation paper on child abduction published in the February 1997 issue of the *British Family Law Journal* reported that in England and Wales the "consistent approach has been to draw a clear distinction between children's objections under article 13b and children's wishes in ordinary domestic custody cases." The English high court has taken a policy decision to approach article 13b with caution (for example, against the risk of indoctrination by an abducting parent) and, even if a child were found to object to a return, to refuse a return only in an *exceptional case.*

Conversely, in countries where convention cases are first heard in local courts without convention expertise, the results can be very different. For instance, in Germany all Amtsgericht (small family courts that can be found in towns that have as few as twenty thousand inhabitants) have jurisdiction to hear convention cases. Cases are heard in the locality where the abductor has taken the children (usually his hometown), and it is impossible to change jurisdictions.*

The risk here is of inexperienced judges, who may misinterpret the meaning of the Hague Convention. The 1996 Lowe report found that in Germany no single Amtsgericht court had heard more than one case, and that *every time the child's objections were raised as a "defense" for abduction or retention, a return order was refused.* Some children were as young as three

---

*This is currently under discussion in Germany, and a proposal has been put forward to reduce the number of courts (at present more than five hundred) eligible to hear convention cases.

and five. Reunite's latest figures show a similar pattern: from their twenty-seven recorded outgoing cases to Germany since 1995, only one child was returned—precisely when article 13b was not advanced as a defense by the abductor.

In my case, the German courts overruled the English High Court order to return the children to the mother in the United Kingdom on the grounds that it was in the children's best interest to be raised in Germany. The judges' view was that the children had suffered in England "because the entire social environment was based on a foreign language since German was spoken neither at home nor at school." In the McHale case (United Kingdom/Germany), similar reasons were given. In Tina Cone's case (United Kingdom/Germany), the judges concluded that her daughter "had learned to trust her father in Germany, whereas in England nasty things were said about Germany." The illegal retention of two children by the wife of Pascal Holdry (France/Germany) was upheld on the grounds that it was the "will of the children" to live in Germany rather than in France. (The children were three and a half and five years old at the time). In the case of Ildiko Gerbatsch (United States/Germany), her illegally retained children were not returned to San Diego in the United States because the environment was deemed healthier for children in Germany. Other examples are available. France has 137 cases outstanding.

A feature of such cases is that they are allowed to become a discussion of the merits of custody arrangements. It is often the case that an abducting parent will, within the framework of article 13b, level allegations against the other parent and request that oral evidence be heard. Judges who are inexperienced treat these article 13b objections as "a merit of custody" argument. This is exactly what the convention was supposed to avoid: such considerations are meant to be reserved to the court of the child's habitual residence, which is best placed to decide on questions of custody and access. But local family courts are too often unable or unwilling to uphold the difference between proceedings under the Hague Convention and arguments over custody arrangements. Underlying this is a distrust of foreign courts.

There is the added risk of a vicious circle, if family court judges are seen to favor local residents. Abductors will be readier to take the law into their own hands if they believe that their judges will ex-post facto legitimize what they have done. It is interesting to note that Madame Thomas Sassier (Direction des Affaires Civiles et du Sceau, French Ministry of Justice) recorded a fourfold increase in the number of outgoing cases from France to Germany between 1993 and 1997.

THE DANGER OF DELAY

The merit of the convention is supposed to lie in the speed of its proceedings. But some countries are markedly slower in dealing with Hague applications than others. This is particularly the case where, as described earlier, court proceedings become in reality an argument over custody. (The problem of delay is compounded when cases are first heard in lower courts and appeals can then be lodged in higher courts.)

In Germany the involvement of the local Jugendamnt, or Youth Authority, plays a major role in proceedings. Local judges tend to rely on their evidence and hold up matters by asking to see welfare reports and the children. While in principle this could give a more complete picture of the children's situation, it is nonetheless a major factor for delay. In the meantime, the child is more and more under the influence of the abducting parent and further alienated from the absent parent. There is another problem. Youth Authority reports are usually based on information available only in the country of retention, and there is little direct investigation into the environment from which the child has been taken. The result, therefore, can be in-built bias in favor of the abductor. Finally, the passage of time will eventually generate a new argument, which favors abductors, namely, that the children are now settled in their new environment and should not be moved yet again.*

PERVERSION OF THE CONVENTION'S INTENT

In a number of countries, therefore, interpretations of the Hague Convention extend its meaning to encompass in practice an unwarranted jurisdiction in custody matters. Certain consequences flow from this, all of them prejudicial to the victim parent when, as is usually the case, the retained or abducted child is not returned.

When a child is not returned, the abducting parent has the advantage of having subsequent proceedings dealt with in the country of retention rather than in the country of the child's habitual residence. Case studies show that these court decisions, dealing with custody and access rights, tend to favor the abducting parent. This tendency, combined with the fact that—for example, in Germany—judges are reluctant to enforce access orders, results in a situation where a parent is often deprived of all contact with the child or, at best, has contact in only the most harrowing circumstances (for example, in a government office with a third party present). On this interpretation of article 13, the Hague Convention becomes in effect the instrument of alienation between child and victim parent—the very opposite of what was intended.

---

*At the Anglo-German Judicial Conference in Dartington (May, 18–20 1997), both sides agreed this was a problem. In England, High Court judges generally made their decision quickly without the child's views being heard. Incoming Anglo-German cases resulting in a judicial return last an average of just over *five and a half weeks,* while the average length of proceedings in Germany is just under *twenty-six weeks.* Similarly, the average time it took for a judicial refusal to be made for incoming Anglo-German cases was *eleven weeks,* while among outgoing cases it was just under *thirty-six weeks.*

CHILD TRAUMA AND
PARENTAL ALIENATION SYNDROME

Children who are abducted will have already suffered from their parents' separation. But in addition, they will experience the trauma of being suddenly cut off from their familiar environment—from a parent, grandparents, school, and friends. This experience is already bad enough, and many children do not understand what is happening or why. But things are often made even worse when the abducting parent is hiding from the police or taking precautions against reabduction—when the child realizes that there is a state of war between his parents. The child has already been traumatized by the loss of one parent; his greatest fear becomes that he will lose the other parent. This fear itself then becomes an obstacle to resolving the situation, since it is central to what is known as parental alienation syndrome (PAS).

Studies of PAS have established the severity of psychological damage done to abducted children who are suddenly separated from a parent. The studies have also shown how susceptible the child is to being systematically alienated by the abductor parent from the victim parent.

This susceptibility bears comparison to the "Stockholm syndrome," when hostages start to identify with their captors. In the case of an abducted child, the identification will be the stronger because of the age of the "hostage" and the child's relationship with the "captor." For fear of losing the abducting parent as well, the child will not only be eager to please but ready to believe allegations that it has been abandoned by the victim parent.

This is fertile ground for systematic indoctrination by the abducting parent and/or a professional psychologist. Since, under some judicial systems, children—sometimes as young as three—may be required to appear in court, it becomes of paramount importance to abductor parents that their children say "the right thing" to judges. This puts an even higher premium on placing psychological pressure on abducted children.

The irony—and tragedy—of this is that the Hague Convention, in judicial systems like these, delivers children into precisely the danger from which it is supposed to protect them. Again article 13b is the crux. It can be invoked only if returning the child would expose him to grave risk of "physical or psychological harm" or place him in an "intolerable situation." What greater psychological harm, what more intolerable situation could there be for a child than to be exposed to systematic indoctrination by one parent against the other? And worse, to carry the main burden of responsibility in adult court proceedings for deciding between mother and father? When placed in this context, "the will of the children" becomes nothing less than a vehicle for legitimizing the actions of the abductor parent.

ENFORCEMENT

Another problem lies in the alarming number of return orders that have not been enforced. In several convention countries abduction is not considered a criminal act. Return orders are not enforceable.

In Germany, for instance, appeal courts have no power of enforcement. A higher court decision can be enforced only by the Amtsgericht judge who heard the case initially. This enforcement process can take several months and does not always end in a return order being made. In 1994, in the *Nusair* case, the appeal court in Cologne had ordered the child's return, but the local Amtsgericht refused to enforce it. The case of Tom Silverster (United States/Austria) is but another example.

LEGAL AID

The lack of legal aid provisions in some countries is another major problem. Victim parents are often unable to bear the costs associated with these expensive procedures. In England and Wales, for instance, the legal aid provisions are extremely generous. But there should be no reason why each contracting